Postcard History Series

Scioto County

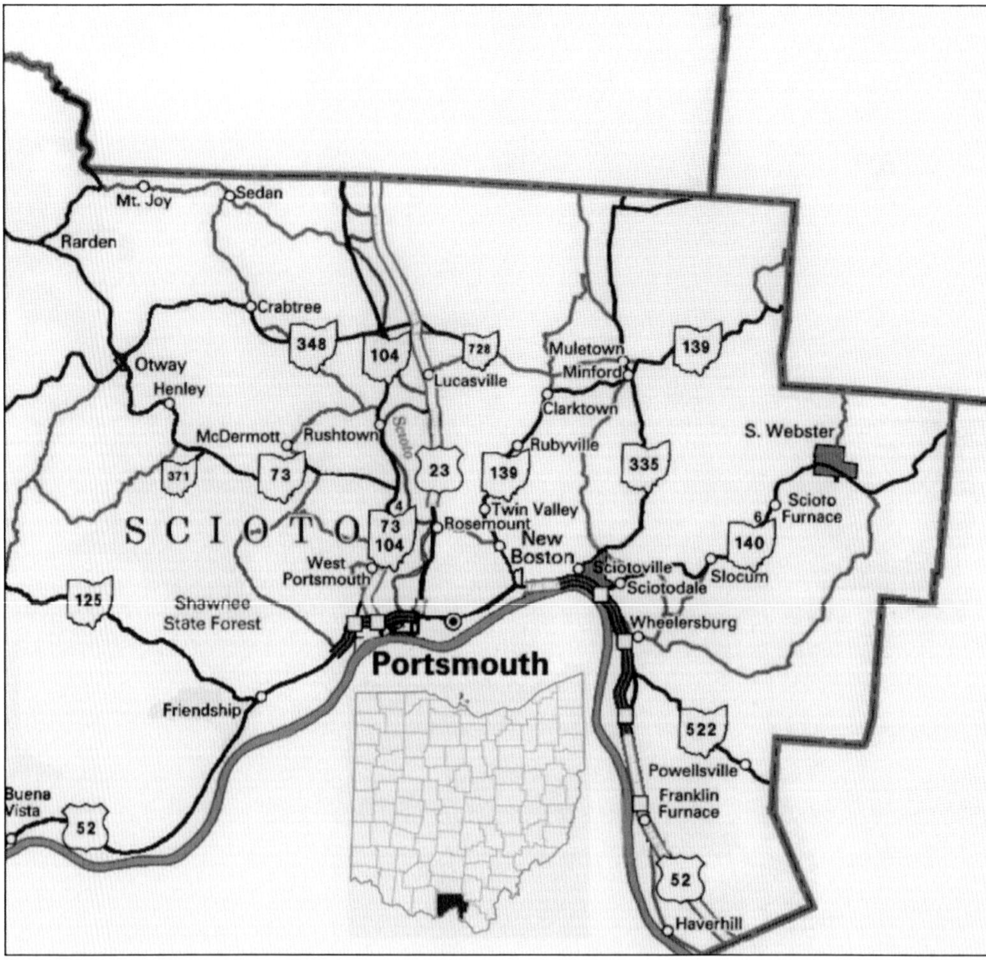

Only three weeks after Ohio became a state, the Ohio legislature designated and named Scioto County on March 24, 1803, taking its name from a Native American word for "deer." The county covers 612 square miles and has a current population of approximately 80,000. Branch Rickey, Roy Rogers, Al Oliver, Larry Hisle, and Gene Tenace are among the many notable people who have called Scioto County home. (James Detty III.)

ON THE FRONT COVER: A picturesque scene between Rosemount and Lucasville is shown on this c. 1918 postcard featuring Scioto Trail. Initially a dirt road extending north from Portsmouth toward Lucasville and beyond, Scioto Trail changed names several times. It was a toll road from the mid-1800s until February 1880 and was reclassified as US Route 23 in 1927. In 1954, a multimillion-dollar project expanded it into a four-lane highway. (Bill Glockner Collection.)

ON THE BACK COVER: Athletic Park, located on Kendall Avenue, was the site for summertime baseball games, including an 1869 contest between the Portsmouth Riversides and baseball's first professional team, the Cincinnati Red Stockings. During the winter, water from the Young Street spring was used to flood the park, creating an ice-skating rink, as shown in this 1908 scene. The park was removed when Dreamland Pool was constructed in 1929. (Paul O'Neill Collection.)

POSTCARD HISTORY SERIES

Scioto County

Jim Detty, David E. Huffman, and Linda Arthur Jennings

ARCADIA PUBLISHING

ISBN 978-1-4671-2517-8

Published by Arcadia Publishing
Charleston, South Carolina

Printed in the United States of America

Library of Congress Control Number: 2016952578

For all general information contact Arcadia Publishing at:
Telephone 843-853-2070
Fax 843-853-0044
E-mail sales@arcadiapublishing.com
For customer service and orders:
Toll-Free 1-888-313-2665

Visit us on the Internet at www.arcadiapublishing.com

We would like to dedicate this book to our families for their encouragement, patience, and understanding during the countless hours spent preparing this book.

Contents

Acknowledgments

Due to the positive feedback on our first Arcadia Publishing book, *Portsmouth*, we decided to write another, this time expanding to include Scioto County. Once again, we relied heavily on the early historians who had the insight to document the history of the county; Nelson Evans, Elmer Swords, and Helen Christian were among the most successful in doing so. Henry Lorberg, Carl Ackerman, and Bill Glockner must also be mentioned, since they had the forethought to preserve local history through photographs and postcards. The authors also found little-known gems of information through hours of searching the *Portsmouth Daily Times* and the Polk city directories.

The compilation of this book would not have been possible without the following individuals and their collections: Susie Beaumont, Sharon Bender, and Sandy Dupuy. We are deeply indebted to Paul O'Neill, who generously gave us access to his vast postcard collection. We would also like to thank Elaine Evans, Janet Humble, Jon Wickline, the Lucasville Historical Society, Portsmouth City School Archives, and the Portsmouth Public Library Local History Department for their assistance.

Every effort has been made to ensure the historical accuracy of this book. Unless otherwise noted, all images are from the collections of the authors.

INTRODUCTION

The Merriam-Webster dictionary defines a postcard as "a card on which a message may be sent by mail without an envelope and that often has a picture on one side." While this definition is accurate, a postcard can be a whole lot more. Beginning in the 19th century, these pieces of thin cardboard not only allowed people to communicate with each other, they unintentionally helped to record history. With the many modern means of communication, it may be hard to imagine sending a 1¢ postcard to a friend or relative, whether they live hundreds of miles or just a few blocks away, just to convey a message. As an added bonus, these cards typically featured artist's drawings or actual photographs of items of interest to the sender or the receiver (or both).

What made early postcards unique was how they inadvertently captured everyday life, allowing future generations to learn about and appreciate the ways people lived. While it was impossible for these few postcards to record everything, we are blessed to view them a century later. Fortunately for us, some of the artists lived and worked in Scioto County, Ohio.

Scioto County was first settled around 200 BC by what was later called the Hopewell Culture. The Mound Builders, which they are more commonly referred to as, were craftsmen who made beautiful objects from bone, metal, shells, and stone. The Mound Builders also created many elaborate mounds of earth in Southern Ohio and Northern Kentucky. Within Scioto County, Portsmouth's Mound Park and Tremper Mound, located northwest of Portsmouth, remain as evidence of their existence.

Later Native American tribes established themselves in the area around 1650, when the Wyandot Indians took advantage of the uninterrupted wilderness for hunting black bear, bison, elk, foxes, wolves, and an abundance of small game. The many creeks and rivers also produced an ample supply of fish. During the mid-1700s, the Shawnee tribe settled in the region with the objective of providing food and shelter for their families while simultaneously protecting themselves from outside intruders. The word "scioto" was created from the language of these tribes—the Wyandot used the term "sci-on-to" to refer to falling or freshwater, while the Shawnee used "sci-o-to" to define deer or the hunting of deer. Although the purpose and goals of the Shawnee were admirable, their presence in the area was relatively brief.

By 1796, the first white settlers arrived in the area, forming a community near the mouth of the Little Scioto River at present-day Sciotoville. In what seemed like the blink of an eye, thousands of white settlers poured into the Ohio Valley and surrounding areas, and the Native Americans, who had lived there for centuries, were soon forced out. As new towns were established and Indian villages were replaced with white settlements, it soon became evident to those in Washington, DC, that the area should be a part of the United States.

When Ohio became the 17th state admitted into the union on March 1, 1803, the name "Scioto County" did not yet exist. The rolling hills and flatlands of the Ohio and Scioto River valleys were part of Adams County, one of only nine counties within the newly formed state. Events moved quickly within the state legislature, which assembled at the first state capital at Chillicothe. On March 24, 1803, the legislature agreed to dissect the eastern portion of Adams County and create Scioto County. With a population of only a few hundred pioneers, Scioto County was born. Two weeks later, Judge John Collins and three of his associates were appointed to organize townships within the new county. During a meeting at Judge Collins's home in Alexandria, the designated county seat (located just west of the confluence of the Scioto and Ohio Rivers), the group formed the townships of Nile, Union, Upper, and Seal.

The townships were further divided over the years from the original four into sixteen. Although Nile and Union Townships kept their names, they changed in size. Green, Jefferson, and Madison Townships were formed prior to 1810. The next decade saw the establishment of Bloom, Porter, Washington, and Vernon Townships. Brush Creek, Morgan, Clay, and Harrison Townships were created during the 1820s and 1830s, while the creation of Valley, Rush, and Rarden Townships did not take place until the latter half of the 19th century.

Early Scioto County primarily consisted of farms and small communities containing businesses to support those farmsteads. Alexandria, which was prone to constant flooding from two rivers, was relocated to nearby Portsmouth and quickly became a major trade center along the Ohio River. By 1830, the county's population had reached nearly 9,000, with most residents living in the prosperous Portsmouth area. The completion of the Ohio & Erie Canal in 1832 opened extraordinary opportunities for the area to flourish; its residents took full advantage of these. The new trade route brought in more money, businesses, and people, which helped the population to triple over the next 30 years. During the second half of the 19th century, railroads and an expanded roadway system helped propel the county to prosperity.

The 20th century proved to be both kind and cruel to Scioto County. Despite disasters such as the floods of 1913 and 1937, the Great Depression in 1929, and locals participating in every war involving the United States, the county continued to thrive in both population and commerce. Unfortunately, a sharp economic downturn and related problems seemed to dominate the area's headlines during the latter part of the 20th century.

Today, Scioto County is rebounding from those losses. While future challenges may seem countless, many feel its best days still lie ahead. Part of achieving that goal is a restoration of pride in one's self and the community that those who live here love. Learning from those who came before and seeing what they accomplished—despite the odds seemingly against them—can give the community the incentive and faith that they can and will obtain these goals.

One

Wheelersburg and Franklin Furnace

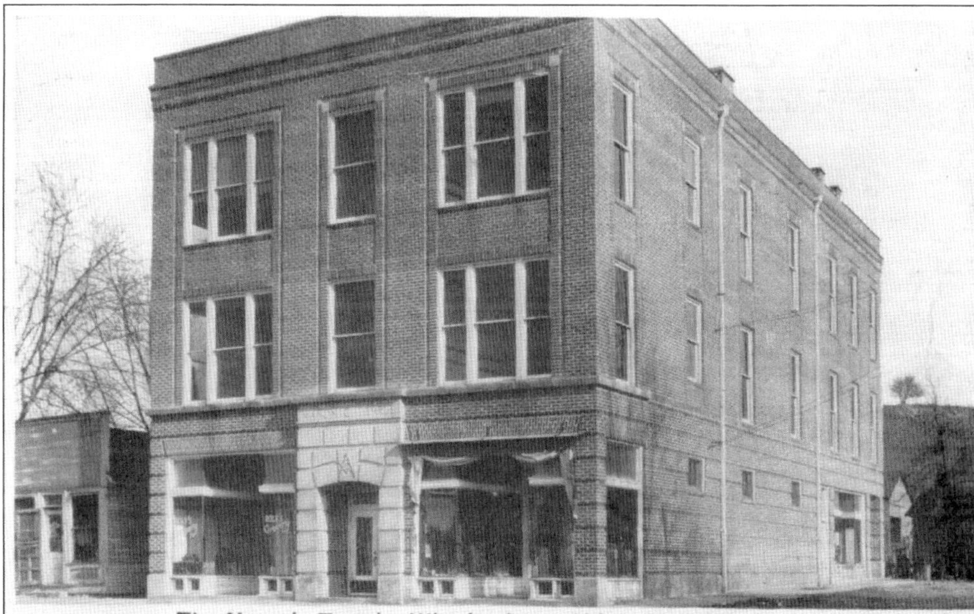

The Masonic Temple, Wheelersburg, Ohio. Cook Photo.

Founded in 1827, the Masonic lodge in Wheelersburg is the oldest such organization in Scioto County. Originally located on Gallia Street at Shela Boulevard, it was relocated three times and was unfortunately the victim of three disastrous fires. In May 1924, the $50,000 brick fireproof structure featured on this postcard was completed at Gallia Pike and Center Street. The money was well spent; the building remains standing today. (Bill Glockner Collection.)

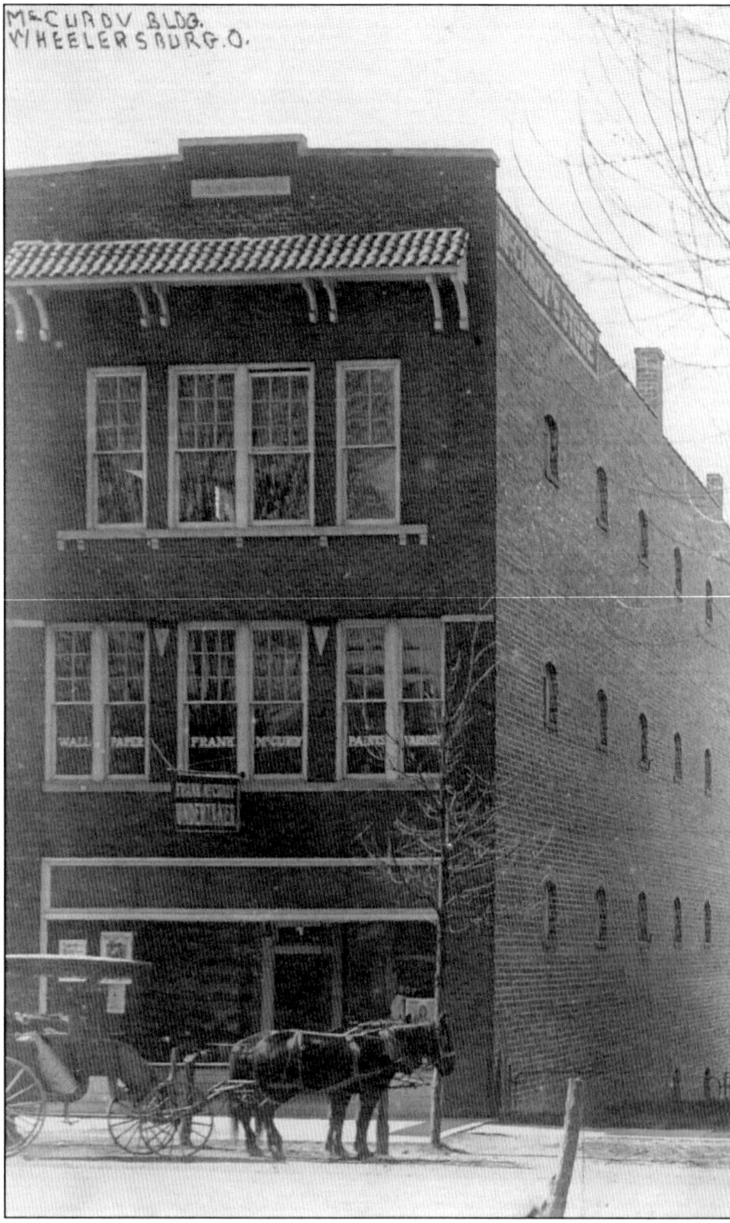

The McCurdy Building was completed in the summer of 1915 at a cost of $8,000. Located on Gallia Pike near Center Street, it was the first three-story building constructed in Wheelersburg and was hailed as a skyscraper by the local press. The *Portsmouth Daily Times* excitedly followed its construction, printing weekly updates on its progress. At 100 feet long and 28 feet wide, the brick structure became a Wheelersburg landmark. When the building was completed, Will McCurdy opened his successful general store in the basement and first floor, while his brother Frank operated an undertaker business and, strangely enough, paint store on the second floor. The third floor was used by local lodges and other civic groups. Frank started one of the first ambulance services in the area in 1925, advertising day or night transport for those who needed it. The funeral home relocated in 1927, while the general store remained for several years longer. At over 100 years old, the building remains standing today. (Bill Glockner Collection.)

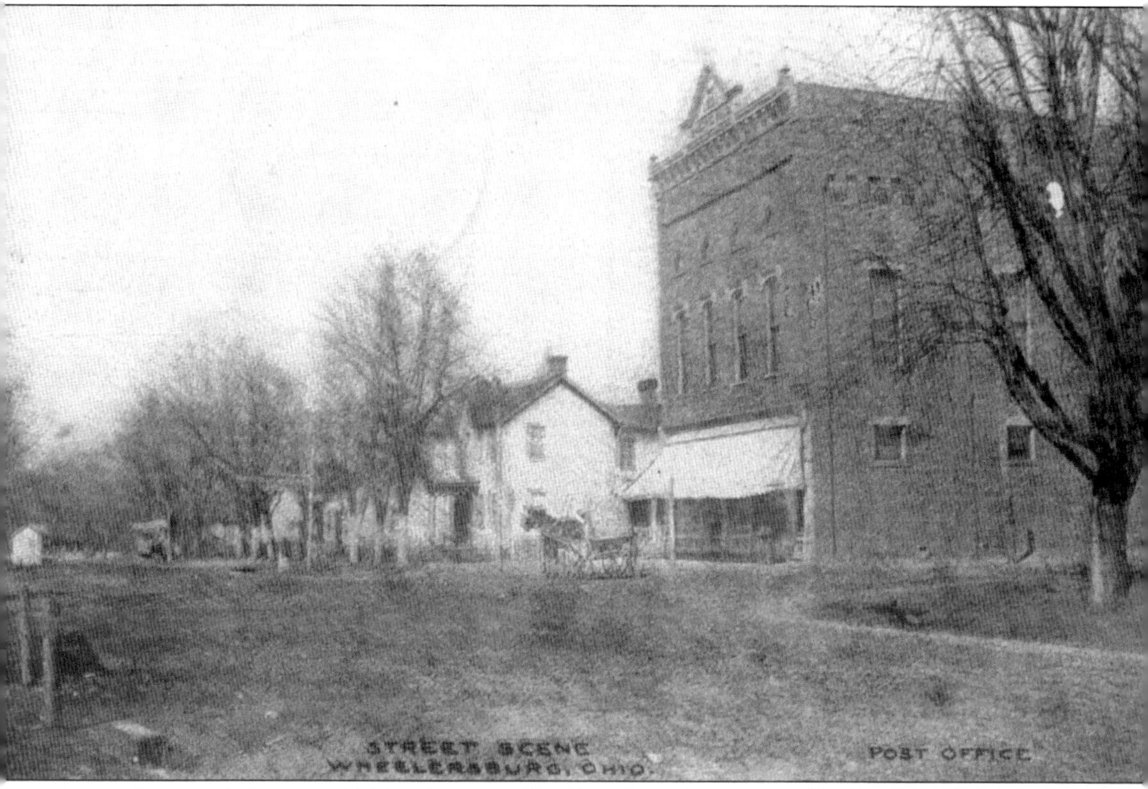

Concord was settled around 1800 and surveyed by Rev. Daniel Young and his brother Johnathon in October 1824. Daniel, who named the settlement after the capital of his native state of New Hampshire, was a Methodist minister and politician in the Granite State. Daniel, who was frustrated with the political corruption in New Hampshire and had a desire to spread his religious beliefs, brought his family and several friends to Ohio in 1820. After purchasing property from early settler Amos Wheeler, Daniel focused his attention on organizing a Methodist church. Johnathon, who focused on establishing a formal education system in the area, started the first school in the growing settlement in 1822. The name "Concord" remained in use until 1833, when the United States decided to establish a post office in the area and learned that a Concord, Ohio, already existed. Town leaders met and decided to change the name to Wheelersburg as a tribute to early settler and War of 1812 veteran Porter Wheeler, whose first name was used to label Porter Township. A typical day in early Wheelersburg is shown on this 1905 postcard. (Sharon Bender Collection.)

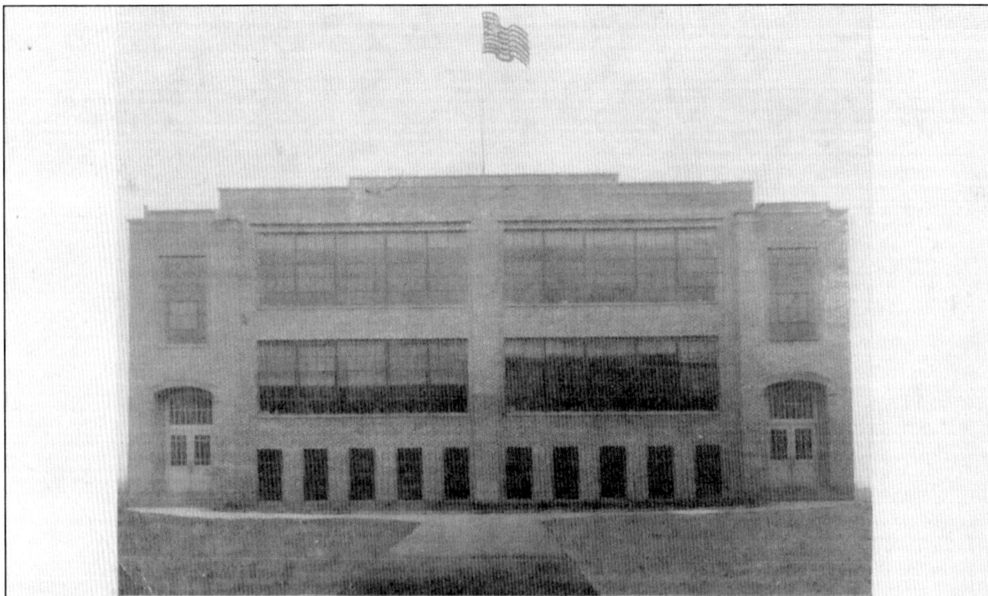

Grade School, Wheelersburg, Ohio. Cook Photo.

In 1924, an eight-room elementary school (above) was constructed on Center Street just west of the current location of Porter Township Fire Department. Offering instruction in grades one through eight, it soon became one of the largest schools in the area, with an enrollment of more than 800 children. In 1939, the elementary school was expanded and converted into the new Wheelersburg High School (below), and the former high school (shown at the bottom of page 13) became the elementary school. Another expansion of the high school in 1951 only delayed the inevitable, and a brand new high school was constructed on Thompson Street in 1958; the old high school was razed shortly thereafter. (Both, Paul O'Neill Collection.)

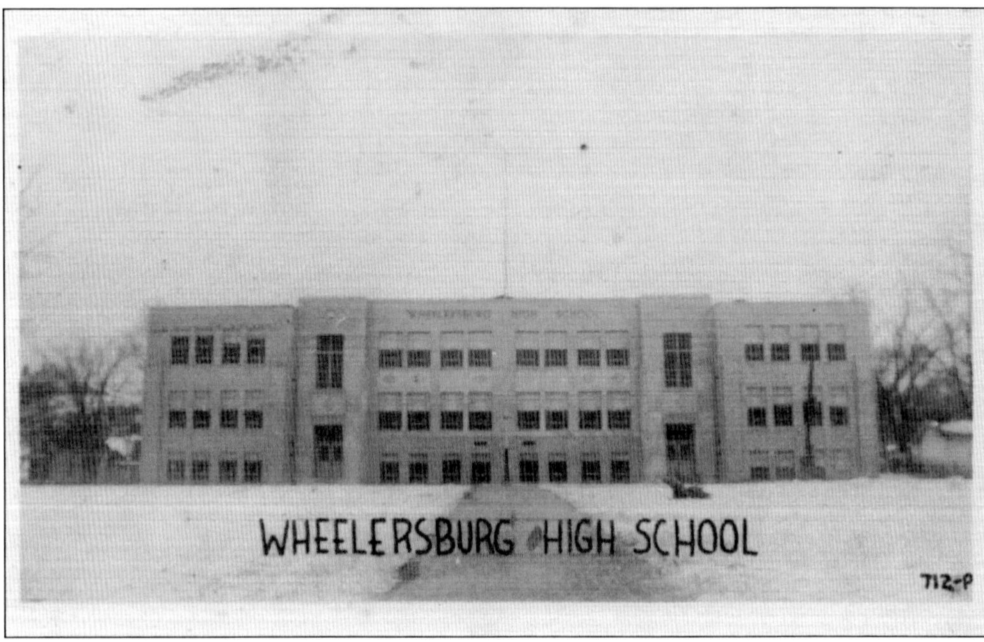

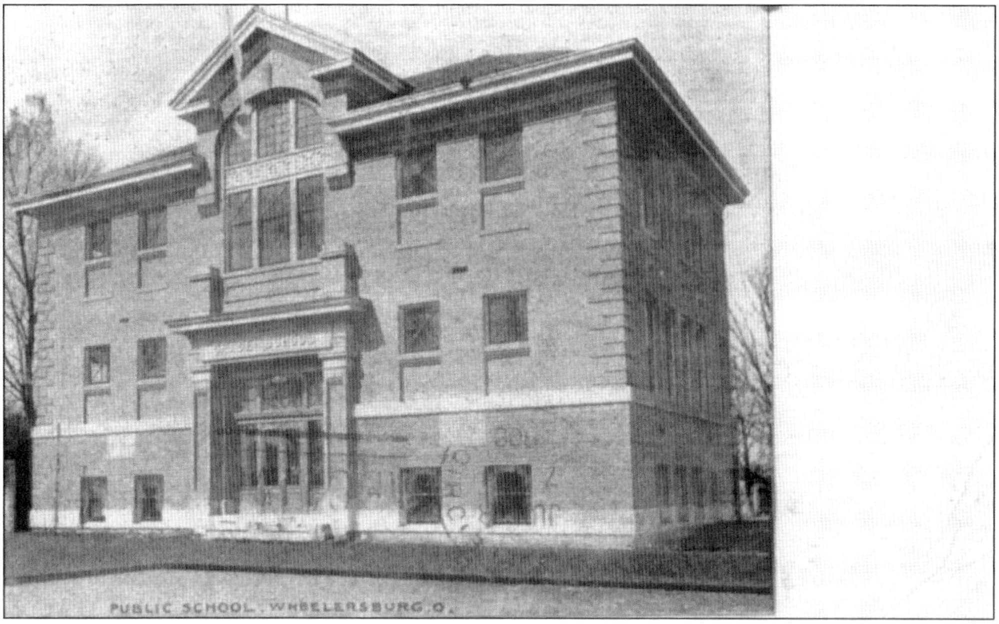

Wheelersburg's school system began in 1822 with a one-room building at Center Street and Hayport Road, where US Bank is now located. John Young was the first teacher and earned $10 per month for a three-month term. In 1907, this three-story brick school was constructed on South Street and considered one of the finest of its time. (Bill Glockner Collection.)

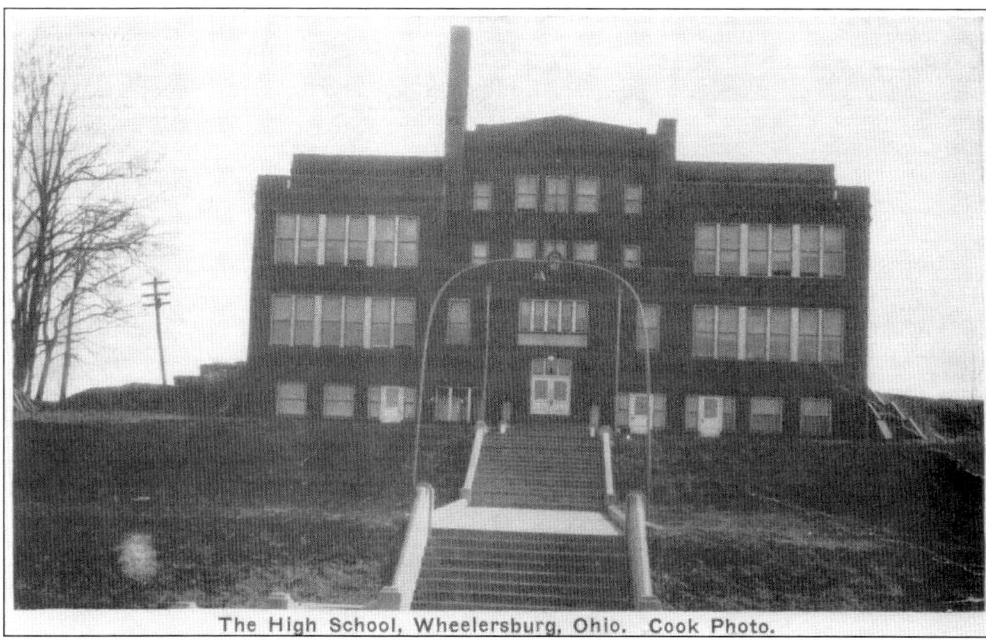

Despite a highly publicized campaign against the costly construction of a new Wheelersburg High School, voters overwhelmingly approved a bond levy in December 1915. The school, which was located on a hill near the current location of Ed Miller Stadium, opened for classes in September 1916 and cost $35,000 to construct. It was converted into an elementary school in 1939. (Bill Glockner Collection.)

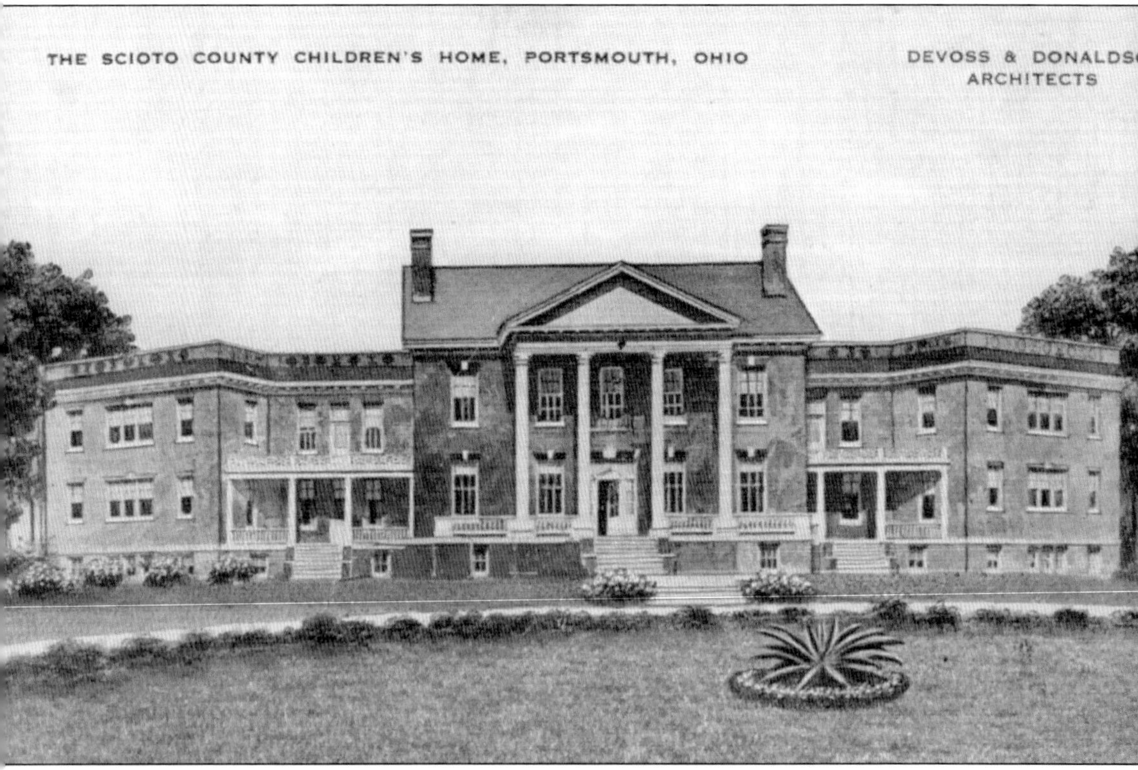

Hillcrest Children's Home, also known as the Scioto County Children's Home, opened in Wheelersburg in April 1921 (replacing the original children's home in Portsmouth's Mound Park) and provided a much-needed home for thousands of orphans over the years. It contained 50 rooms on 17 acres of property and could house, feed, and clothe over 100 children at any given time, more than doubling the capacity provided by the original children's home. During the home's nearly 50 years in operation, each Christmastime, the employees of the phone company and the Kiwanis Club, with the help of and donations from other area businesses and citizens, purchased and delivered toys to the Hillcrest children. With foster homes becoming more popular, in addition to the increasing expense of operating the large house, county commissioners closed the structure in the early 1970s. After vandals and thieves destroyed the building, it was sold at auction and razed to make room for residential development. Today, hundreds of former residents attend annual reunions, with many traveling from several states away. (Bill Glockner Collection.)

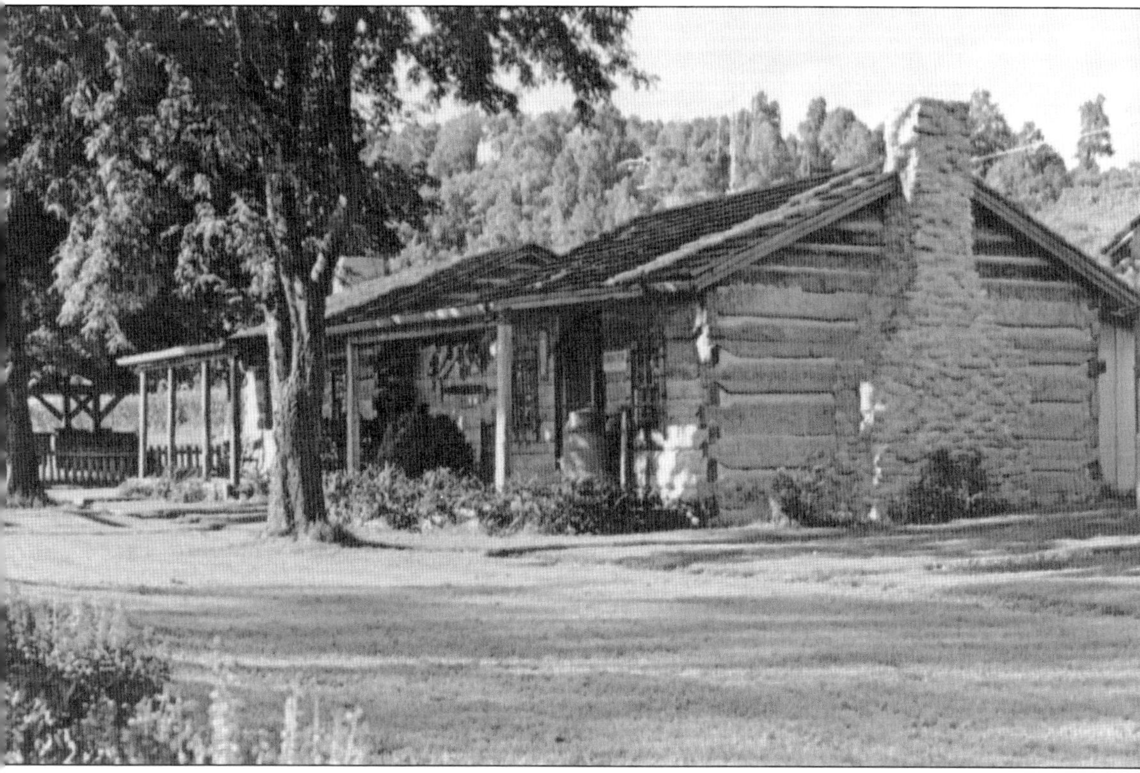

Few people impacted a town as much as Ray Litteral did in Wheelersburg. Litteral, a former fire chief with the Porter Township Fire Department, always gave to his community. Born in 1909, he opened his first grocery store in 1937. He later owned two grocery stores named after his daughters—the Nancy Rae in Wheelersburg and the Anna Lou in South Shore, Kentucky. From 1964 until 1985, he gave one percent of all sales at the stores to nonprofit organizations. In 1972, he opened the Pioneer Village of Wheelersburg, Ohio, on Ohio River Road as a way to represent and document life in Scioto County between 1800 and 1935. Litteral purchased, dismantled, relocated, and reconstructed several original vintage log buildings found throughout the county. After completion of the village, he filled the buildings with various antiques and historical displays for people to enjoy. Following his death in December 1998, a dedicated group of volunteers continued the preservation of Pioneer Village, and in August 2014, their group, Pioneer Village of Wheelersburg, Ohio, was certified in Ohio as a nonprofit organization. This devoted organization remains active in pursuing the goal of complete restoration of the village and the realization of Litteral's dream of educating visitors about appreciating the past. (Paul O'Neill Collection.)

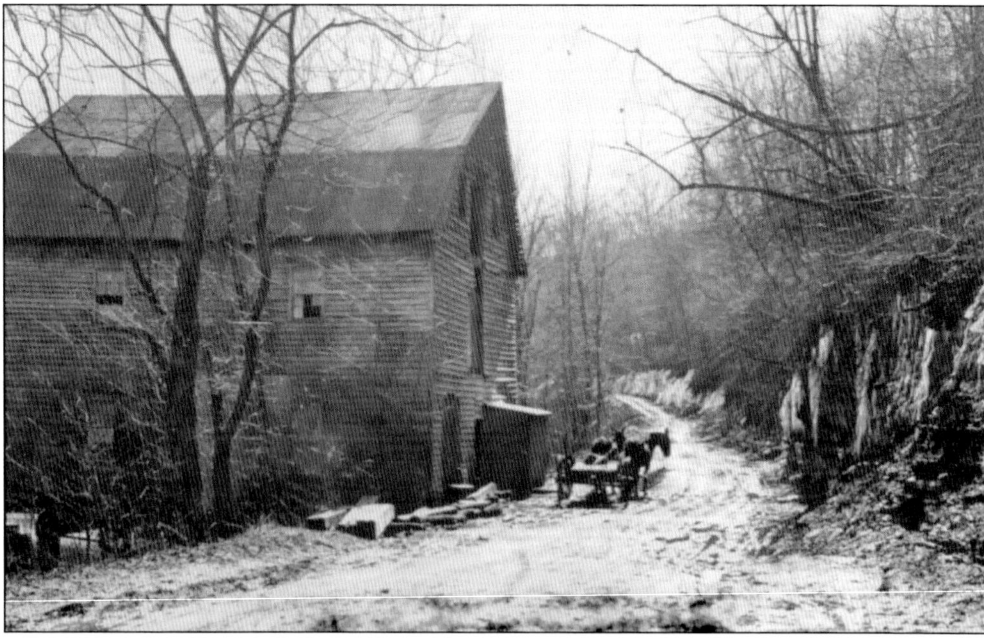

During the 1800s, several mills were built in southeastern Scioto County and produced a variety of products ranging from flour to wool. In the c. 1900 postcard above, a mule-pulled wagon waits at the rear of a mill along Pine Creek, now known as Giant Oaks Mill Road. The mill shown the 1930 scene below is a short distance downstream, near Wizard Oil Bridge, on what is now Mill Road. In the mid-1800s, the bridge in the photograph was covered and made of wood, and the Wizard Oil medicinal company supplied the paint for the structure in exchange for the company's name being painted in 10-foot-tall letters on the side of the bridge. The original bridge was replaced in 1888, but the name remained and is still in use today. (Both, Bill Glockner Collection.)

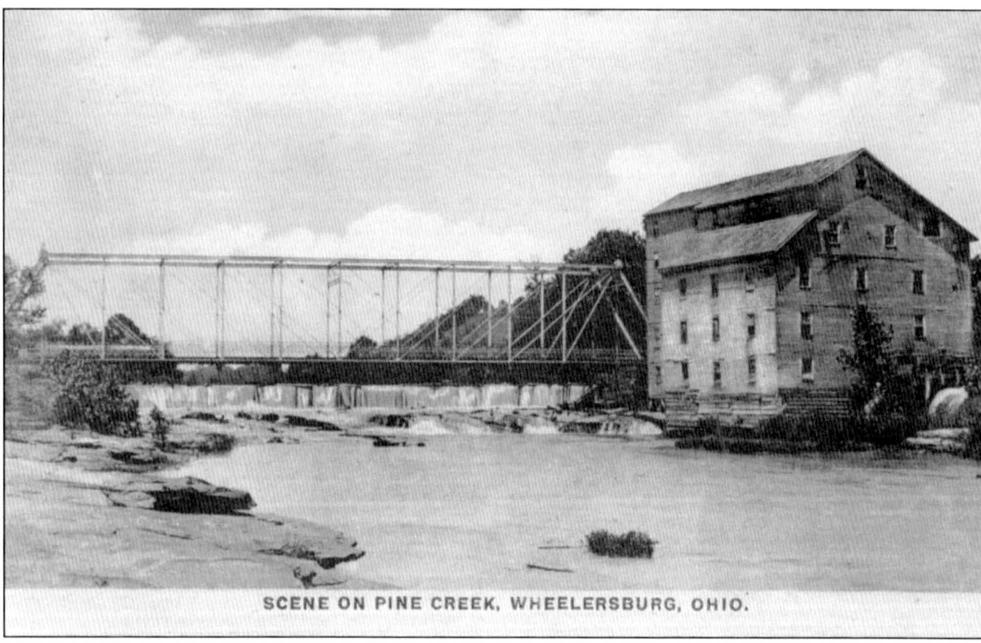

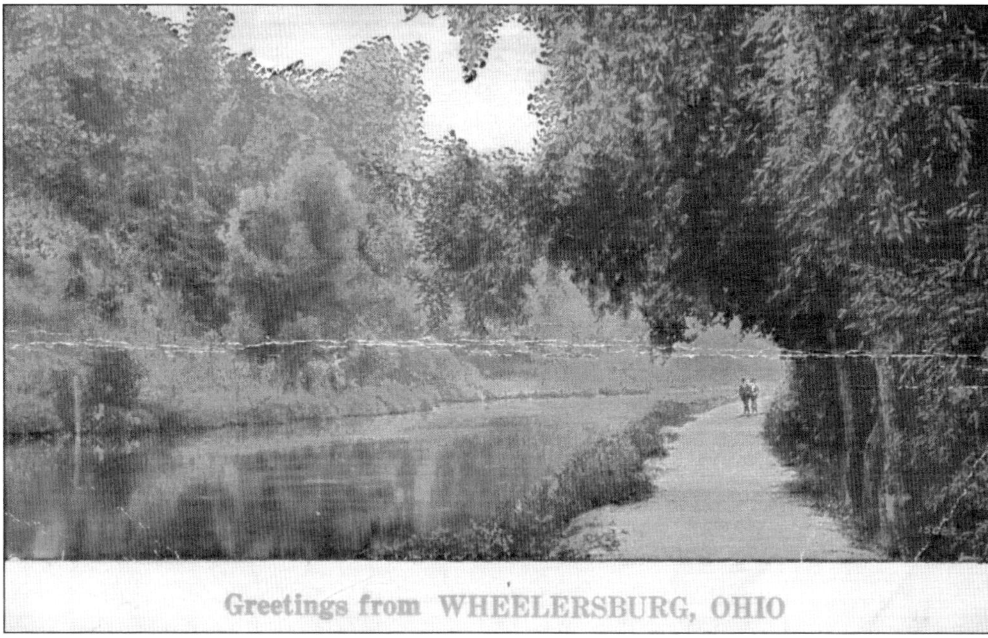

Pine Creek, near Wheelersburg, was occasionally used for recreational purposes. During the mid-1870s, it was a popular location where local men organized for fox hunts, and dozens would arrive with foxhounds and whiskey. When the intoxicated hunters returned home with only groundhogs and skunks, the true reason for the "hunt" was revealed. (Bill Glockner Collection.)

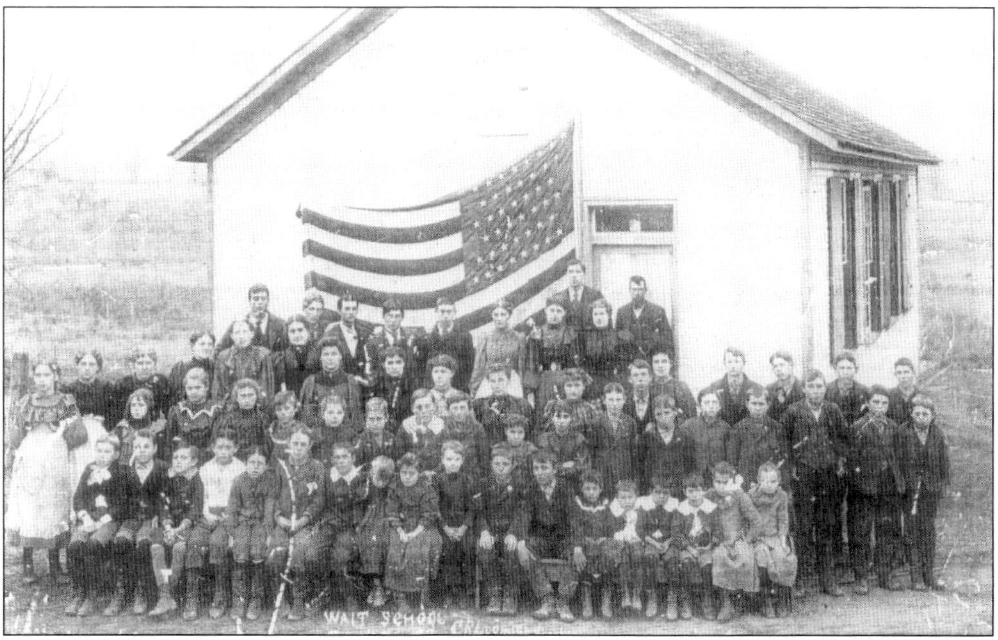

Wait's Station School, constructed in the early 1840s, was located along current State Route 140 near Slocum. Sunday church services began here in 1913, giving the building a dual purpose. It ceased being a school in 1928, when students were transferred to the new Lindsay School. After many renovations, it is still used as Wait's Missionary Baptist Church. (Portsmouth City Schools Archives.)

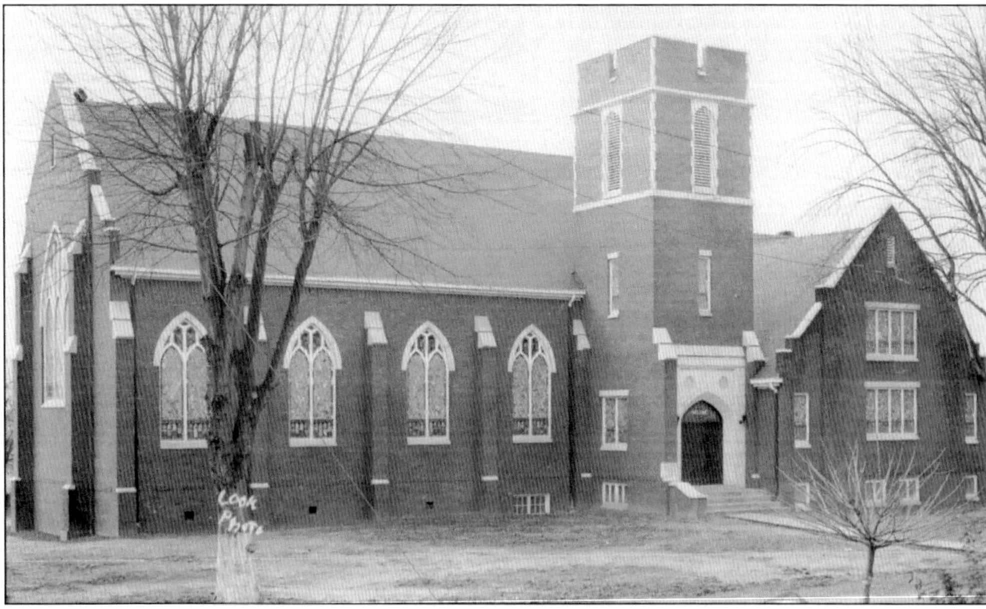

Wheelersburg United Methodist Church members built their first church on Gallia Street in 1838. Due to growth, a larger building was erected in 1883 on the site of the present church, costing $4,000. In 1917, the congregation united with German-speaking members of Zion Methodist Church of Lang Slocum and became the Wheelersburg Methodist Episcopal Church. A new brick church (pictured) was built in 1926 at a cost of $60,000. (Bill Glockner Collection.)

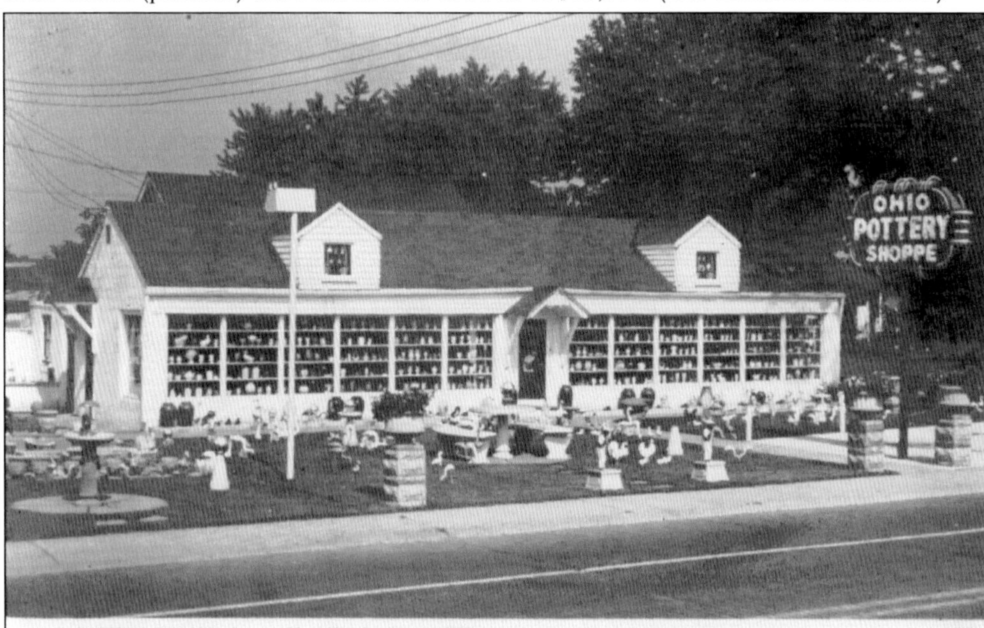

Michael Conklin, a car repairman for Norfolk & Western Railroad, opened the Ohio Pottery Shoppe in the mid-1930s. Located on busy Route 52 in Wheelersburg, it advertised a wide variety of ceramic and concrete decorations, as well as 20-piece dish sets for $1.79. After Conklin passed away in 1941, the business continued successfully for another 20 years. (Paul O'Neill Collection.)

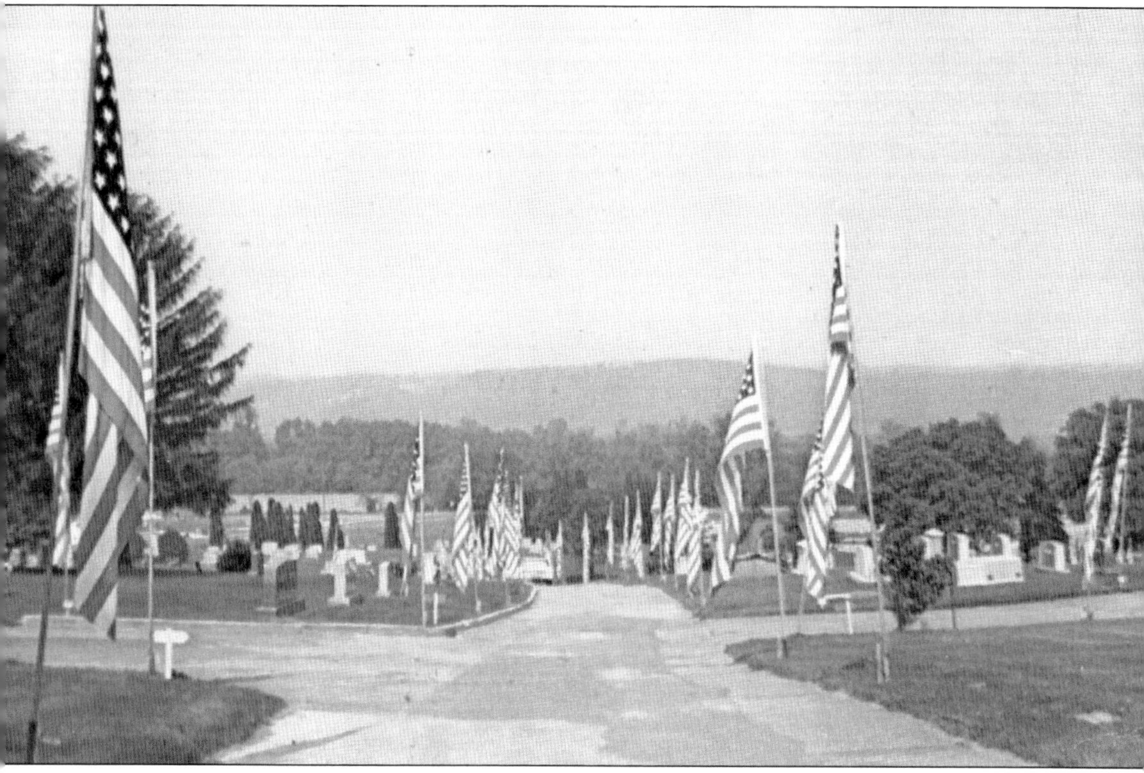

Established in late 1925, Memorial Burial Park in Wheelersburg is the final resting place for thousands. Located on Gallia Pike, the beautiful hillside property was originally farmland owned by Portsmouth business magnate Levi York. After York's death in 1920, Ray Bishop of Columbus purchased the land with the intent of opening a much-needed public cemetery. Thomas Stitt was hired to oversee the complete grading of the nearly 80 acres of property in addition to supervising the design of roads and the beautification of the park. Stitt and his wife, Elizabeth (Louise), remained as caretakers, living in a house located within the cemetery. The memorial park was immediately well received by the public for its sheer splendor and peaceful atmosphere. One popular annual event is the Avenue of Flags, which honors veterans on Memorial Day. In this early-1990s postcard, over 500 large American flags are proudly displayed along the roadways in tribute to those who bravely served this country. (Bill Glockner Collection.)

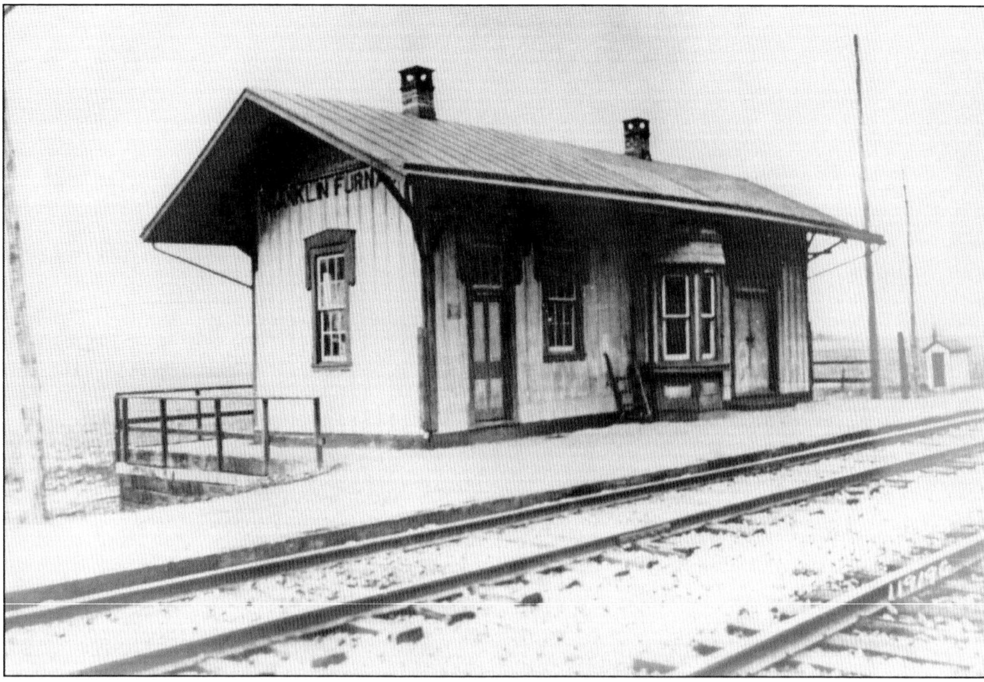

Franklin, one of the earliest settlements in Green Township, was founded around 1800 and named after Benjamin Franklin. "Furnace" was added to the settlement's name in 1827 to publicize one of the iron ore mills in the area. The Franklin Furnace Norfolk & Western depot, where passengers, freight, and mail arrived and departed many times daily, is shown in this 1918 image.

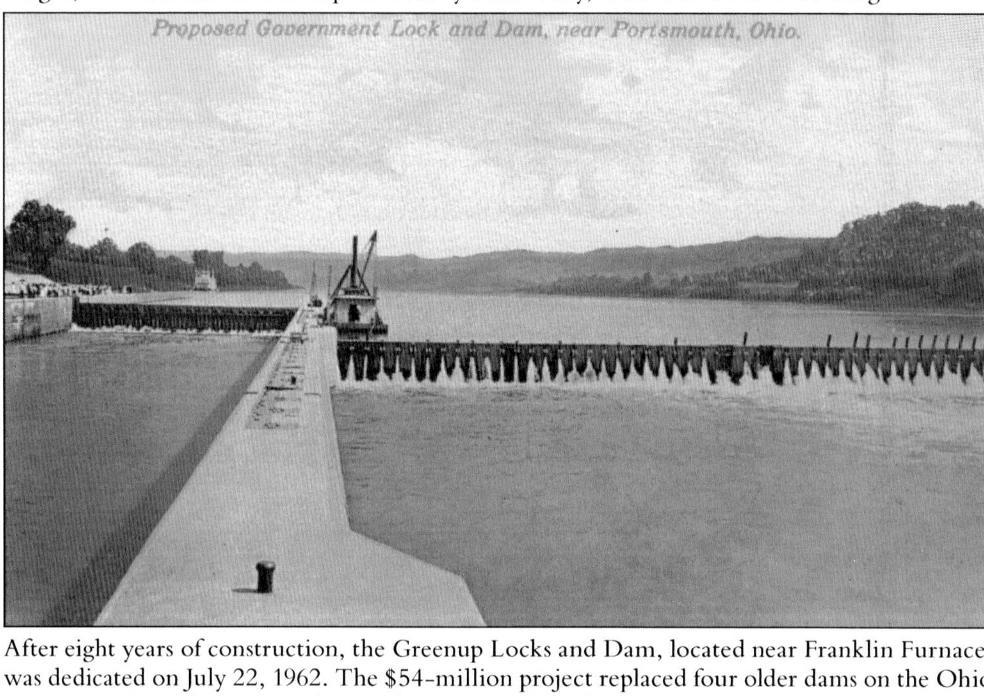

After eight years of construction, the Greenup Locks and Dam, located near Franklin Furnace, was dedicated on July 22, 1962. The $54-million project replaced four older dams on the Ohio River, greatly reducing travel time for river traffic. The Jesse Stuart Memorial Bridge was completed on top of the dam on January 23, 1987. (Paul O'Neill Collection.)

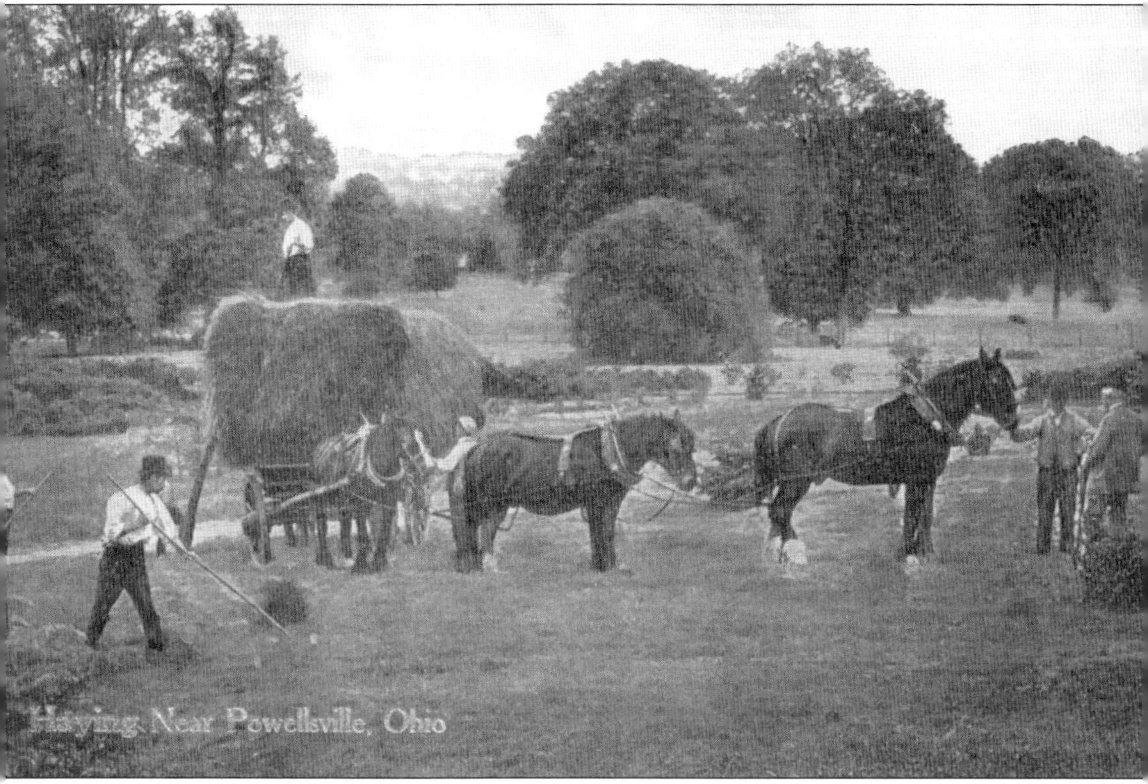

The community of Powellsville, located along present-day State Route 522, was first surveyed in July 1846 by William Powell and brothers John and Washington Irving. Powell's three sons operated separate businesses in the area when the town was formed, which led to the name "Powellsville." Although farming was the primary means of income in the early years of the village, as shown on this c. 1900 postcard, it also contained a blacksmith, a carpenter, a buggy manufacturing and repair shop, a hotel, three churches, and a school for grades one through eight. Powellsville also had three doctors, including one female, which was rare at the time. When the village began to get a reputation as a rough town of drunks and slackers, the citizens decided to hire a law enforcement officer to make the community more civilized. During the late 1800s, St. Lutheran Church, located on Junior Furnace Road, held ice cream socials for the entire community. Today, Powellsville is known as a farming and residential area, and many of its early buildings remain standing. (Paul O'Neill Collection.)

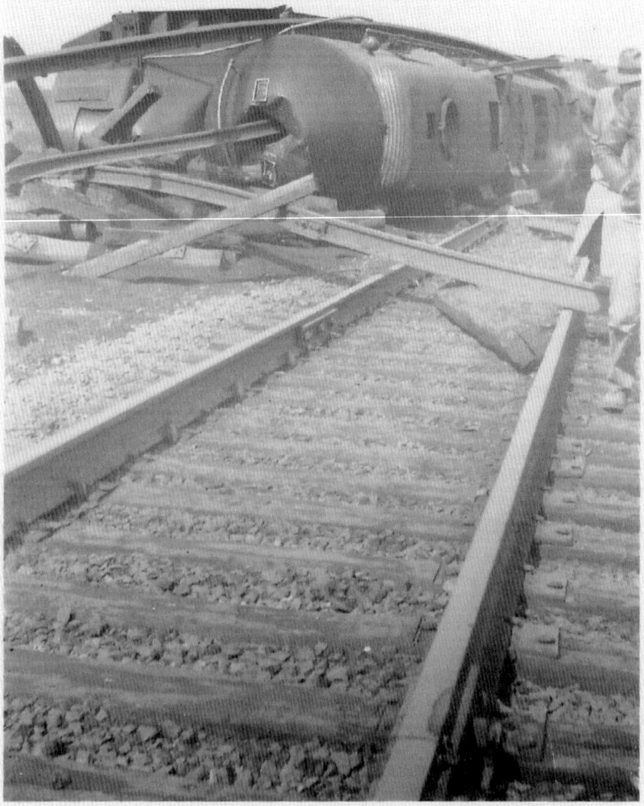

The Norfolk & Western Railway's most celebrated passenger train, the *Powhatan Arrow,* was involved in a rare and tragic accident near Franklin Furnace on February 20, 1948. While traveling eastbound from Portsmouth, the train consisted of Class J locomotive No. 607 and six passenger cars containing 54 occupants. While attempting to enter a middle passing siding in order to pass a stopped eastbound coal train, the locomotive entered the siding at 77 miles per hour—more than twice the recommended speed. The 247-ton locomotive fell to its side and skidded nearly 150 feet. A broken rail penetrated through the headlight and exited short of the locomotive's cab, missing the explosive boiler by mere inches. The passenger cars became uncoupled when the series of events began, no doubt saving countless lives. Unfortunately, the train's fireman was killed, and 44 passengers and crew members were injured. Locomotive No. 607 was repaired and put back in service; it was permanently scrapped in 1959 at a Sciotoville scrapyard.

Two

McDermott and Lucasville

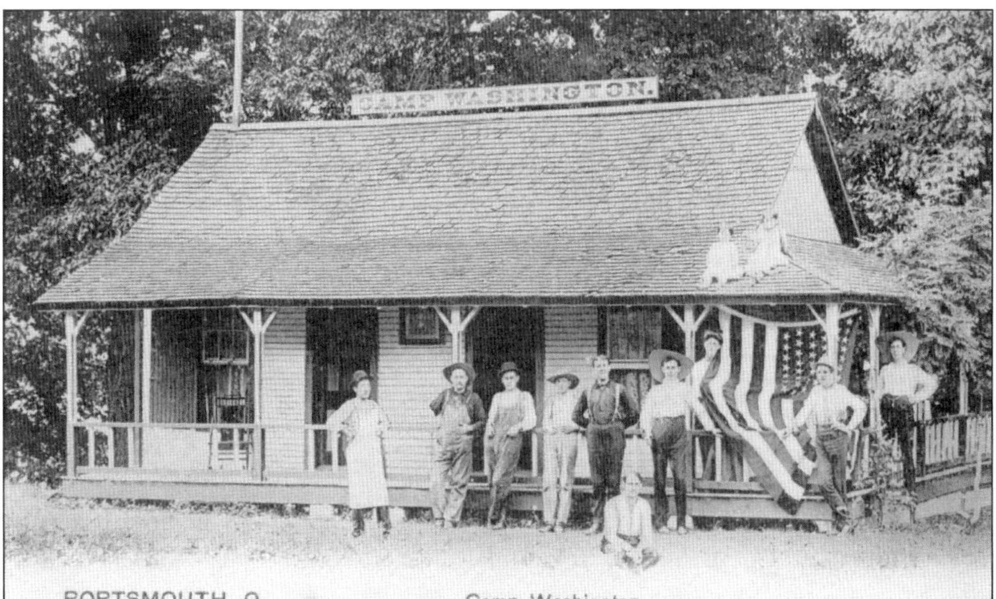

Camp Washington was situated a short distance north of Crichton Inn in Rushtown. The campground, pictured here in 1907, stood adjacent to four transportation routes: the Scioto River, Ohio & Erie Canal, Galena Turnpike (later State Route 104), and Norfolk & Western Railway (N&W). This popular destination for campers and fishermen was within walking distance of the N&W railroad depot. (Bill Glockner Collection.)

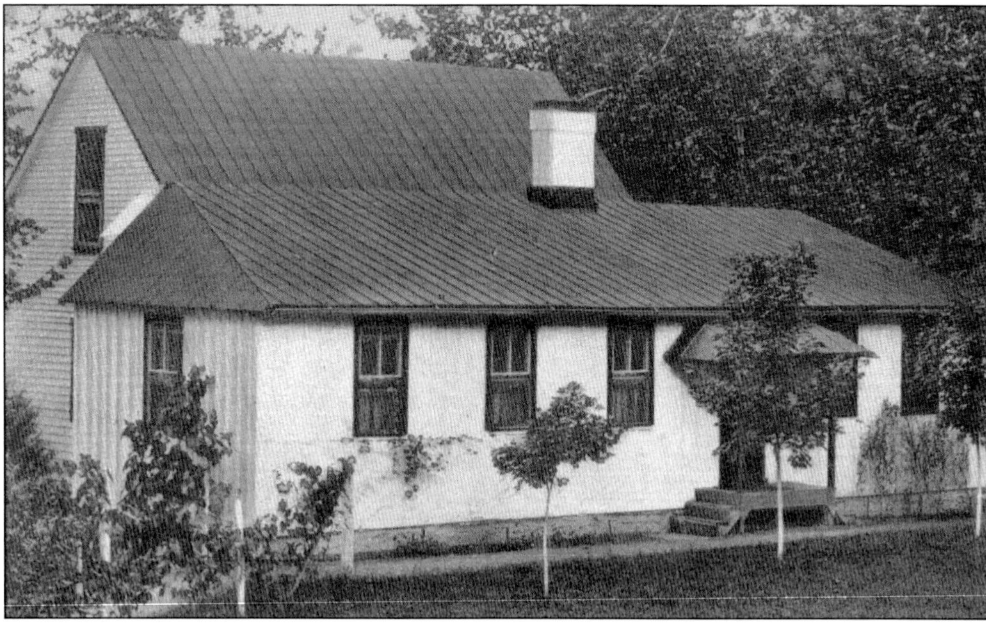

Camp Arion, located west of McDermott along Scioto Brush Creek, was one of the many recreational facilities in early Scioto County. From the early 1890s through the 1940s, its cottages and campgrounds were a vacation destination for many who came to fish or play baseball and tennis. Local veterans of the Spanish-American War used Camp Arion for their reunions, which featured live bands and chicken dinners. (Bill Glockner Collection.)

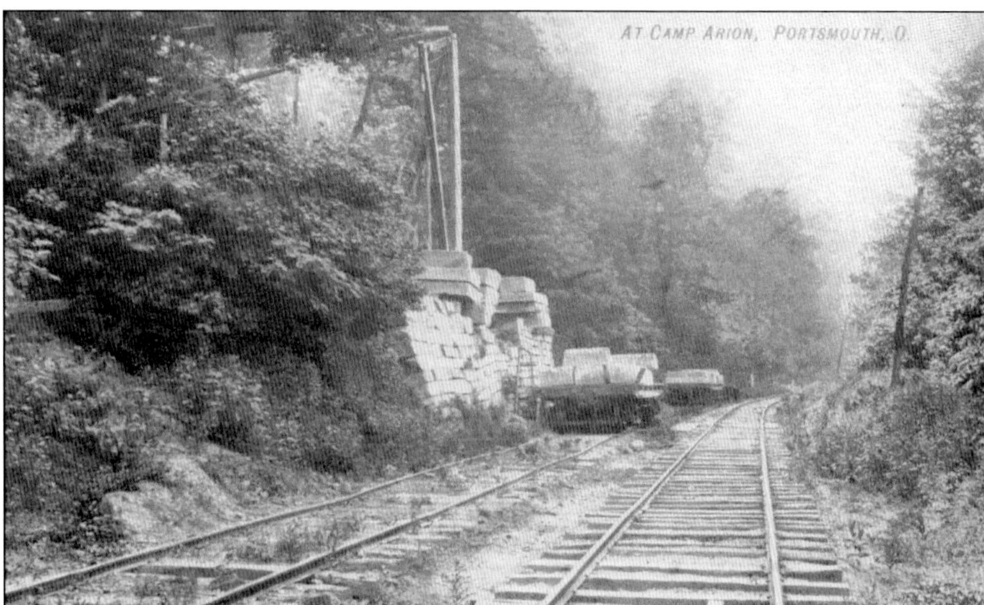

In 1886, Milburn Coe opened a stone quarry near Camp Arion. Benefiting from a vast supply of quality stone in the region, Coe and his 30 employees had customers throughout the eastern United States. In this 1898 image, a steam-operated hoist loads cut stones onto a flatcar for eventual shipment via the Cincinnati, Portsmouth & Virginia Railroad. (Sharon Bender Collection.)

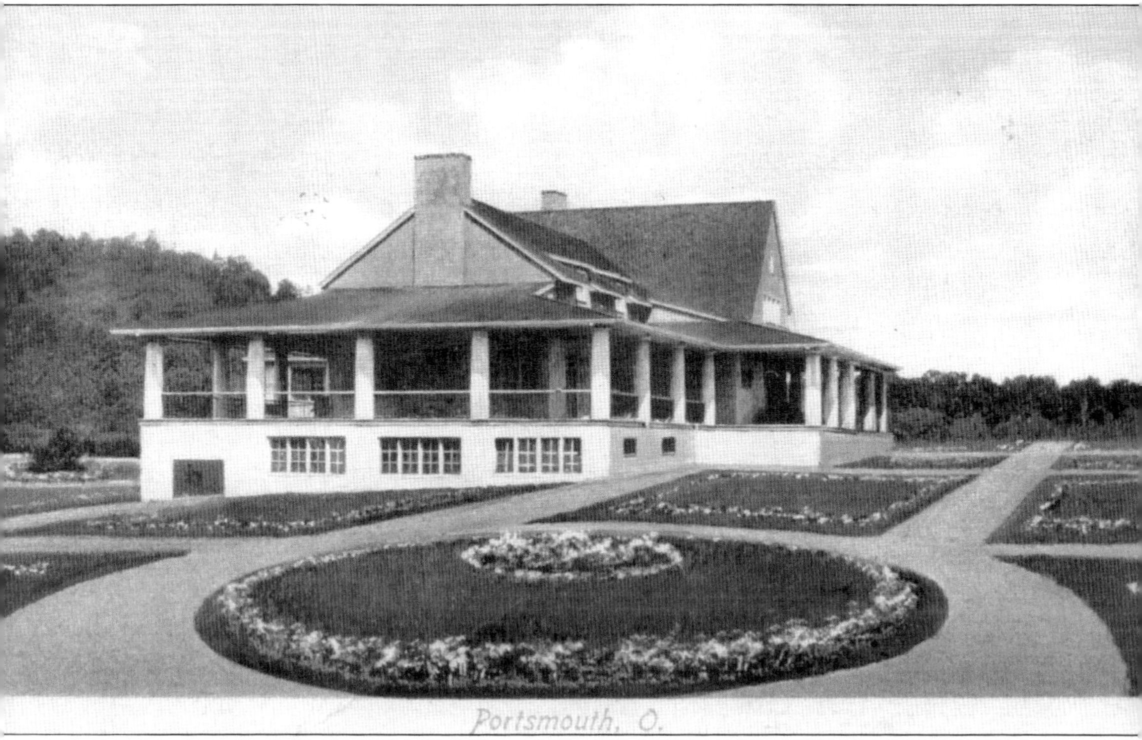

One of the most popular recreation areas in Scioto County developed on land originally known as the Lucas farmstead, which dated to the early 1800s. After opening in September 1924, Portsmouth Country Club quickly became one of the finest golf courses in Southeastern Ohio. Designed by golf course architect Donald Ross, who planned golf courses on the PGA Tour, it has been the scene of thousands of tournaments and social gatherings over the years. On July 16, 1932, golf legends Gene Sarazen and Tommy Armour were featured in an exhibition match attended by thousands. Unfortunately, plagued by financial problems, Portsmouth Country Club was sold in June 1937 and renamed the Valley View Country Club. On May 15, 1941, the local Elks club acquired the property; it has been known as the Elks Country Club ever since and has remained a popular destination for outdoor leisure. The spacious lodge is shown on this 1925 postcard. (Sharon Bender Collection.)

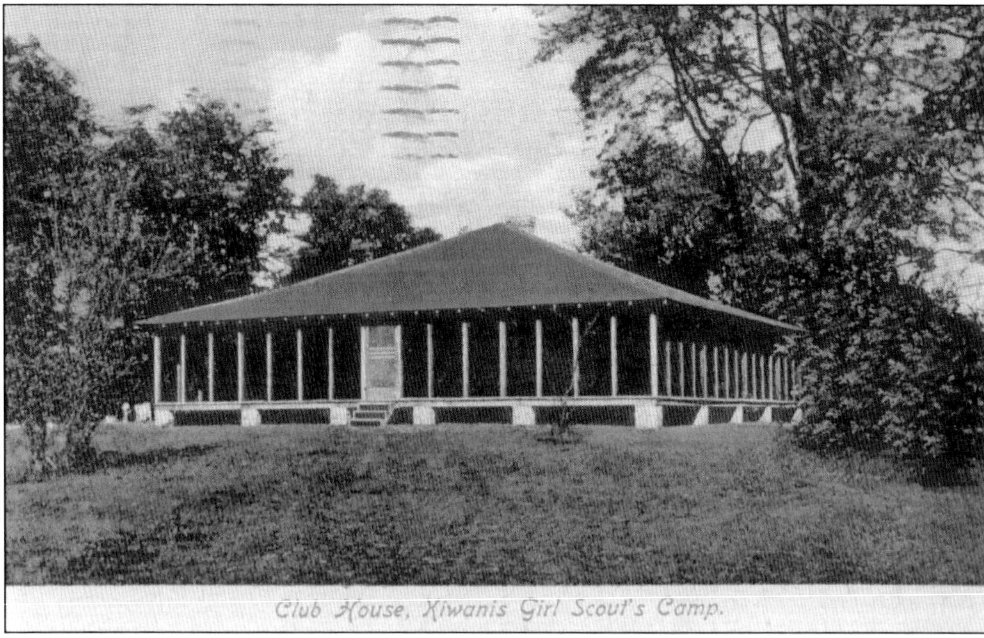

Club House, Kiwanis Girl Scout's Camp.

The first Girl Scout camp in Scioto County opened in 1920 on donated property near Arion along Scioto Brush Creek. In July 1923, the site was moved to a farm on Pond Creek Road across from the Portsmouth Country Club golf course. The facility was named Kamp Kiwanis in tribute to the organization that sponsored it. A large dining hall (above) was constructed on the 125 acres of land. By 1930, the Girl Scouts were looking for a new location, so local widow Mary "Molly" Lauman agreed to generously donate 100 acres of her property on Bear Creek Road. Facilities constructed on the new site included a swimming pool (below), which was built in 1933 and funded through proceeds from Girl Scout cookie sales. Camp Molly Lauman is still in operation today. (Above, Bill Glockner Collection; below, Paul O'Neill Collection.)

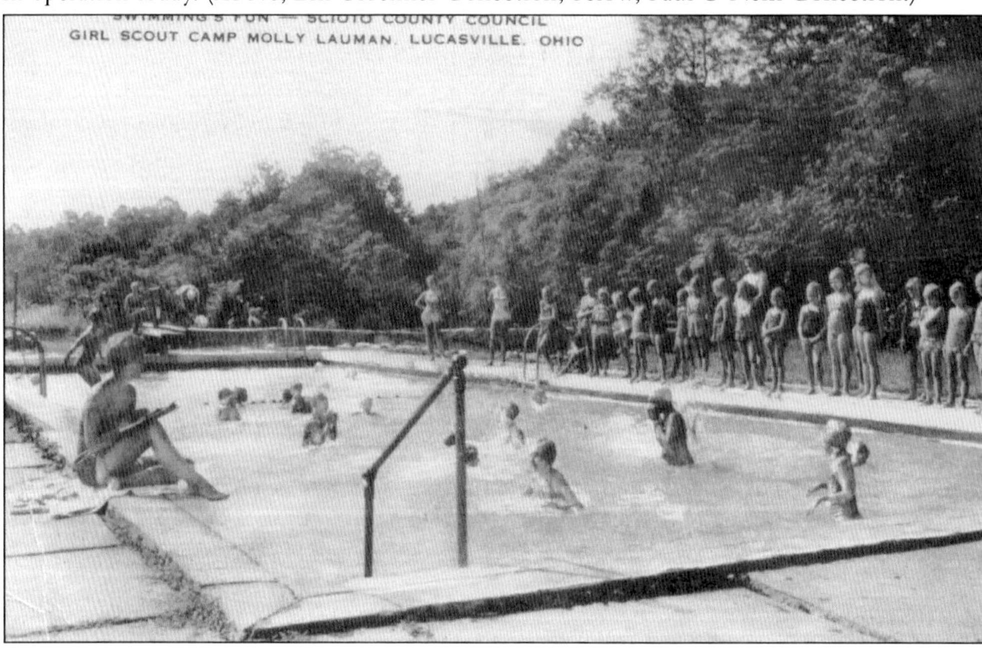

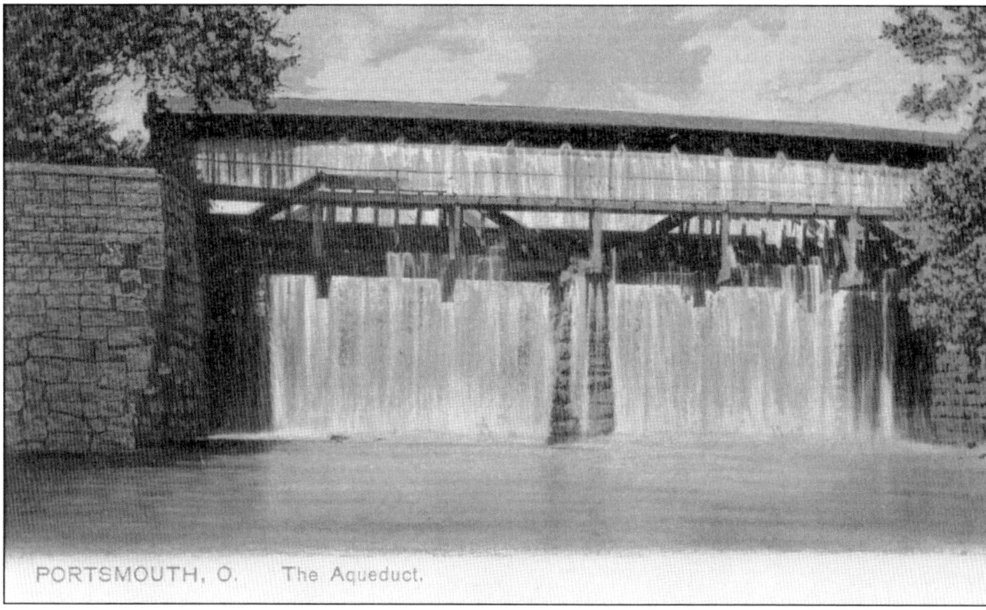

The only aqueduct in Scioto County is located along the Ohio & Erie Canal spanning Brush Creek, near Rushtown, and is shown in this 1906 postcard. These manufactured waterways allowed uninterrupted travel along the canal where it crossed natural streams. The waterfall shown here was created by the construction of the aqueduct. This covered bridge was used by horses and early automobiles and later became part of State Route 104.

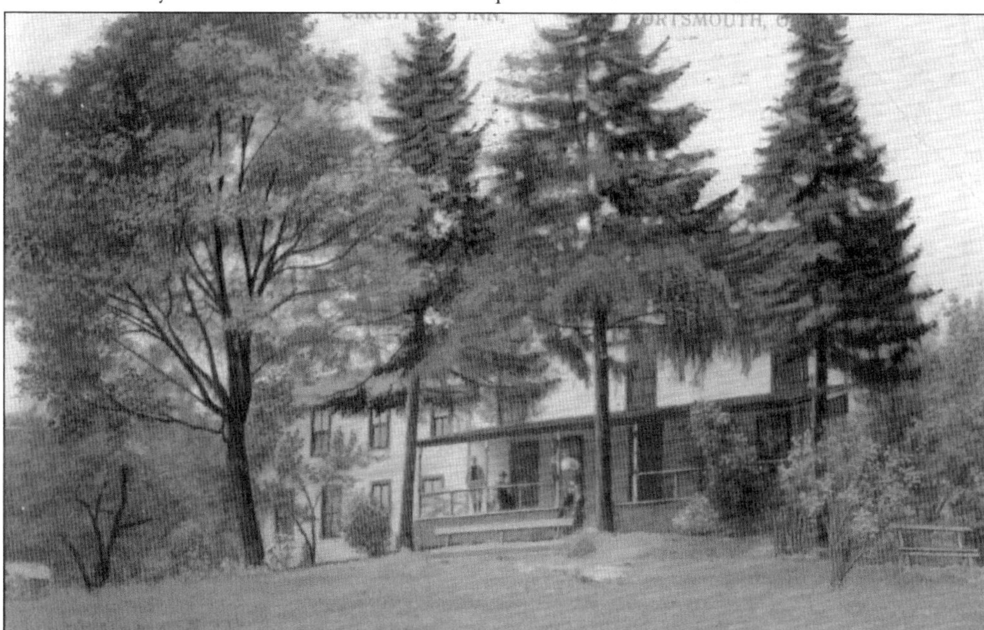

During the early 1900s, William Crichton operated the Crichton Inn on a hillside at Rushtown. Shown in this 1909 postcard, the resort was a popular stop for hunters, who utilized nearby wooded areas; fishermen, who fished in the nearby Scioto River; and families and groups, who used it for picnics and social gatherings such as moonlight dances. The Young Women's Christian Association (YWCA) sponsored summer camps here for high school girls.

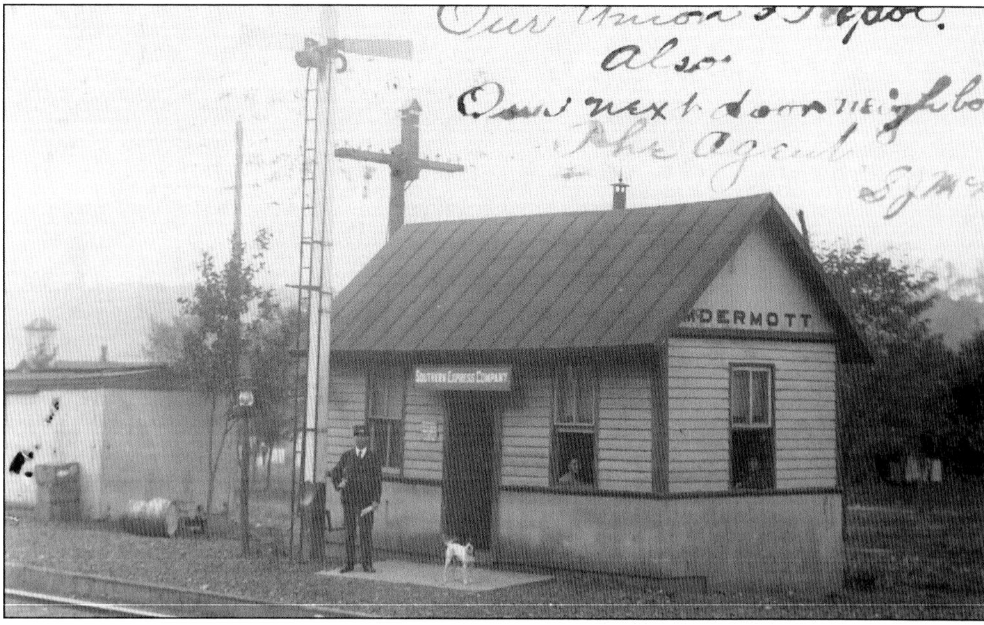

On July 28, 1898, the town of McDermott was named after William and Michael McDermott, who owned the nearby McDermott Stone Company. A railroad depot was constructed in 1903. On May 8, 1912, Pres. William Howard Taft stopped here on a special campaign train. This station was replaced in September 1915 with a larger one built with materials from the nearby McDermott Stone quarries. (Paul O'Neill Collection.)

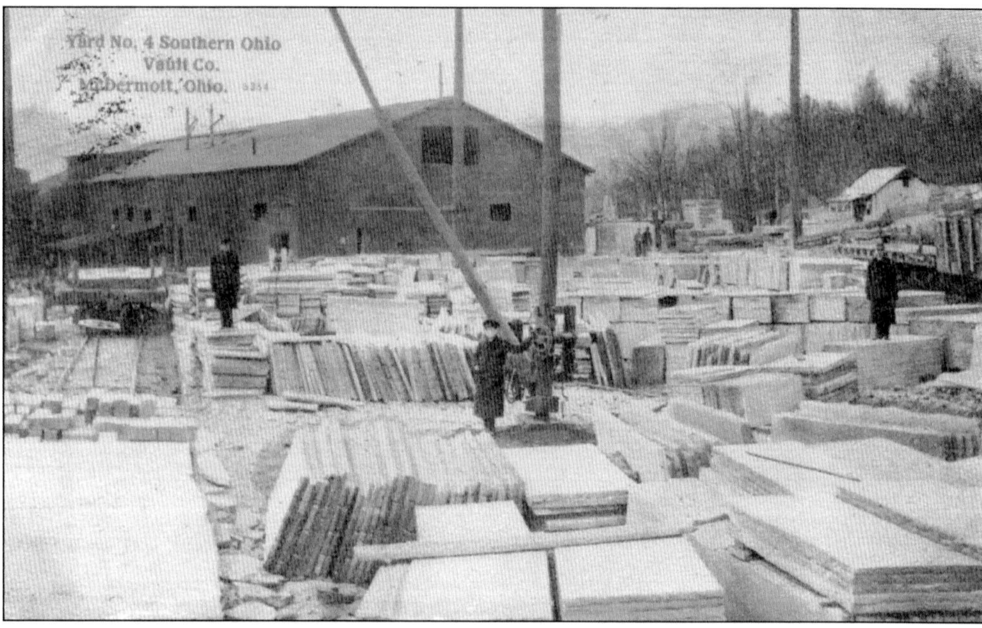

The Southern Ohio Vault Company in McDermott was one of several stone businesses in western Scioto County. Shown in this 1909 postcard, this company provided cemetery vaults for hundreds of funeral homes throughout the United States, largely thanks to the adjacent Norfolk & Western Railway. In April 1915, it became a part of the McDermott Stone Company and employed over 100 workers. (Bill Glockner Collection.)

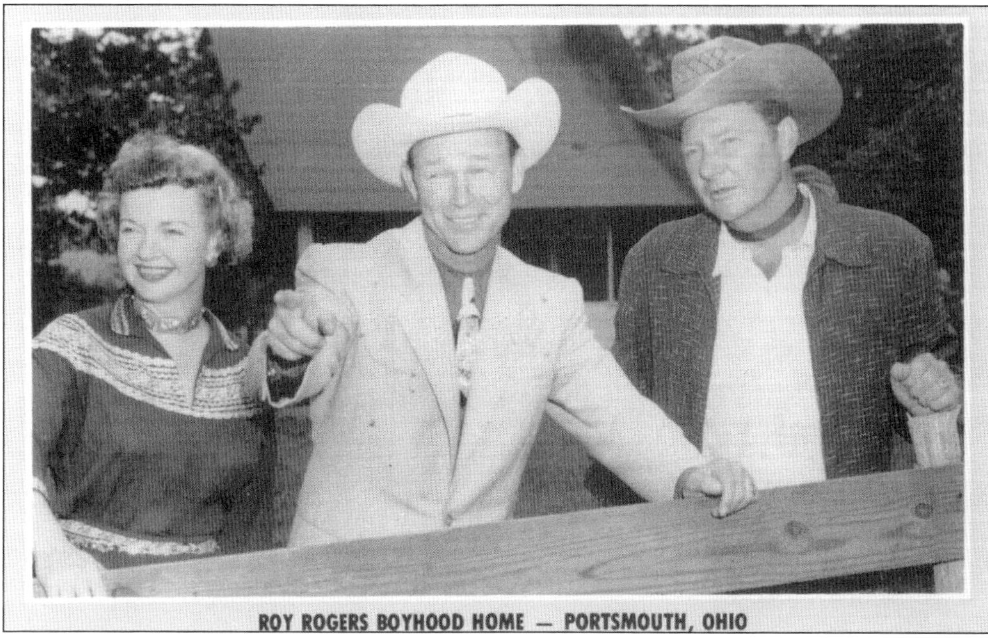

Leonard Slye was born in Cincinnati in 1911. He and his family moved to Portsmouth the following year, then to Duck Run in 1919. Slye relocated to California in 1930, and by 1937, he had become the legendary Roy Rogers. Rogers (center), with his wife, Dale Evans, and longtime friend Pat Brady, visited his Duck Run boyhood home in 1956. (Paul O'Neill Collection.)

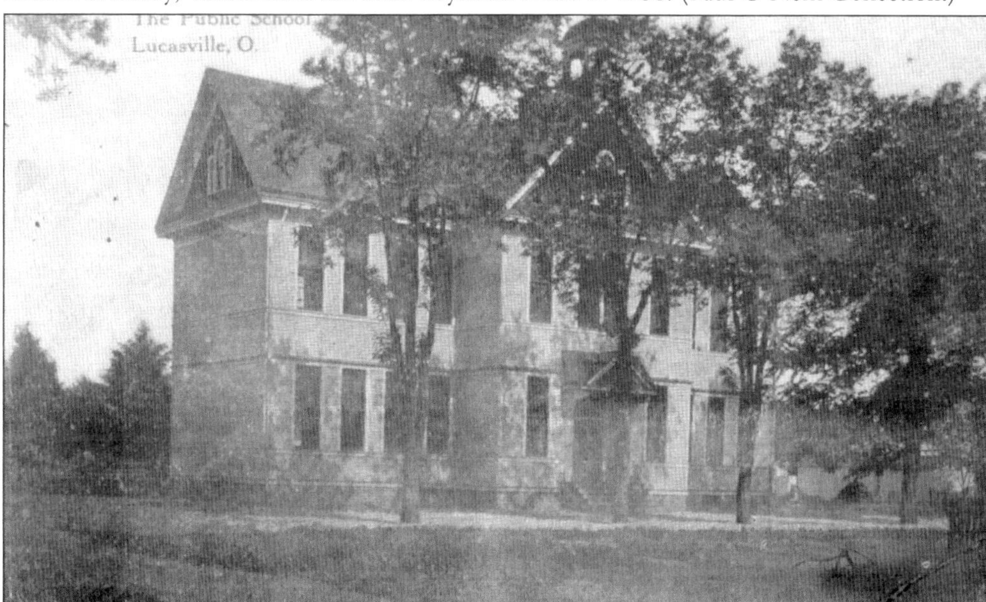

By 1910, most one-room schoolhouses scattered throughout the Lucasville area had been consolidated into Lucasville Public School, a wooden structure (pictured) with multiple floors located on the corner of Scioto and West Streets. Hundreds of children were educated here, including future baseball legend Branch Rickey. By the 1920s, modern brick schools had been constructed nearby, making this building obsolete. A private residence and American Legion log cabin occupy the property today. (Bill Glockner Collection.)

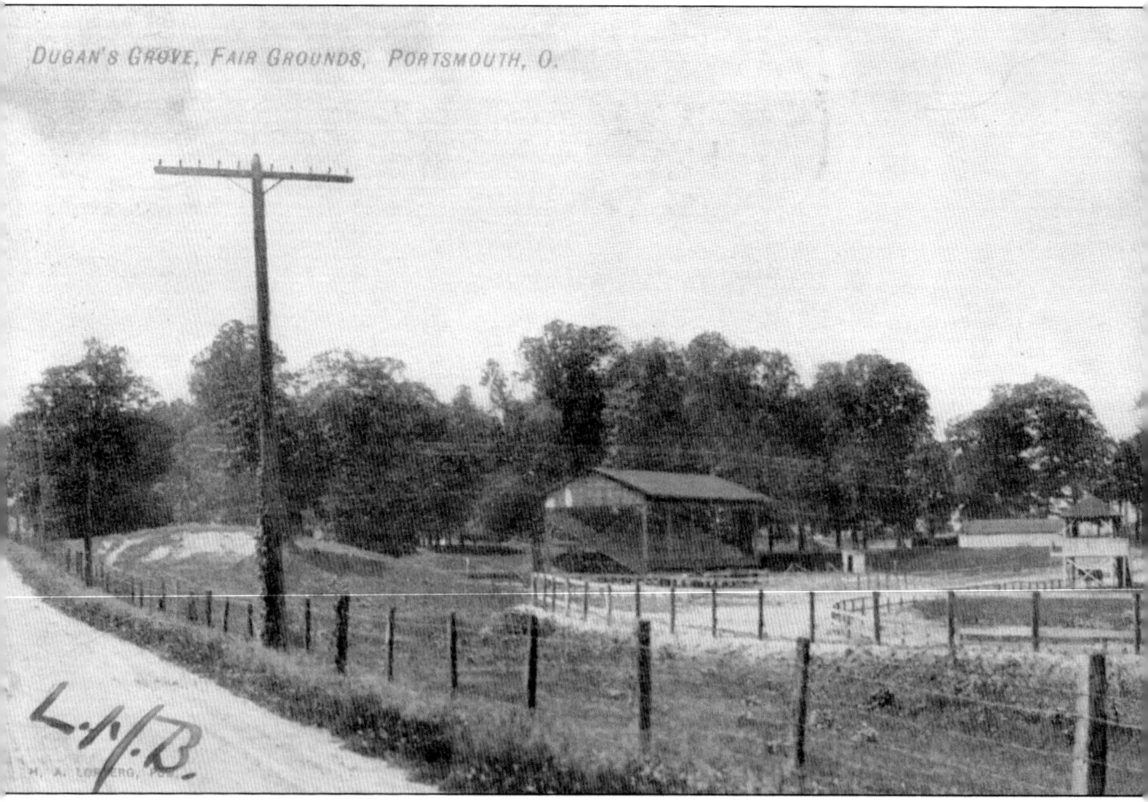

The popular Scioto County Fairgrounds in Lucasville began as a simple meadow known as Dugan's Grove. Owned by Portsmouth banker Thomas Dugan, the field was a popular spot for Civil War veterans' picnics. It was later frequently used by civic and political groups, churches, school classes, and businesses for hosting picnics, music concerts, and gatherings. In 1900, the first fair was held on the property, and it became one of three fairgrounds operating in Scioto County each year. By 1908, the three fairgrounds had merged and agreed to hold the annual festival in Lucasville. Continuously growing in size and popularity, the early fairs featured horse and motorcycle races, hot-air balloon rides, airplane rides, displays by area businesses, and exhibitions of livestock and small animals. A major improvement took place in 1925, when lights were installed throughout the property, allowing the fair to operate past sunset. The first sponsored automobile race in the county occurred here on August 23, 1936. (Bill Glockner Collection.)

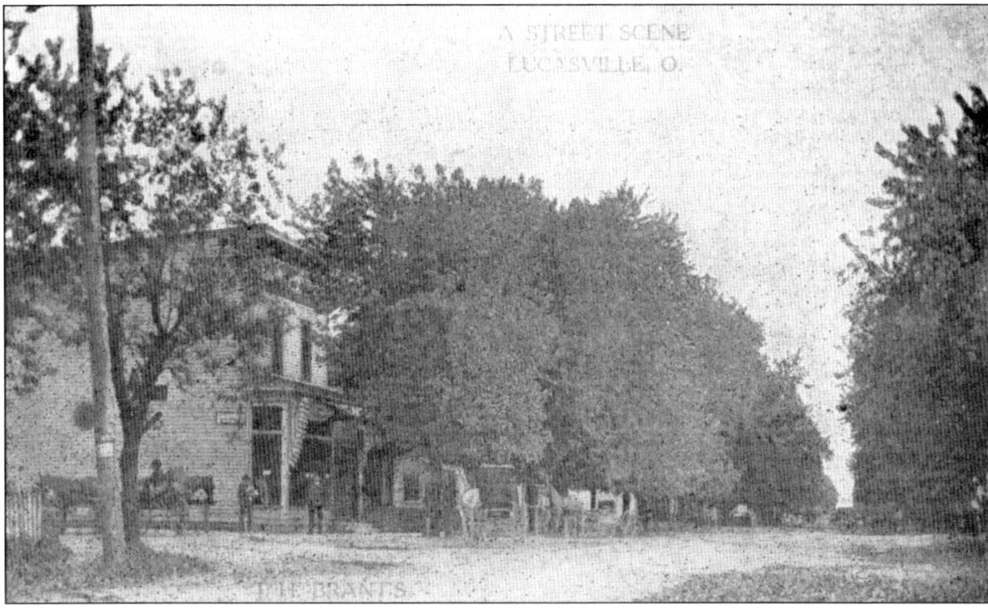

Settled in 1795 by Hezekiah Merritt, Lucasville was surveyed and named by John Lucas in 1819. This 1903 postcard shows Joseph Brant's store on Main Street, which advertised selling "everything from coal oil to hairpins." Brant's served as the town center of business and local gossip around its large potbellied stove for many years. (Bill Glockner Collection.)

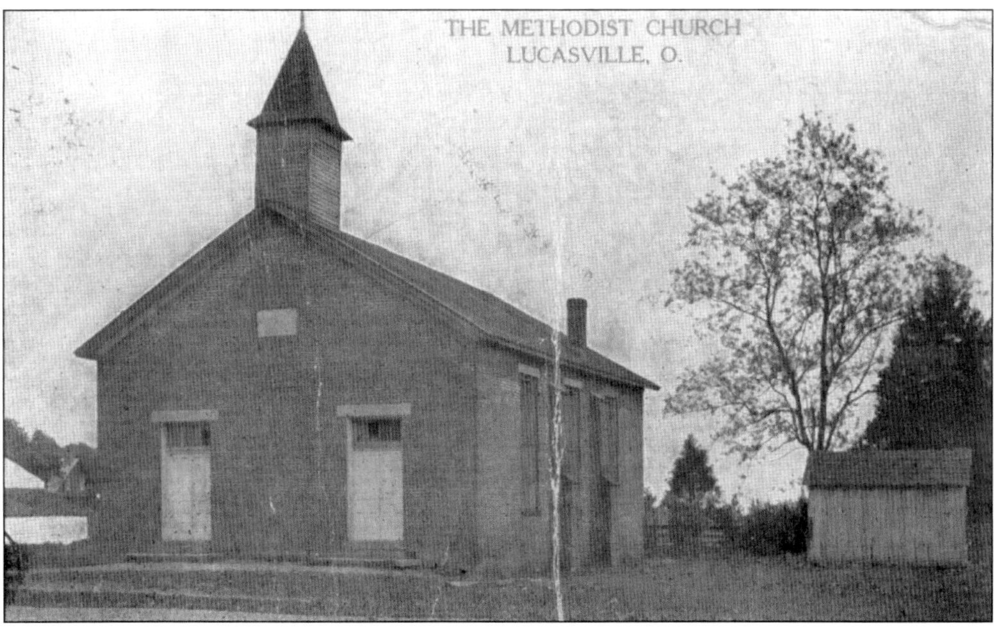

Lucasville was still in its infancy when the Methodist Episcopal church was organized in October 1849. For nearly eight decades, this brick church on Scioto Street served worshippers well. A growing congregation required a larger building, which was constructed nearby and dedicated on July 1, 1928. The bell and other items from the original church were saved for the new building, which remains standing today. (Bill Glockner Collection.)

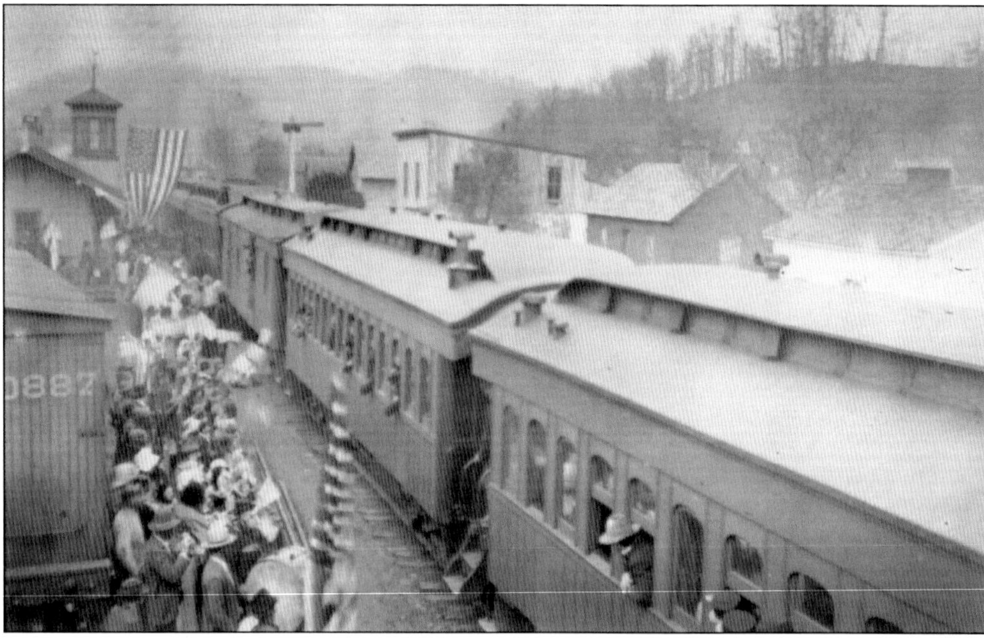

Nearly the entire town of Lucasville gave an appropriate send-off to a train filled with soldiers during the Spanish-American War in 1898. The four-piece band was comprised of local Civil War veterans, one of whom had been a prisoner of war. The Norfolk & Western depot is visible on the left, while directly across the railroad tracks is the Lucasville Hotel (the building with the flat roof).

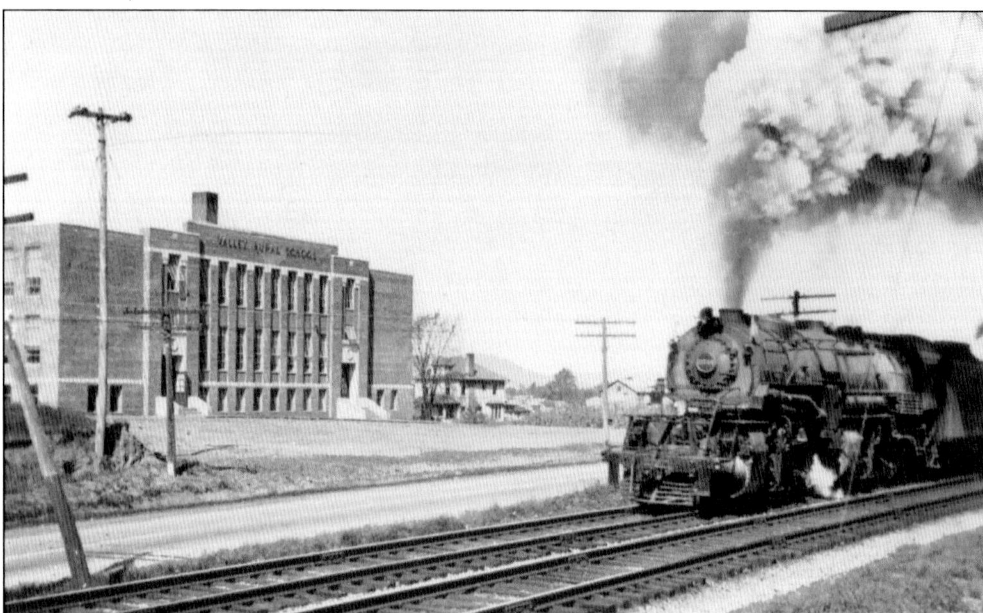

One can almost feel the ground tremble as a Norfolk & Western train roars past Lucasville's Valley High School in 1950. This everyday scene was dramatically altered when the two-lane Route 23 expanded to four lanes in 1954. This steam locomotive was replaced by diesels and scrapped in 1958. The school was converted into a middle school in 1956 and razed in February 2003.

Three

Friendship and West Portsmouth

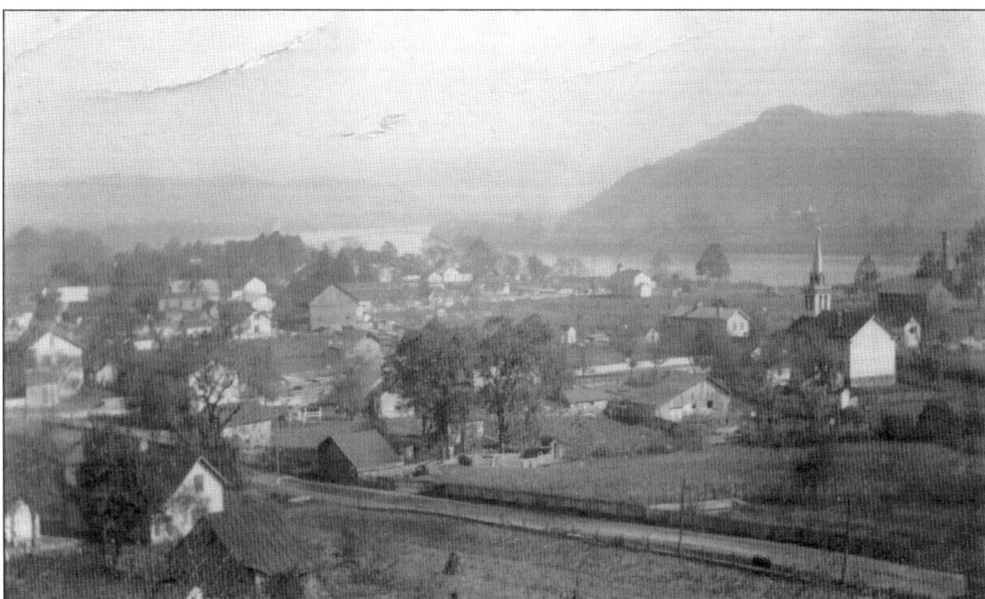

In 1846, the United States began a two-year war with Mexico over boundary disputes in the southwest. One of many battles was fought near the village of Buena Vista, Mexico, and ended in an American victory. In 1850, when this Ohio River settlement was planned, a vote was cast to honor the victors of the battle with the name Buena Vista, which remains today. (Bill Glockner Collection.)

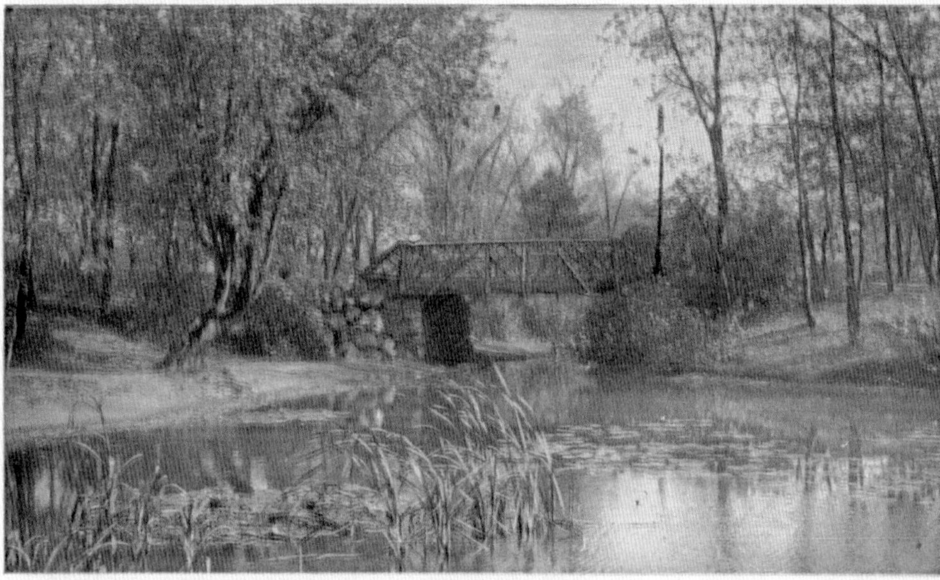

Greetings from FRIENDSHIP, Ohio

The pleasantly named community of Friendship began soon after the creation of Nile Township in August 1803. Its early businesses consisted of a blacksmith shop, cooper shop, and a gristmill. In 1835, a Methodist church was built. By 1900, the township contained 10 one-room schoolhouses scattered throughout the area. Famed Major League Baseball legend Branch Rickey taught at a school near Turkey Creek for two years for a salary of $35 per month. Friendship native Al Bridwell also claimed fame on the baseball field, playing for several professional teams in the early 1900s, including the Cincinnati Reds, New York Giants, and Chicago Cubs. Both Rickey and Bridwell are buried within their native Scioto County. (Both, Bill Glockner Collection.)

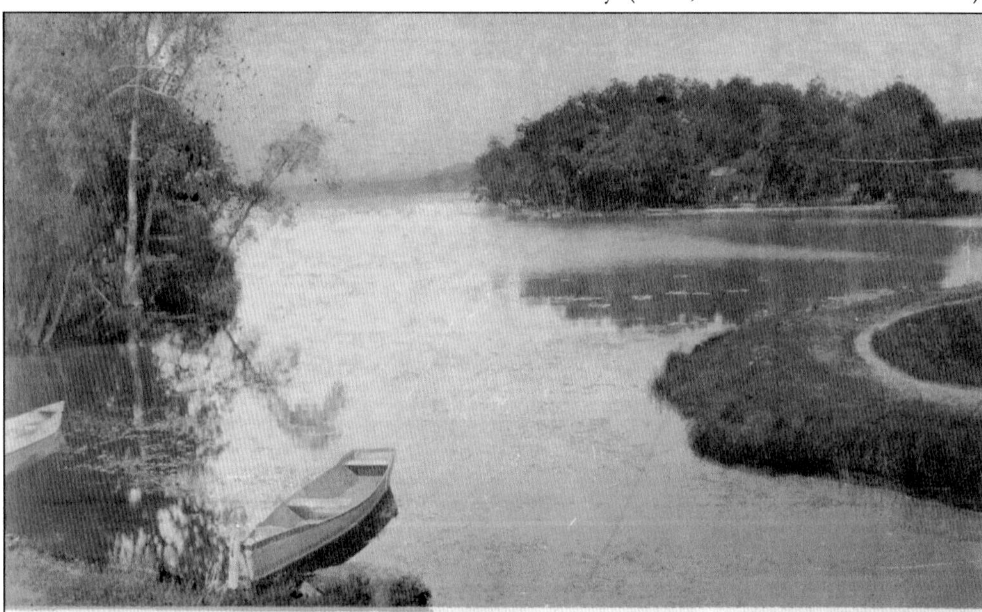

Greetings from FRIENDSHIP, Ohio.

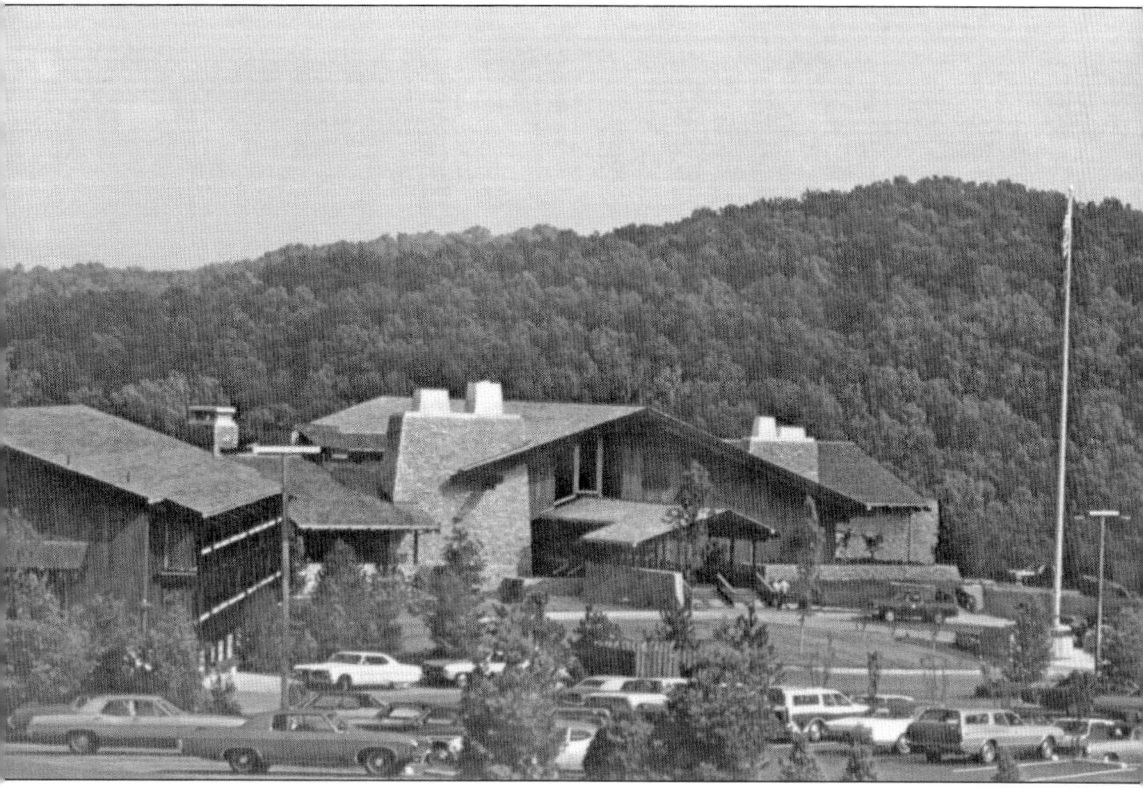

Over 5,000 people attended the grand opening festivities of the impressive Shawnee State Lodge on January 14, 1973. Constructed at a cost of $3.4 million, the lodge was part of a nearly $5-million expansion of the recreational facilities at Portsmouth State Park, later renamed Shawnee State Park. In addition to the 50 guest rooms, the lodge's interior included a spacious lobby with fireplaces, meeting and banquet rooms, a coffee shop, an indoor pool, a game room, and a restaurant that can compete with any in the entire region. The murals and furnishings decorating the lodge reflect the Shawnee culture. The exterior featured a separate outdoor swimming pool, tennis and basketball courts, shuffleboard, and badminton. Shawnee State Park—which is tucked inside the 63,000 acres of Shawnee State Forest, the largest state forest in Ohio—is one of the best parks in both Scioto County and Ohio. (Paul O'Neill Collection.)

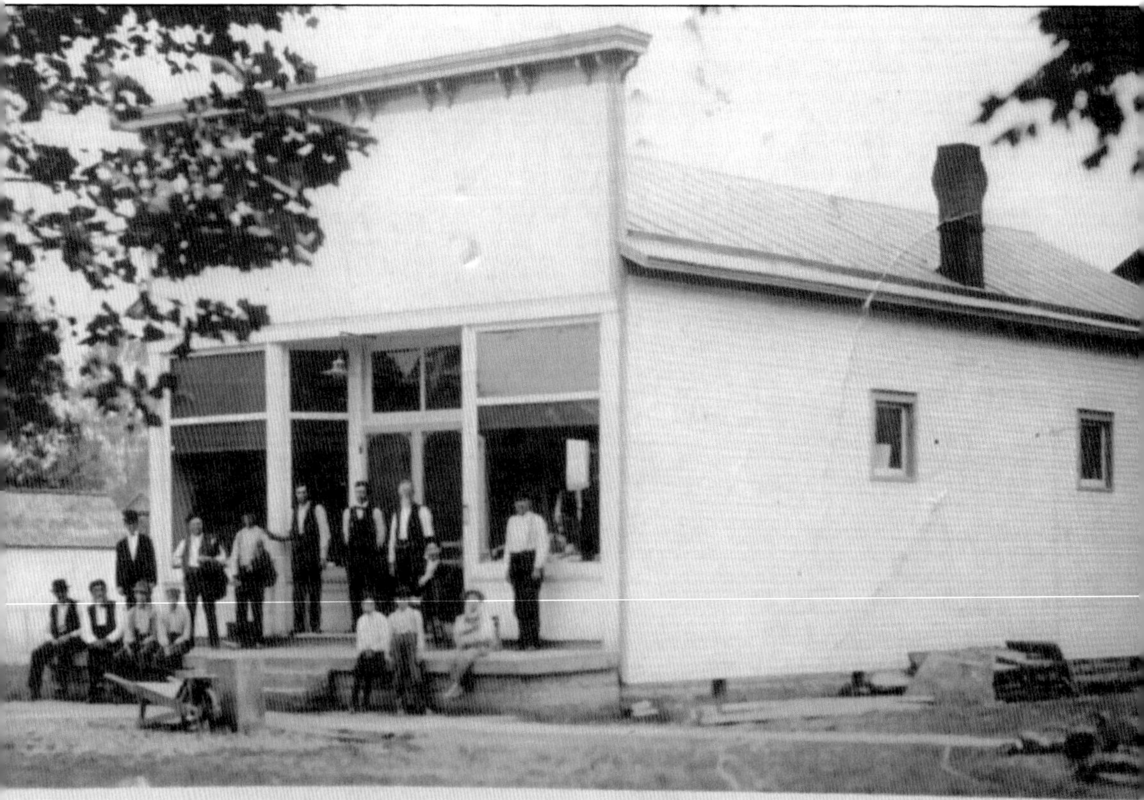

J. J. Pieper & Co's Store, Buena Vista, O.

John Pieper was already a successful tobacco farmer in Otway when he, along with James Blackburn, opened a general store in Otway in 1896. In January 1910, Pieper opened a mercantile store of his own on Main Street in Buena Vista. The store is shown on this postcard, which depicts it shortly after opening. While still living in Otway, Pieper continued to operate both stores successfully until the one in Otway was destroyed in a fire in April 1916. After reopening the Otway store six months after the fire, Pieper enjoyed continued success. In addition to operating two stores, he served on the Otway village council, was vice president of the Otway Savings Bank, and was a cosponsor of an Otway basketball team that traveled throughout the area challenging other communities for bragging rights as to which town was the most athletic in the mid-1920s. (Sharon Bender Collection.)

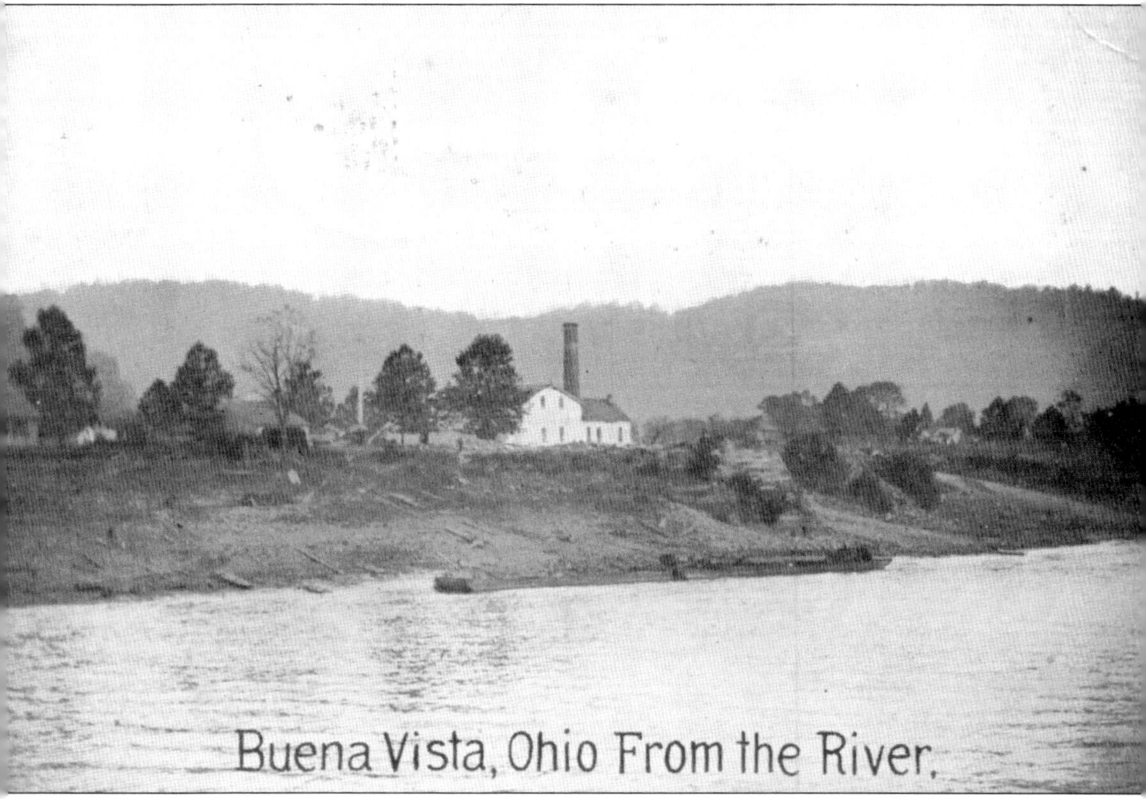

Soon after Buena Vista was settled in 1848, an enormous amount of undisturbed stone was discovered beneath hundreds of acres of virgin forests. By the mid-1850s, several stone quarries began operating throughout the many hilltops in the area. Stone was removed and sent for processing to larger buildings like the one shown here. Tramways transferred stone from the hills either by mechanical means or by mules and wagons. Large pieces were cut to the desired size here or shipped by flatboats on the Ohio River and then cut at the construction site. The excellent grade of rock was used for many buildings and sidewalks in Cincinnati as well as the piers for the famous Roebling Suspension Bridge. Concrete, a less expensive construction option, became more popular near the end of the 19th century, which led to the closing of the area's last quarry in 1903. (Bill Glockner Collection.)

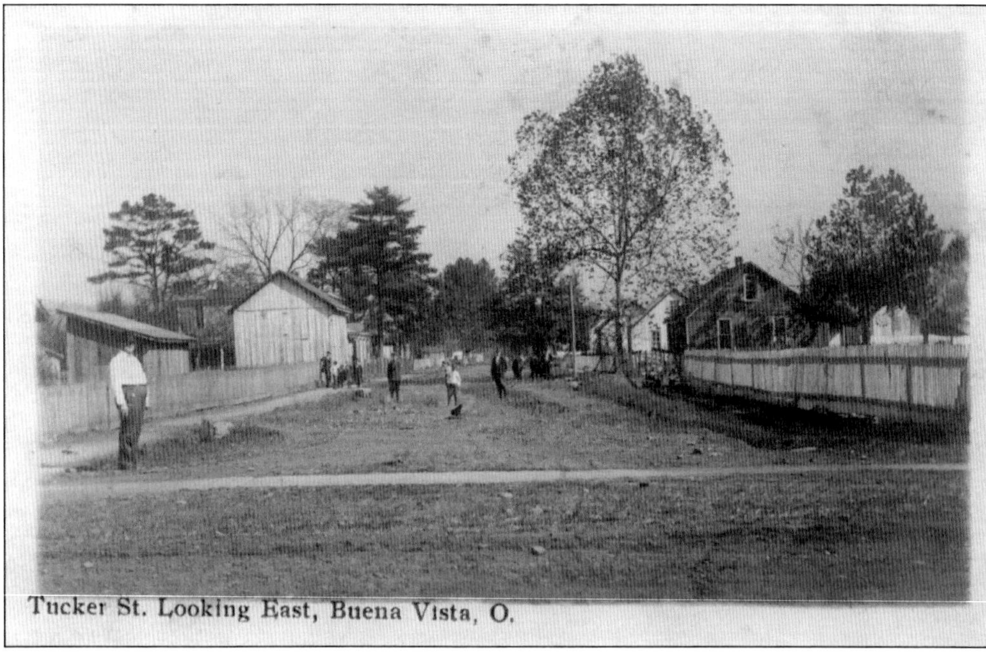

Nearly a dozen people stopped to pose along Tucker Street in Buena Vista in this c. 1910 postcard. In 1848, Cyrus McCormick, who built the first house in Buena Vista, also operated the community general store. A blacksmith, livery stable, hotel, and railroad-tie manufacturer soon followed. The town doctors, W.A. Frizell and his son James, were proprietors of the town drugstore. (Bill Glockner Collection.)

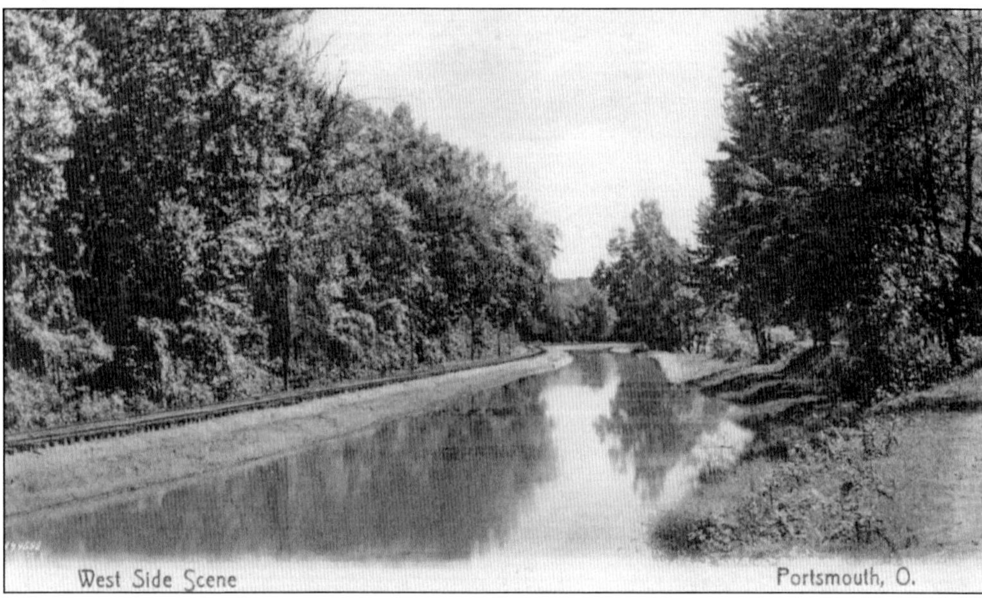

Looking southward near West Portsmouth in this picturesque c. 1890 postcard, one can see the Ohio & Erie Canal and the rails for the Cincinnati, Portsmouth & Virginia Railroad. The towpath for the canal is barely visible on the far right. In 1895, Portsmouth High School decided to use this image in their invitations for that year's commencement ceremonies at the Grand Opera House in Portsmouth.

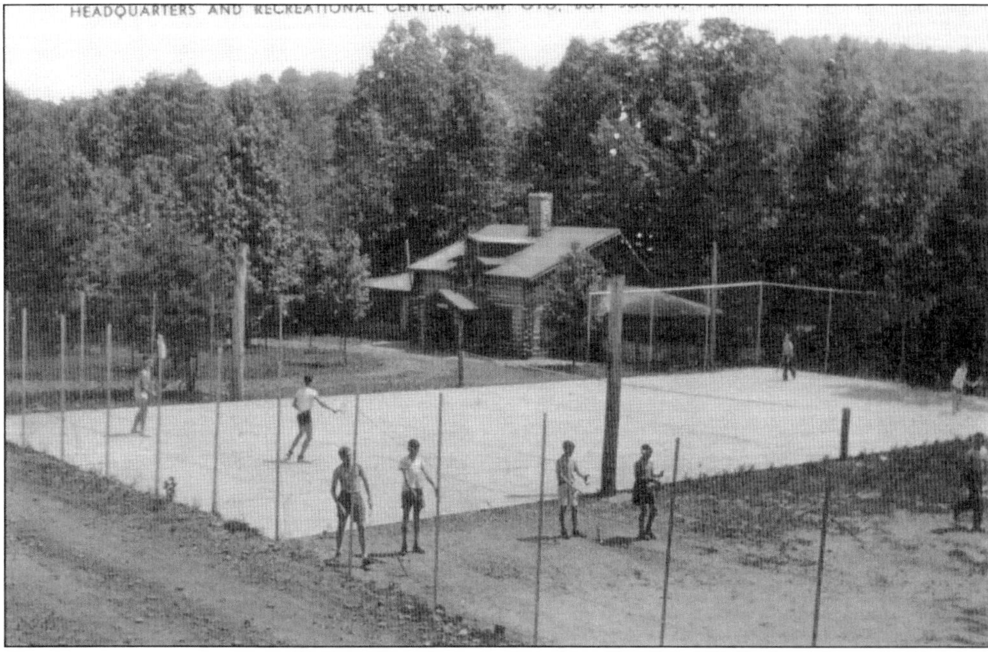

The Boy Scouts of America Camp Oyo, located near State Route 125, opened in August 1926. Named after a local Indian tribe's term for the Ohio River, Oyo provided early campers with numerous activities thanks to donations from many local businessmen. The successful first summer saw over 200 Scouts enjoying hiking, swimming, and sleeping outdoors in large Army tents. Meals were served in a large dining hall that could seat 100. Camp Oyo expanded in the 1930s to include horseshoes and tennis courts (above), additional log cabins with fireplaces, and a swimming pool (below) built in 1938. Multiple expansions and improvements have continued in the years since. Camp Oyo is still very active today, and thousands of area Boy Scouts and dedicated volunteers have enjoyed unforgettable experiences during its 90-plus-year history.

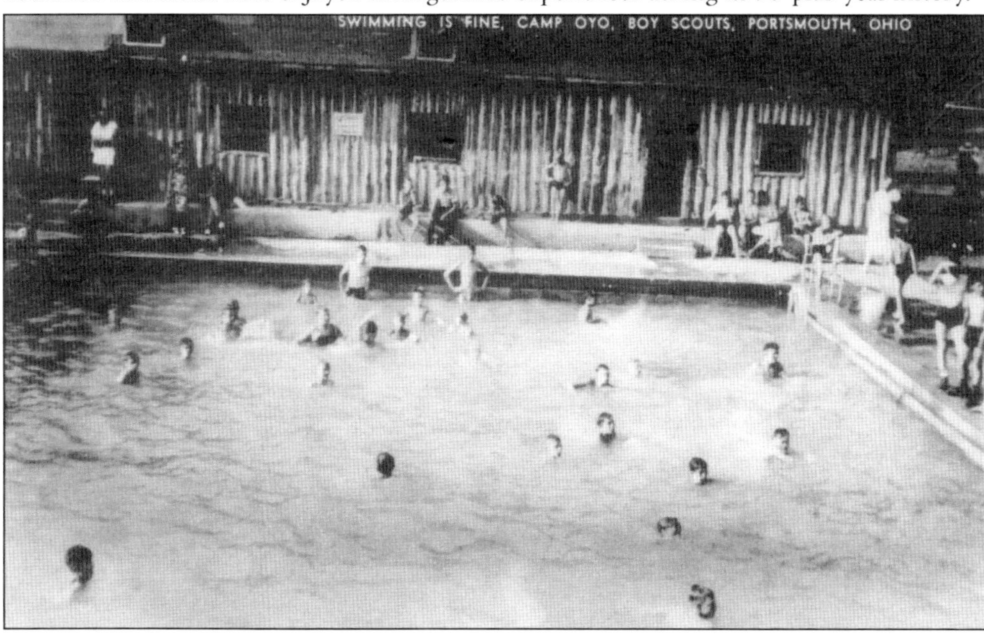

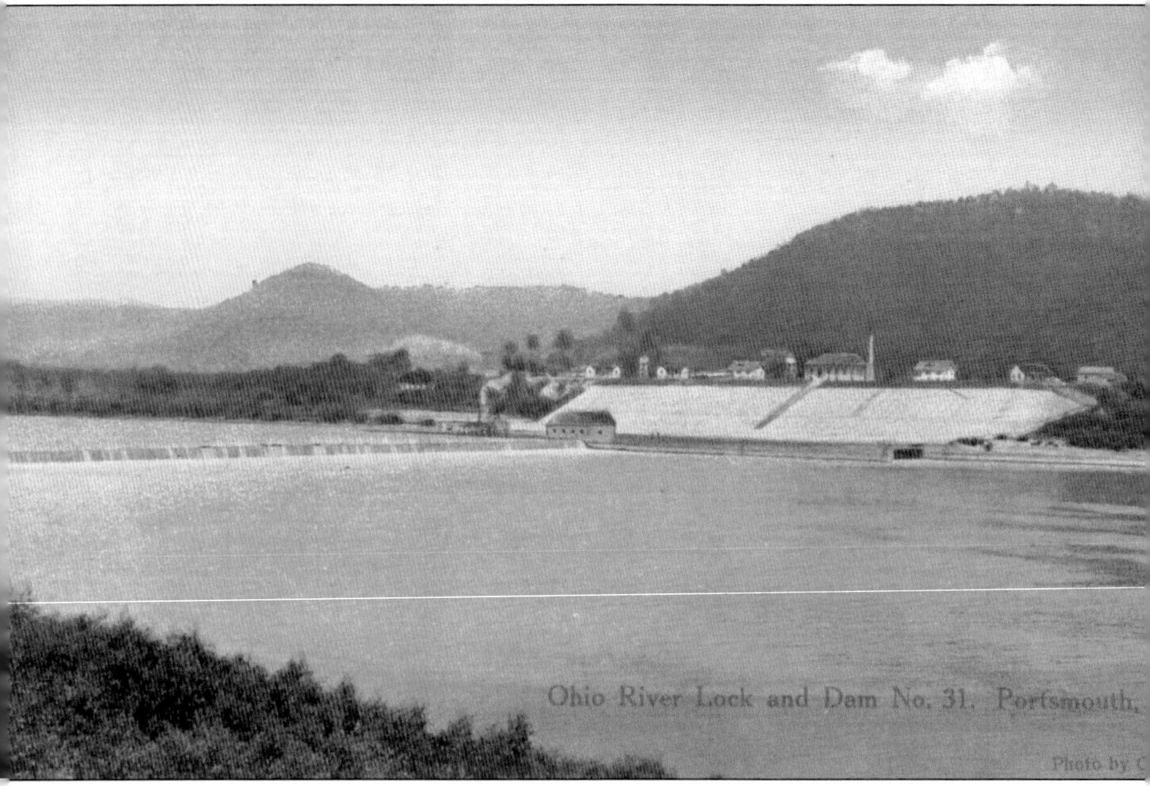

Ohio River Dam No. 31 was located near the current site of the Washington-Nile Schools complex in West Portsmouth. Dedicated on July 15, 1920, the dam was one of 53 locks and dams built by the federal government between Pittsburgh and Cairo, Illinois, between 1879 and 1929. Shown in this c. 1920 view looking toward Kentucky are buildings used as living quarters for the employees, a power-generating plant, a blacksmith shop, and other maintenance buildings. For nearly 50 years, Dam No. 31 was a vital facility for riverboats traveling the mighty Ohio River. In the early 1960s, the more modern Meldahl Locks and Dam began operating downstream and made Dam No. 31 obsolete. The last towboat went through Dam No. 31's locks on August 14, 1964, and the dam was dismantled almost immediately thereafter. The structures survived and were acquired by local businessman Edward "Ebby" Glockner in March 1967. The Glockner family still owns the property, and thanks to their preservation efforts, it was listed in the National Register of Historic Places on May 12, 1987. (Paul O'Neill Collection.)

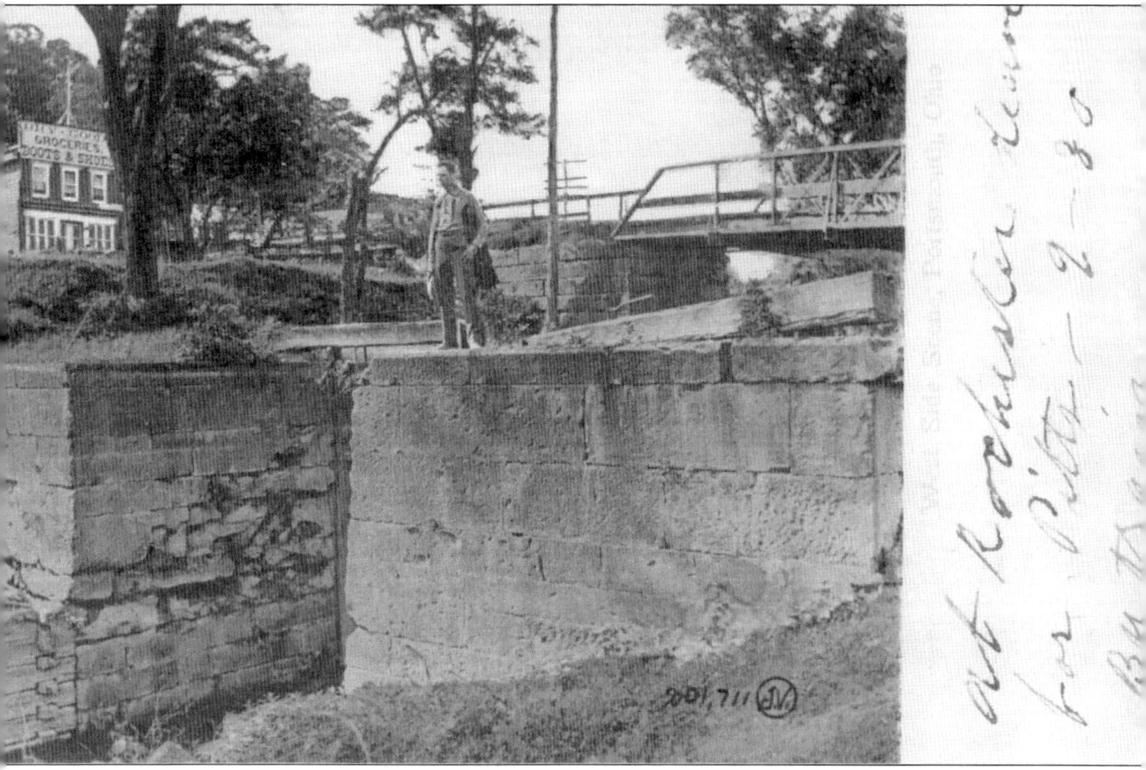

An unidentified man stands near Lock No. 50 in this 1908 postcard of Union Mills, located near present-day West Portsmouth. Perhaps he was envisioning his next fishing trip on the extremely slow-running water of the Ohio & Erie Canal, where locals bragged of catching bass weighing in at five pounds or more. The general store and post office for Bertha (the previous name of West Portsmouth) is visible in the background at left. The structure, which was destroyed by fire in 1911, was rebuilt only to be nearly destroyed a second time by a 1913 flood, but the building was reconstructed once again. However, the Ohio & Erie Canal, which was already suffering from low revenue due to the railroads and rapidly improving highways, was delivered one last devastating blow by Mother Nature and ceased to operate following the flood. (Paul O'Neill Collection.)

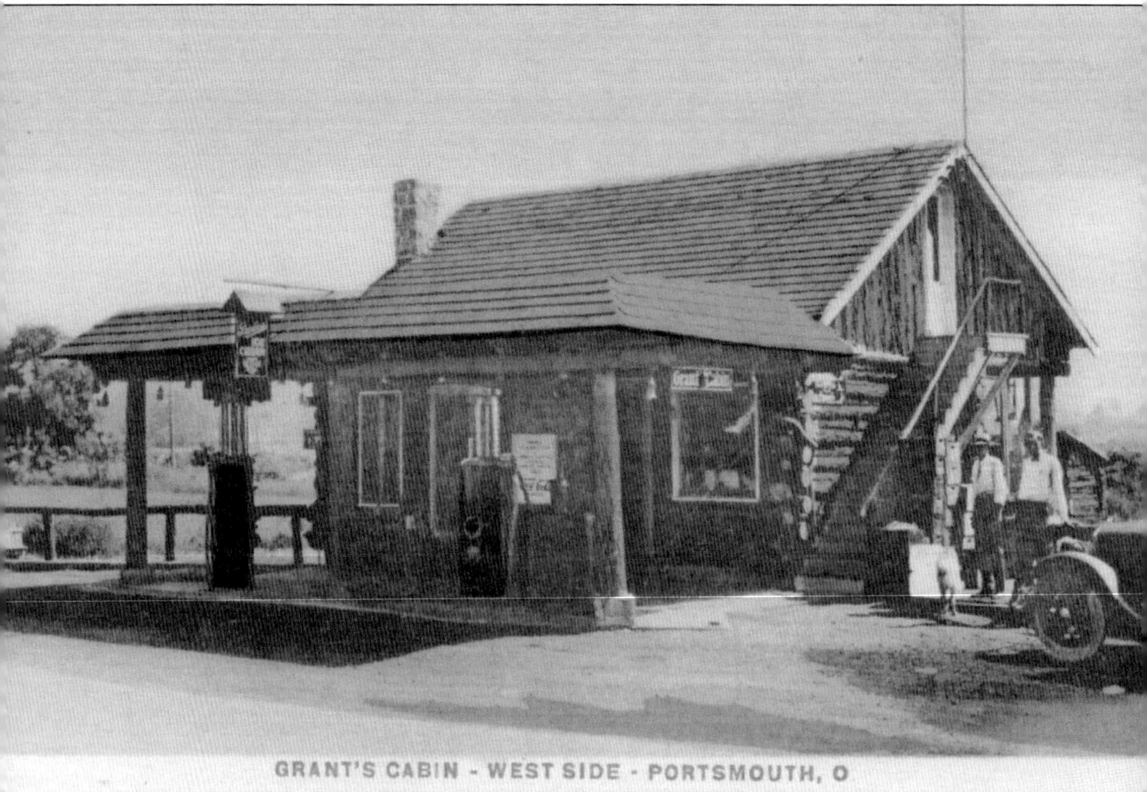

Grant's Cabin was located on Galena Pike at Coles Park, along present-day State Route 73, on the same property as tanneries operated by Orville Grant, brother of Gen. Ulysses S. Grant, during the mid-1800s. The re-created log cabin featured a gas station, along with a small restaurant specializing in barbecue, fried chicken, spaghetti, and beer. Grant's Cabin presented live entertainment nightly from local bands and also hosted square dances in an outdoor pavilion on special occasions. Financial difficulties forced the business to be sold in September 1935, but money problems continued for the new owner. In September 1939, it was purchased by a New Boston magistrate. Oddly enough, less than one year later, the magistrate was arrested for having an illegal gambling device within the building. After pleading guilty, he served one year of probation. Grant's Cabin continued to operate into the early days of World War II. (Bill Glockner Collection.)

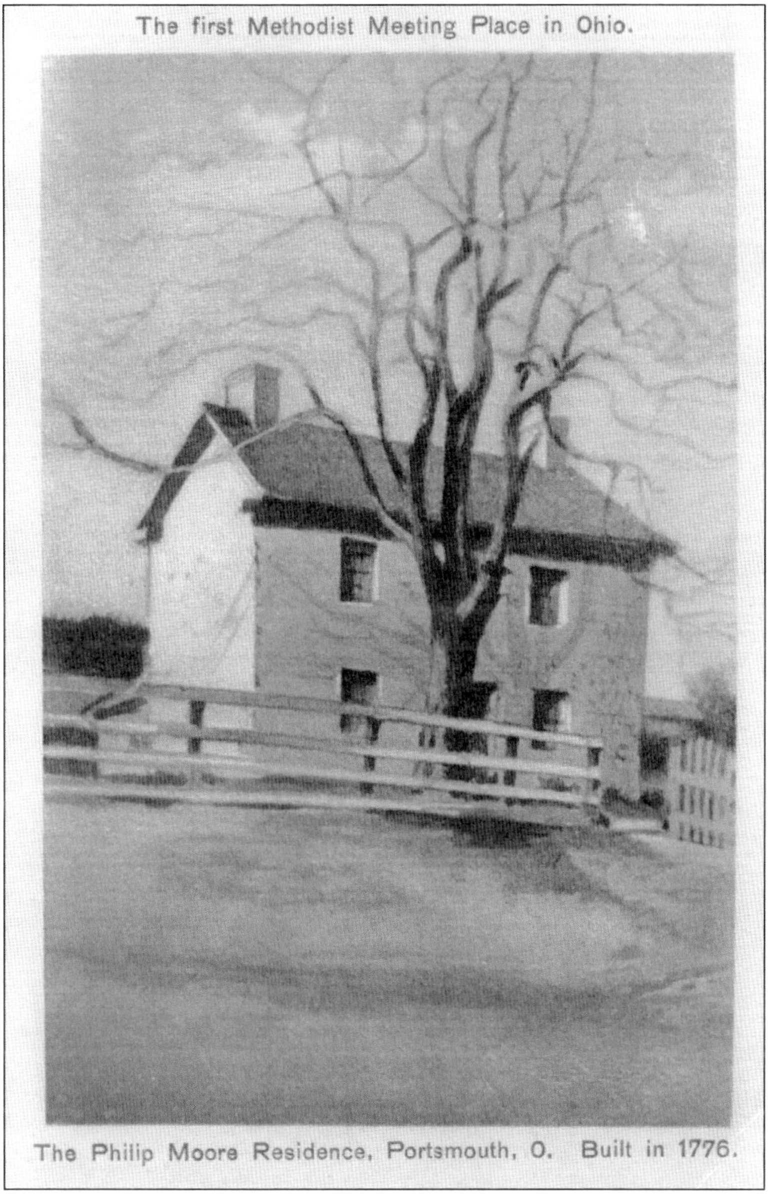

Revolutionary War veteran Philip Moore brought his family from Pennsylvania to Alexandria in 1797, six years before Ohio became a state, erecting a stone house constructed from local sandstone and placed at a high elevation. Moore's house survived the multiple floods that eventually destroyed the settlement. The first church services held in Scioto County were conducted in Moore's stone house, and it soon became an important stop for traveling Methodist ministers wanting to expand their church. It is widely believed that this was the birthplace of the Methodist church in Ohio. Considered the oldest house in Scioto County, this structure changed owners several times. In the 1930s, it became the Stone House Tavern, which featured nightly entertainment, sandwiches, and beer. The property was purchased by Dr. Louis and Ava Chaboudy in 1973, and the beautifully restored home was listed in the National Register of Historic Places in 1975. Local radio personality Steve Hayes purchased the property in 2005 and has successfully maintained the historic home. (Bill Glockner Collection.)

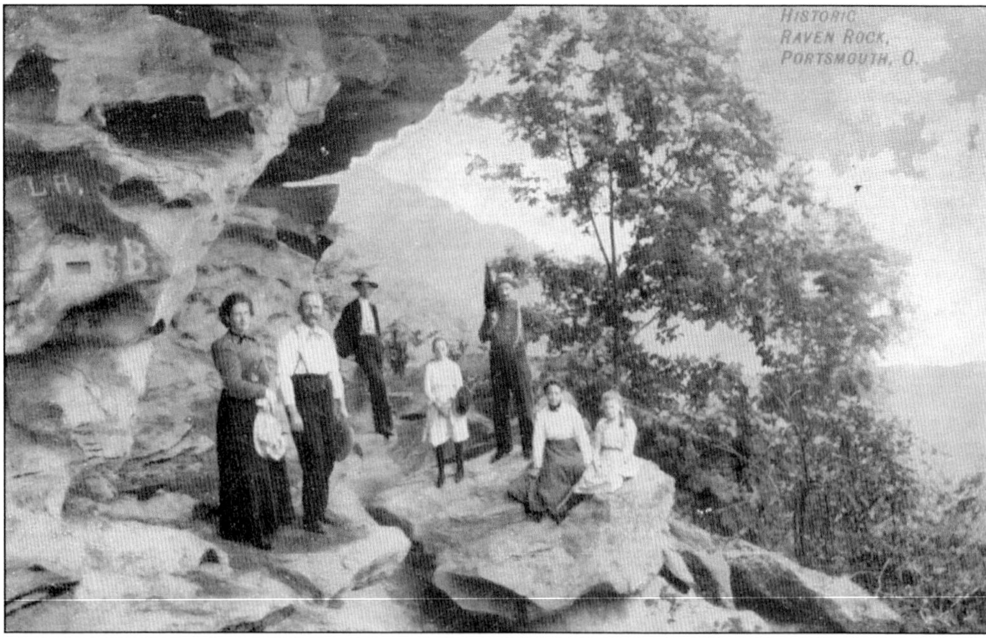

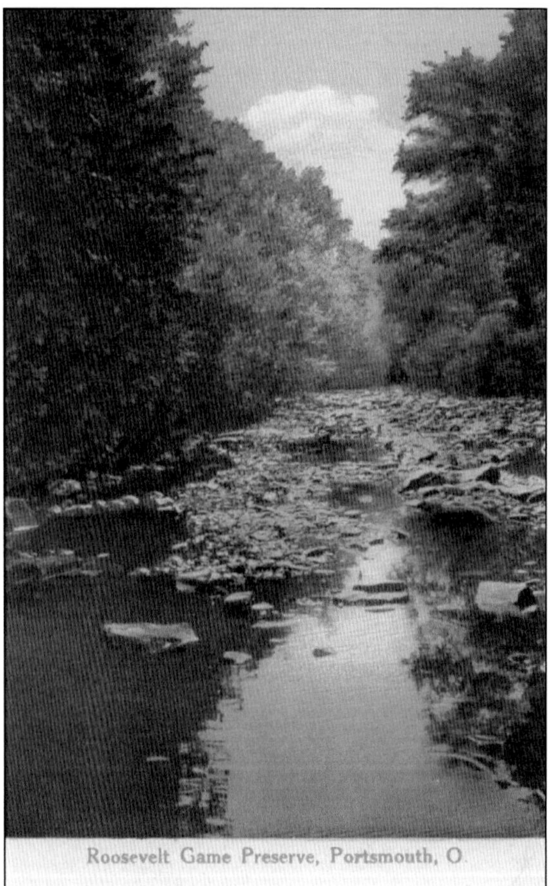

Initially used by Native Americans as a lookout, Raven Rock, shown in this c. 1910 postcard, became popular for those wanting to enjoy nature's wonder. The stone promontory is nearly 500 feet high, and approximately 14 miles of the winding Ohio River and its surroundings can be viewed from its vantage point. The Ohio Department of Natural Resources requires visitors to acquire a special permit to access the landmark. (Paul O'Neill Collection.)

Turkey Creek, likely named for the many feathered friends that used it, is located within the Theodore Roosevelt Game Preserve, which opened in 1922 and became part of Shawnee State Forest in 1951. Although the preserve was picturesque, it kept local game wardens busy in the 1920s due to poachers taking advantage of animals drinking from streams and moonshiners operating stills in the wilderness area. (Paul O'Neill Collection.)

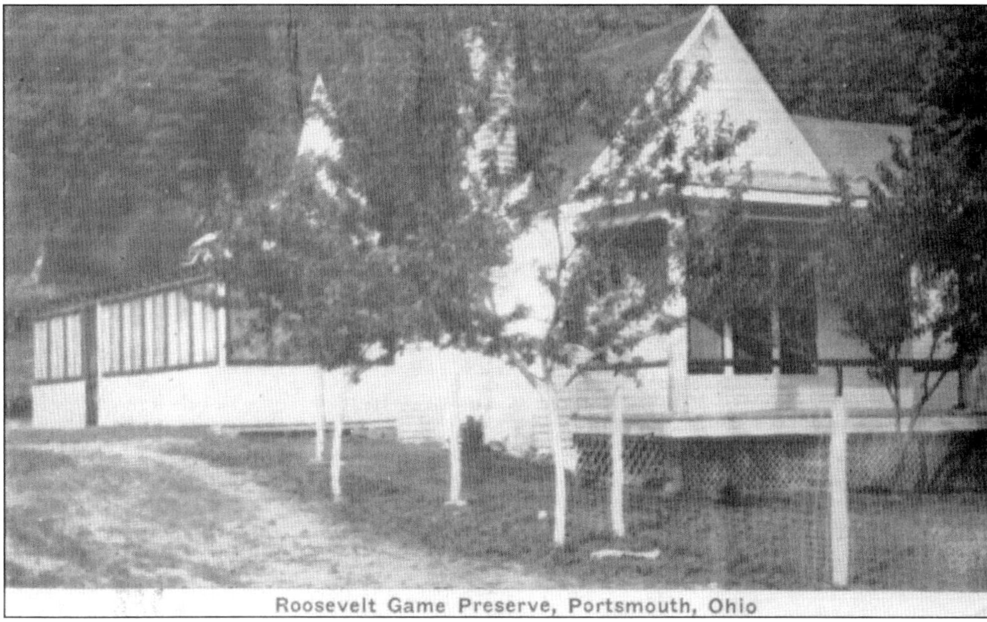

The Theodore Roosevelt Game Preserve opened in 1922 and was located in the forests of southwestern Scioto County. Encompassing over 20,000 acres, the sanctuary protected wildlife that was becoming rare in Southern Ohio. The Theodore Roosevelt Game Preserve headquarters cottage contained dining areas for guests and offices for park rangers assigned to protect the animals. The preserve became a part of Shawnee State Forest in 1951. (Bill Glockner Collection.)

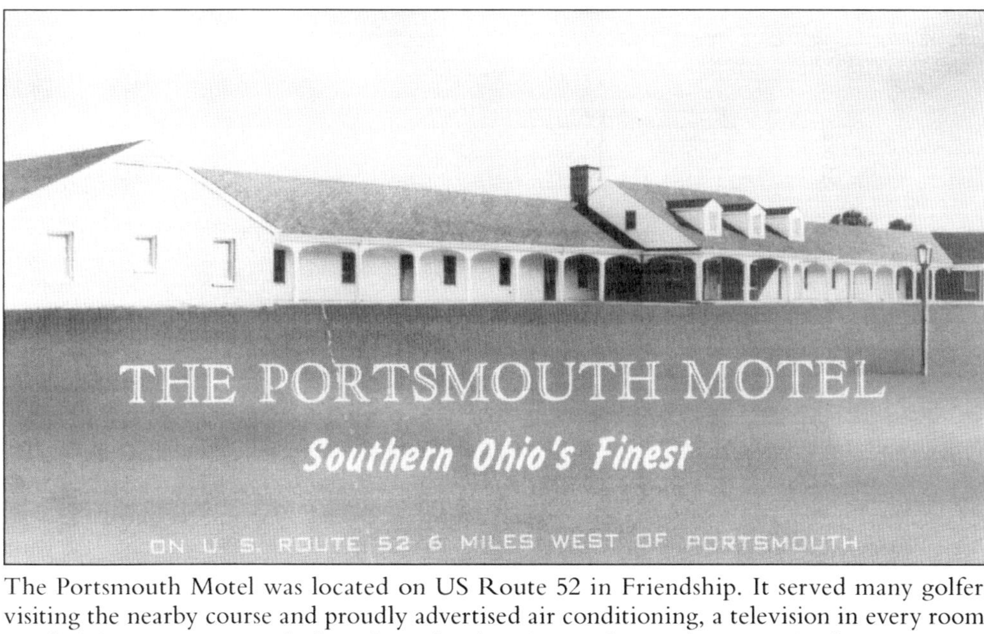

The Portsmouth Motel was located on US Route 52 in Friendship. It served many golfers visiting the nearby course and proudly advertised air conditioning, a television in every room, an adjoining restaurant, and a large heated swimming pool. Later known as Buckeye Inn Motel and Quality Courts Motel, the building remains in use today as the Country Living Assisted Living Center. (Paul O'Neill Collection.)

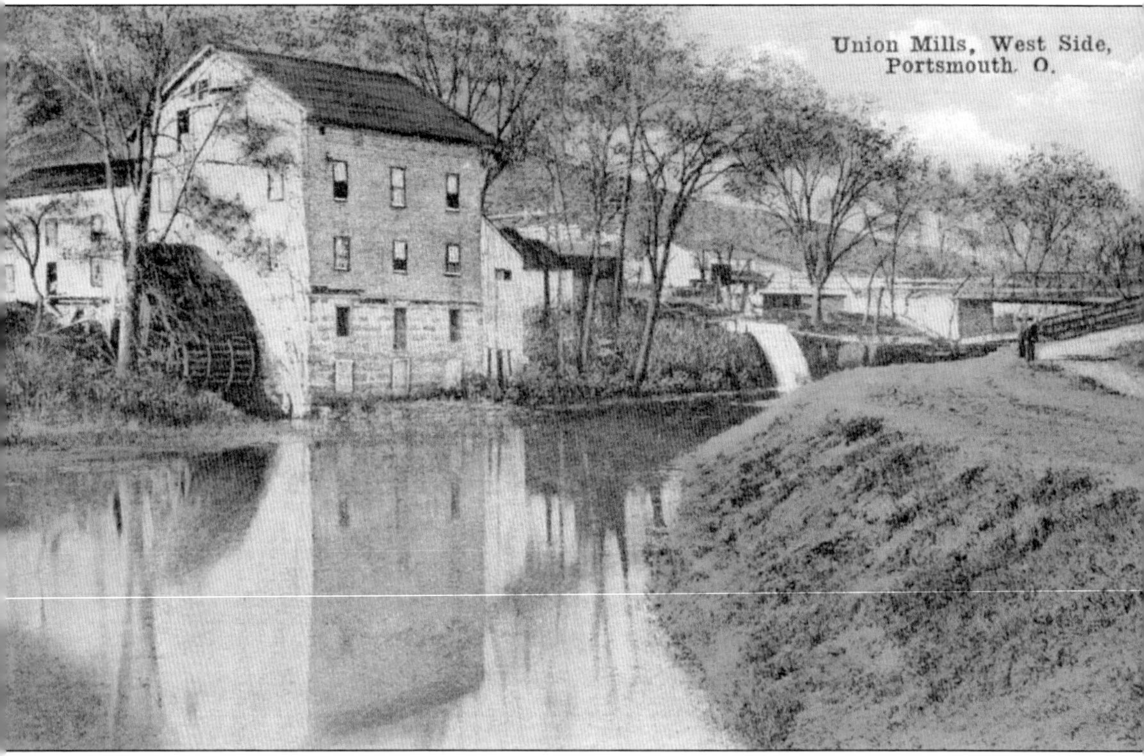

The importance of the Ohio & Erie Canal in the early development of both Ohio and Scioto County cannot be overstated. Completed in December 1832 after seven years of construction, the 308-mile waterway stretched between Cleveland and Portsmouth. Built for an initial cost of $2.3 million (an extraordinary sum in 1832), the canal featured 146 locks along its system. Since the canal allowed only one boat at a time to pass through a lock in a process that took nearly 15 minutes, bottlenecks would frequently occur, with boats sometimes waiting for hours. Taking advantage of the circumstances, entrepreneurs along the canal soon opened shops and other businesses for the benefit of temporarily stranded boat crews and passengers. Small communities such as Union Mills (pictured) were soon formed. Union Mills featured a gristmill and distillery that could grind 600 bushels of corn and produce 2,000 gallons of whiskey per day. Union Mills Confectionery now stands on this site located near the historical Lock No. 50. (Bill Glockner Collection.)

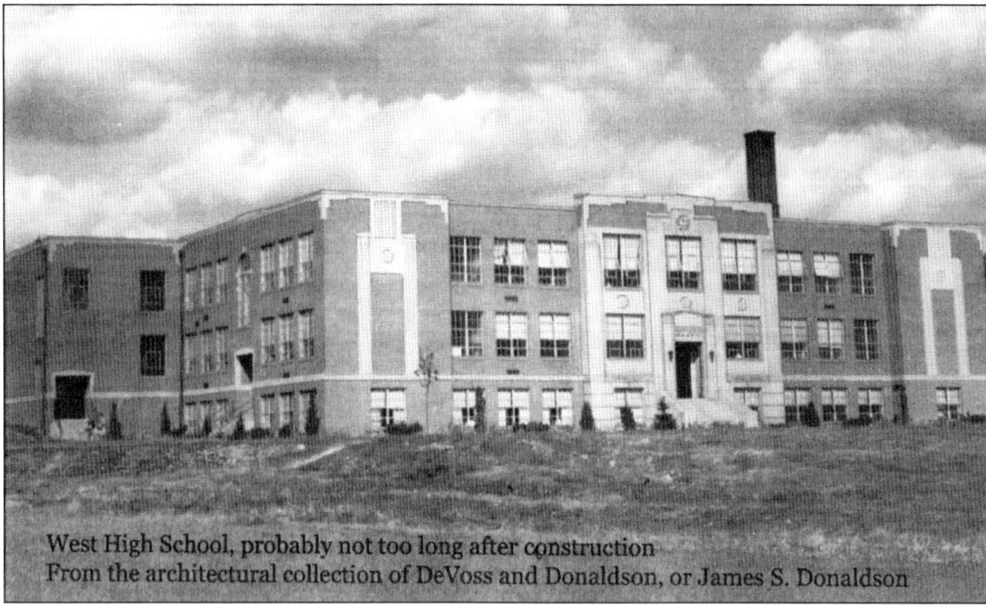

Washington High School (later renamed West High School) opened in 1939 at Fifth Street and Calverts Lane and was the first high school in West Portsmouth. Student enrollment increased in the 1950s due to the booming economy. The building was converted to Nauvoo Elementary School in 1969 and remained as such until 1998, when new schools were built along US Route 52. The building was razed shortly thereafter.

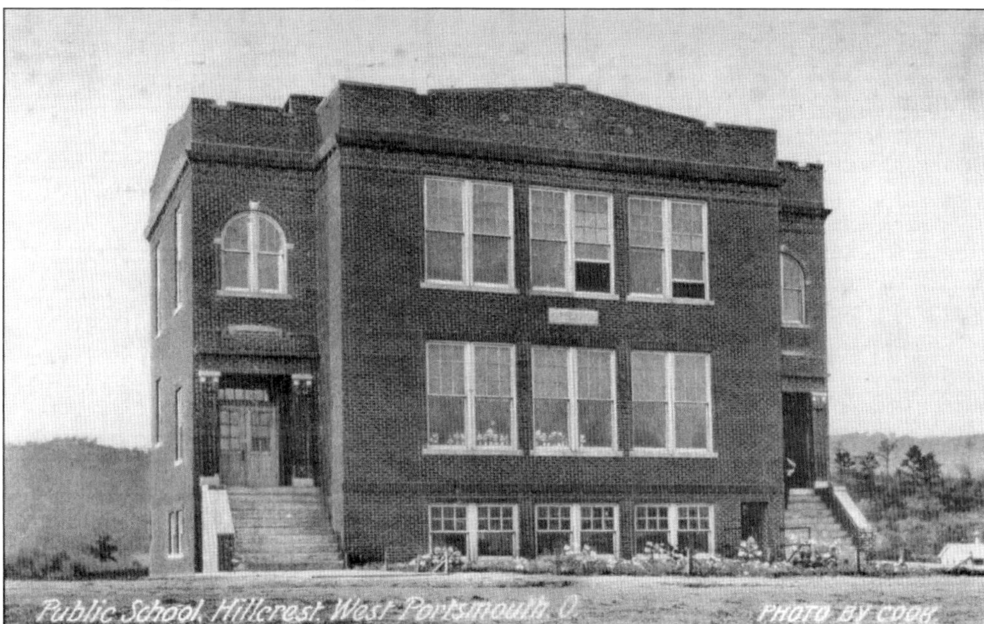

Constructed around 1921, Hillcrest School was located on Calverts Lane and was a part of the early Nauvoo school system. This brick structure replaced a wooden one-room building and housed an average of 200 students per year in grades one through eight. Due to the school being located at a high elevation, it served as a temporary home for refugees during the 1937 flood. (Bill Glockner Collection.)

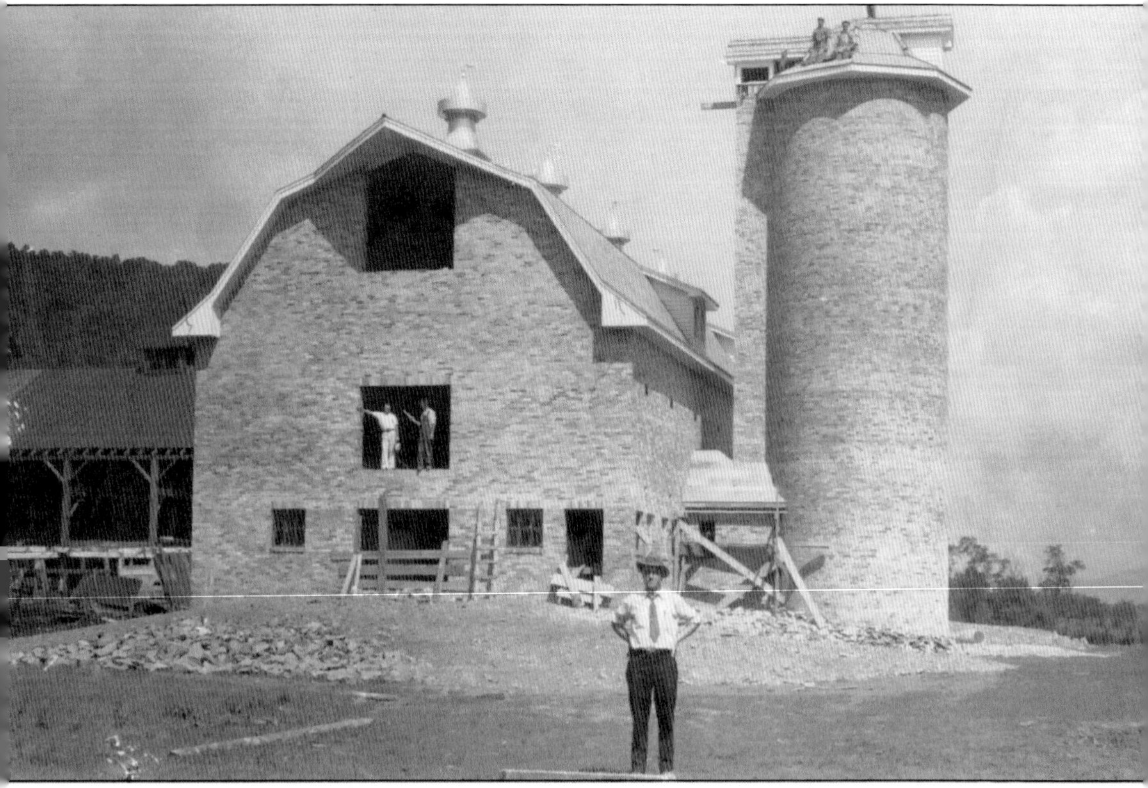

Constructed in 1847 and overseen by Scioto County commissioners, the Scioto County Infirmary was located at present-day US Route 52 and Carey's Run Road. It provided long-term housing for the poor suffering from various physical or mental illnesses. The patients were housed in separate buildings depending on their conditions and were often referred to as "inmates" by insensitive outsiders. The massive operating costs were offset by a self-sustaining 30-acre farm located across the road that supplied wheat, corn, hogs, and cattle for use at the infirmary. In 1936, the federal government's Works Progress Administration supplied funds to replace the old wooden barn with a modern brick storehouse and grain silo. In July 1936, construction workers posed for this photograph. The infirmary remained operational until the late 1960s and was razed shortly after it ceased operations. A cemetery containing nearly 200 graves of former patients is located inside what is now Earl Thomas Conley Park. (Bill Glockner Collection.)

Four

Sciotoville and New Boston

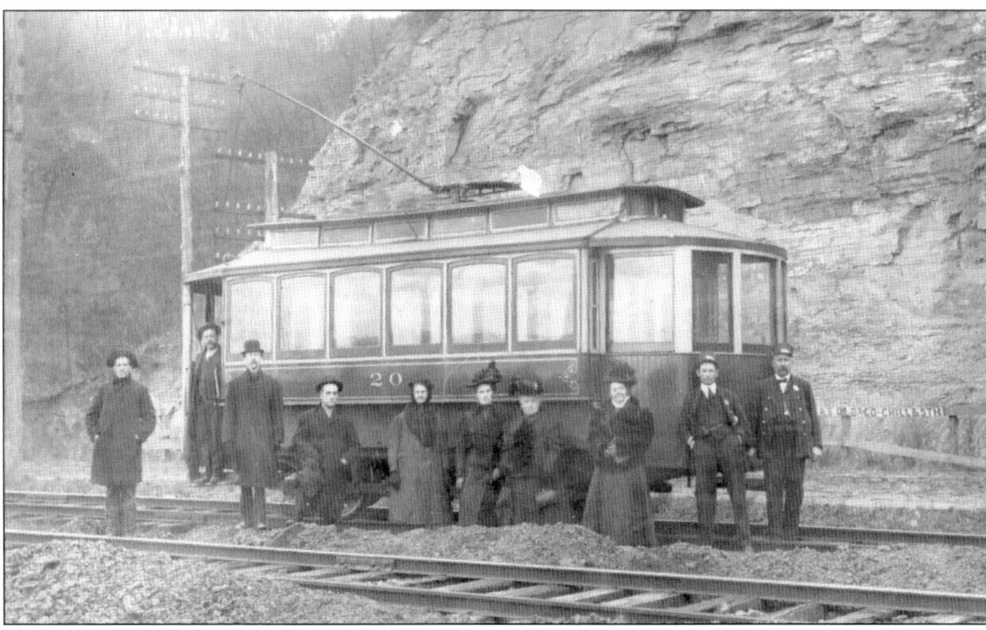

Beginning in late 1903, citizens could travel between Portsmouth and Sciotoville on a newly completed extension of the Portsmouth Street Railway. For 15¢, a person could ride round-trip between the two communities in one the most modern means of transportation available at the time. This postcard features a photograph taken outside New Boston and shows employees and passengers on one of the first trips on the line. (Paul O'Neill Collection.)

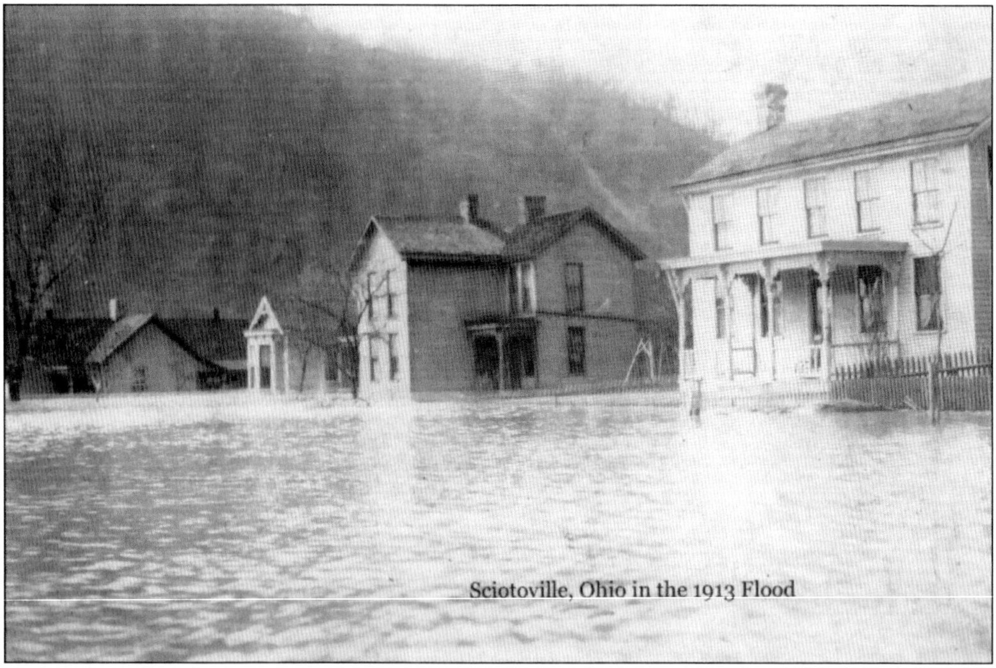

Misled by inaccurate weather forecasts, these residents on Gallia Street in Sciotoville were ill-prepared for the massive flood of March 1913. Due to persistent heavy rains in the region, the Ohio River at Portsmouth rapidly rose an extraordinary 35 feet in a 24-hour time span. All of these houses remain standing after surviving both this flood and a more devastating one that struck 24 years later.

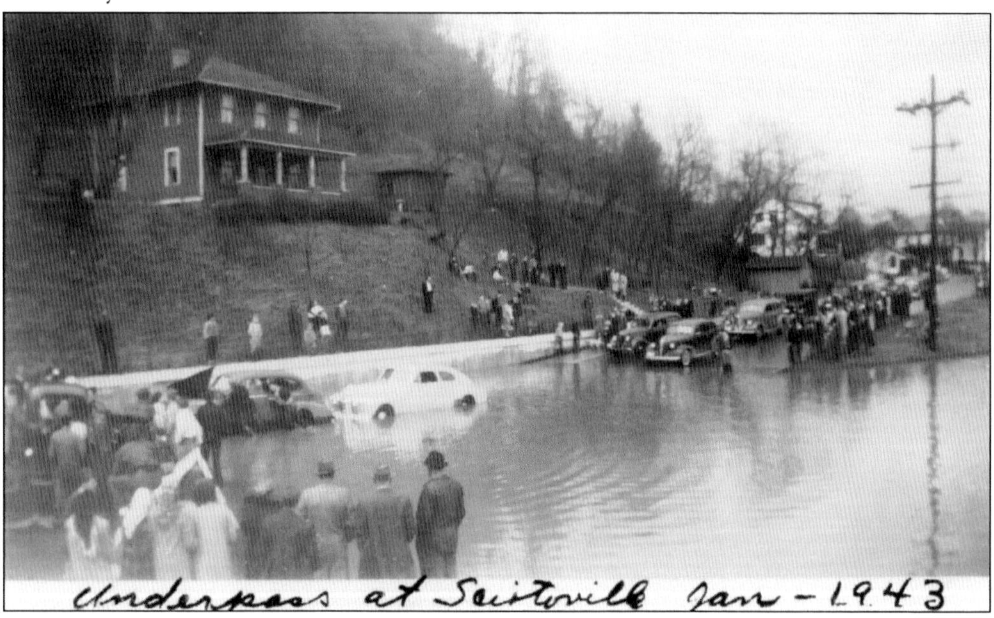

In this January 1943 image, Sciotoville residents withstand Mother Nature's wrath. Persistent rains caused the Ohio River to crest at 61.2 feet, the highest it had risen since the well-known 1937 flood. This was the sixth-highest Ohio River flood on record. The drivers of the partially submerged cars learned too late of the water's depth. (Paul O'Neill Collection.)

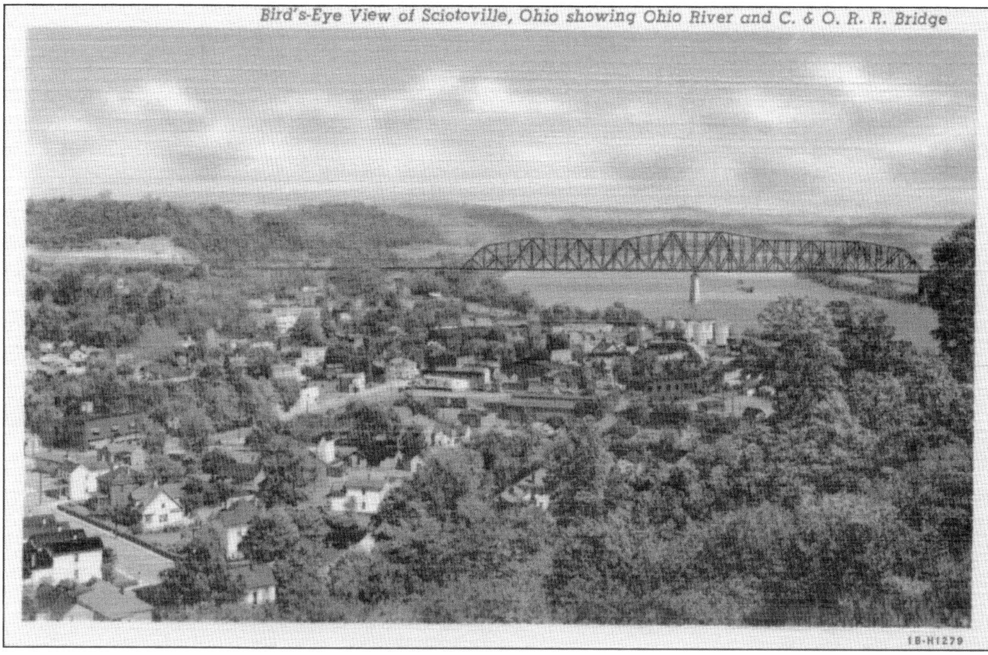

Sciotoville began in 1795, when Maj. Isaac Bonser from Pennsylvania cleared land at the mouth of the Little Scioto River for a homestead. Upon arriving with his family the following year, he found the families of Samuel Marshall and John Lindsey had just arrived. The group became friends and combined their talents to start building what would later become Sciotoville, which was platted in January 1841. (Bill Glockner Collection.)

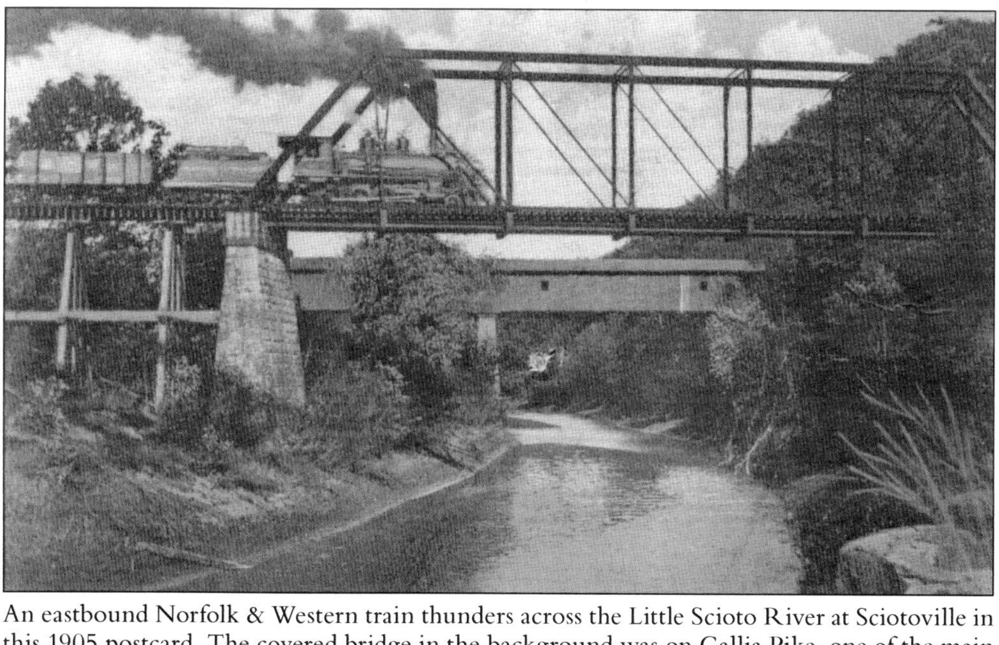

An eastbound Norfolk & Western train thunders across the Little Scioto River at Sciotoville in this 1905 postcard. The covered bridge in the background was on Gallia Pike, one of the main thoroughfares between Portsmouth and eastern Scioto County. After nearly collapsing in 1926, the wooden bridge was replaced one year later with a concrete one. US Route 52 is now situated between these two bridges. (Paul O'Neill Collection.)

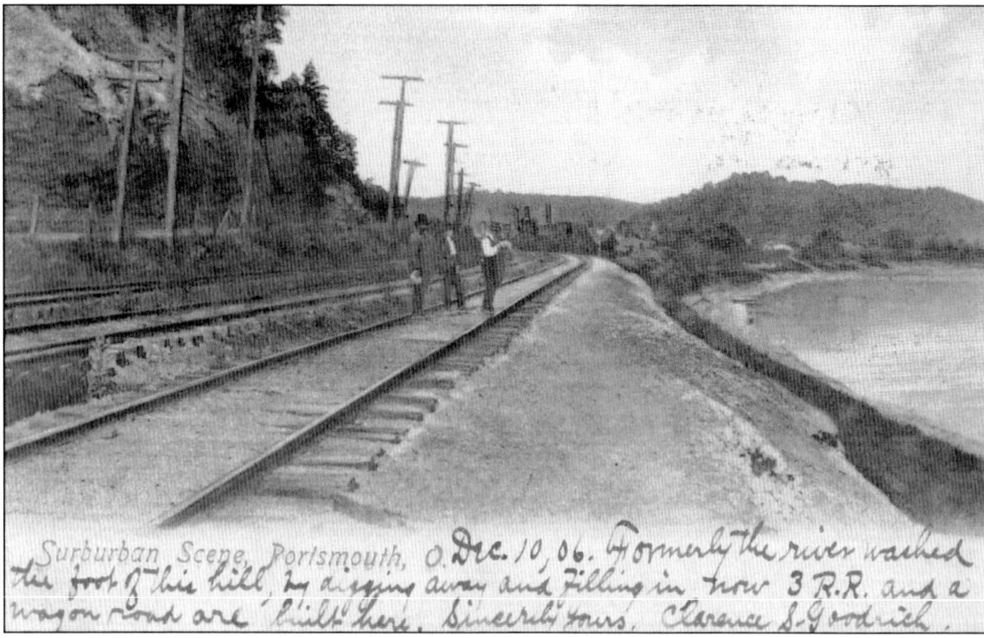

The short distance between New Boston and Sciotoville offered a paradise for train enthusiasts. In this 1906 postcard, the Ohio River is on the right, and next to it are the rails of three major lines. From right to left are the rails of Norfolk & Western Railway, the Baltimore & Ohio Railroad, and the Ohio Valley Traction line. At farthest left is the roadway that later became US Route 52.

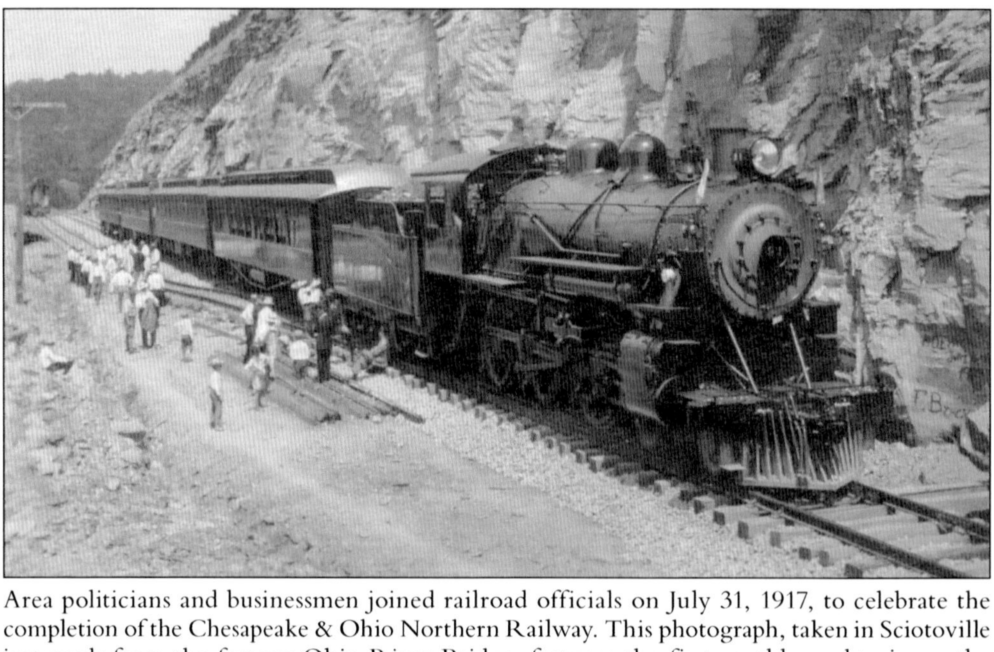

Area politicians and businessmen joined railroad officials on July 31, 1917, to celebrate the completion of the Chesapeake & Ohio Northern Railway. This photograph, taken in Sciotoville just yards from the famous Ohio River Bridge, features the first southbound train on the $4.5-million route. This train later met the first northbound train on the center of the bridge to officially open the rail line. (Paul O'Neill Collection.)

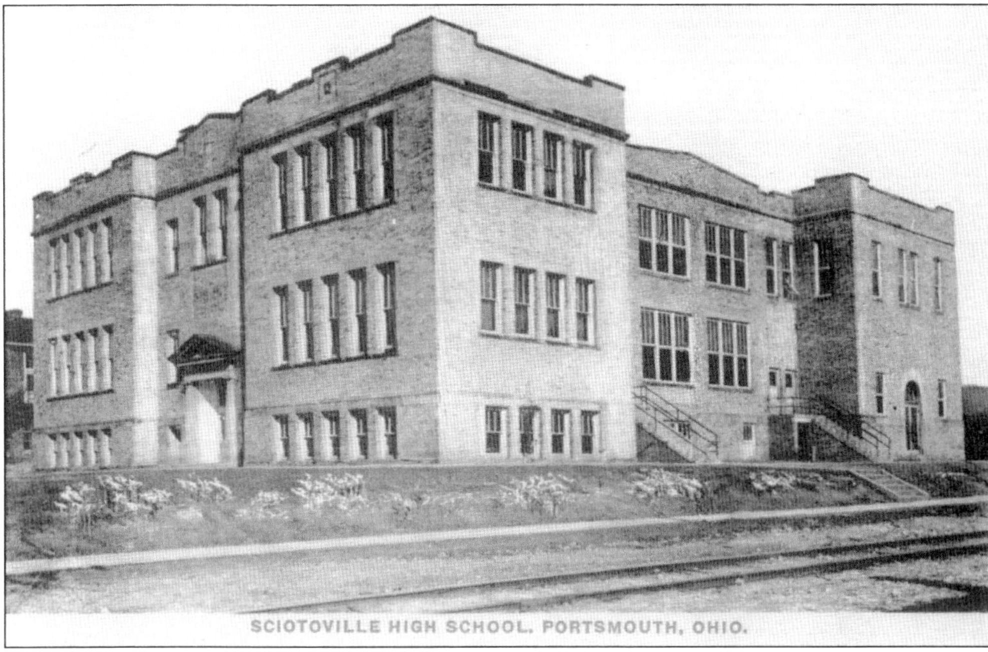

This Sciotoville High School building was constructed in 1915 on the northeast corner of Marshall and Farney Avenues. It was built next to the old school, which was razed in 1938 to create space for a new addition. The school's name was changed to East High School in 1940. Improvements made in 1957 included the additions of a large gym and music and science rooms plus the conversion of the auditorium into a cafeteria. (Paul O'Neill Collection.)

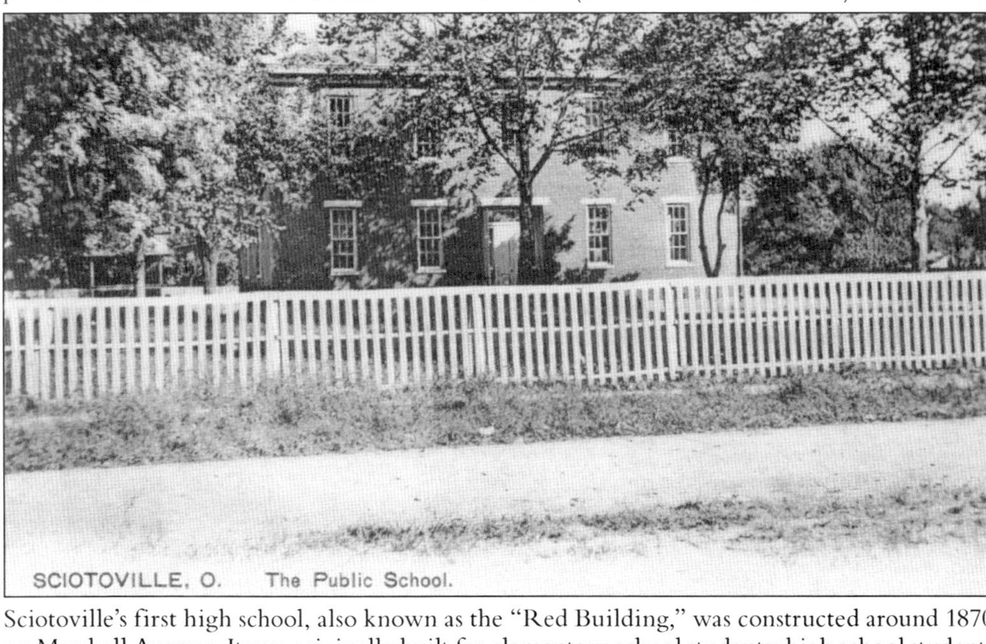

Sciotoville's first high school, also known as the "Red Building," was constructed around 1870 on Marshall Avenue. It was originally built for elementary school students; high school students began attending in 1911. From 1913 to 1915, classes were held in an old hardware store on Winchester Avenue due to overcrowding. A new Sciotoville High School was built in 1915 at the corners of Marshall and Farney Avenues. (Paul O'Neill Collection.)

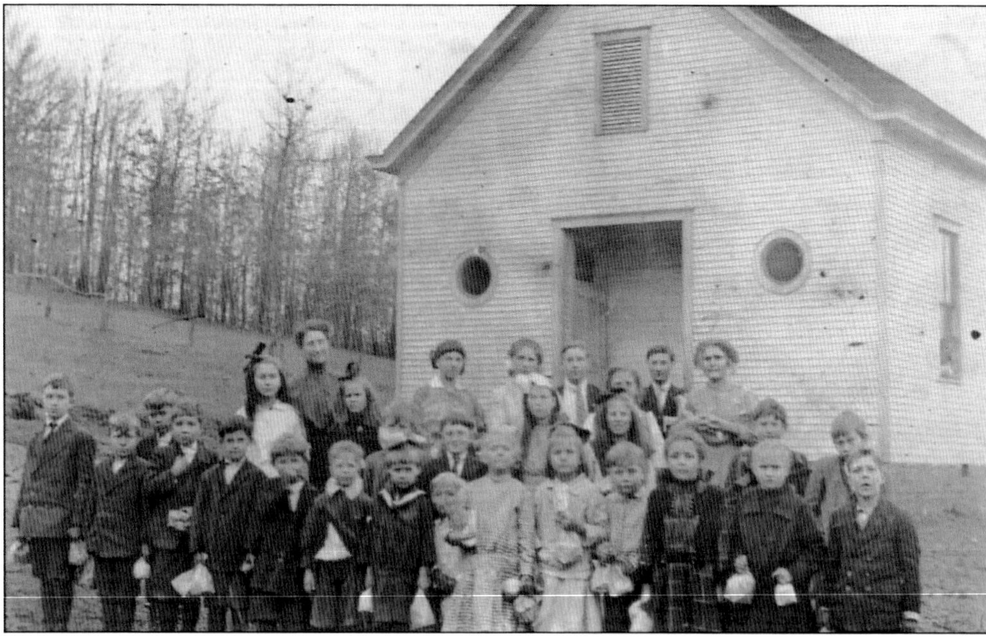

Located where Hartley Road and Dogwood Ridge intersect, the Hartley School was built in the late 1800s and housed grades one through eight. The school was closed in 1929 despite protests from parents, and students were bused to the new Lindsay School. This building was converted and used as a family home for many years; it was razed in 2008. (Portsmouth City Schools Archives.)

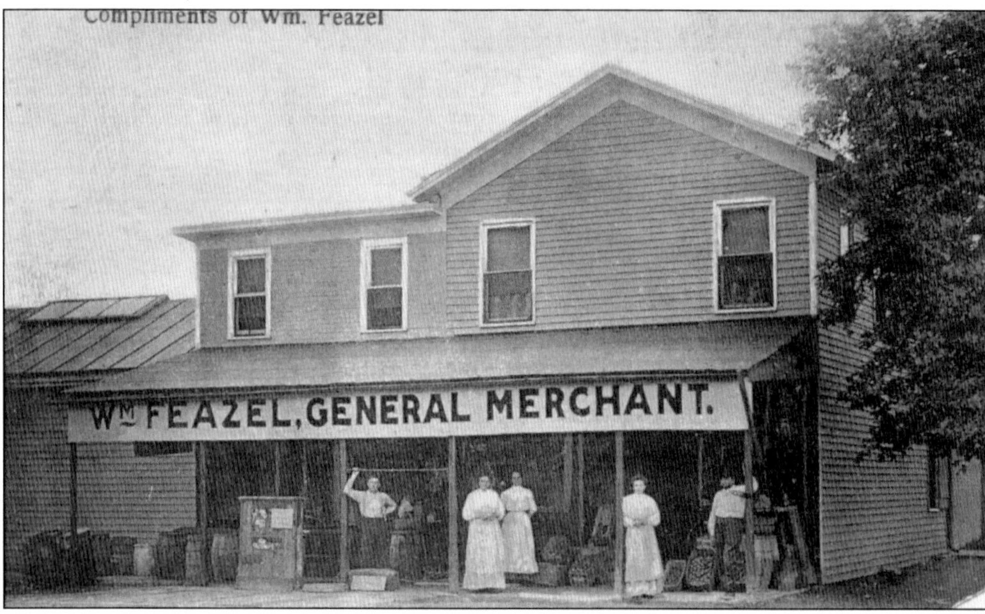

William E. Feazel operated a general store at Harding and Winchester Avenues in Sciotoville around 1895. Feazel's store carried a wide range of products and became even more popular in August 1916, when it became one of the first in the community to sell gasoline. By 1920, Feazel had relocated to Florida and became a successful orange farmer. (Sharon Bender Collection.)

The Sciotoville Christian Church (also known as the Church of Christ) was organized in 1867 with 17 charter members. After originally meeting in their homes, they worshiped in the old Marshall Hall for the next 15 years. In 1880, a wooden structure costing $2,090 (right) was built on land (donated by Mrs. Jeff Davis) at Third and Bloom Streets. As the congregation continued to grow in the early 1920s, the structure was moved to the rear of the lot and an auditorium (below) was built. After a devastating fire in 1941, the congregation held meetings at East High School while the church was being restored. Attendance began to increase again in the late 1940s, and the educational building was constructed. This church has helped establish churches in Wheelersburg and Minford and has sent young men into the ministry. (Both, Paul O'Neill Collection.)

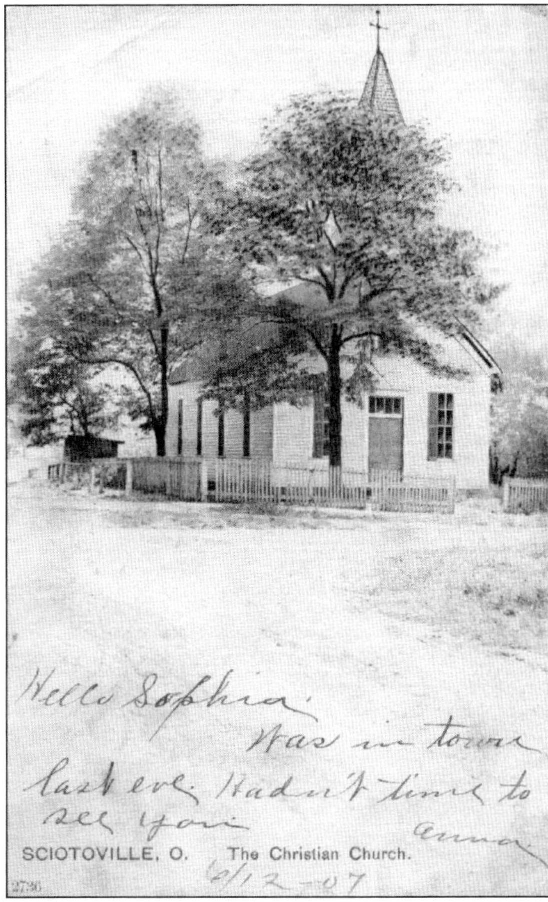

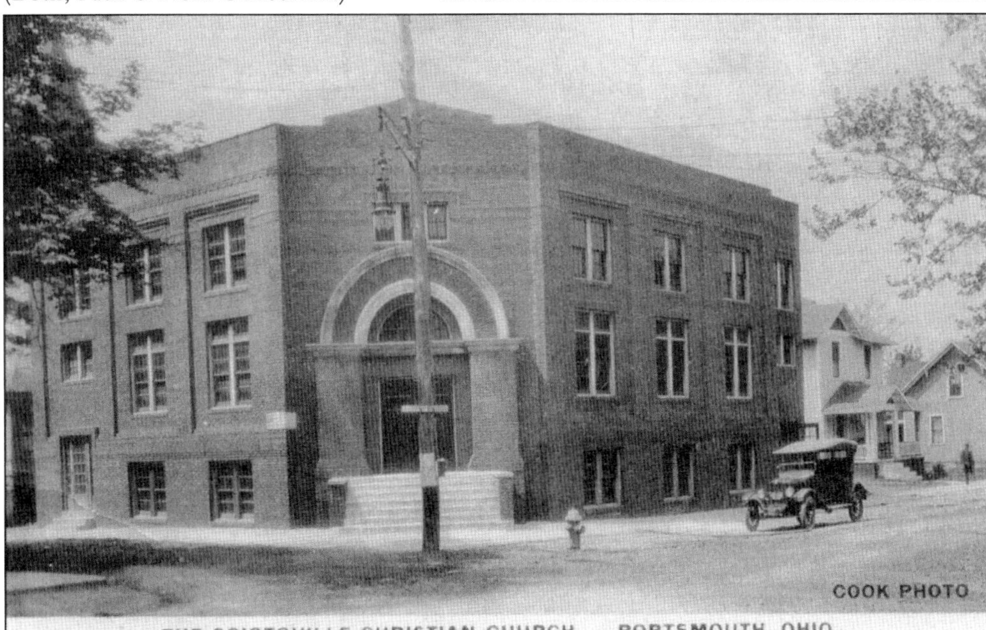

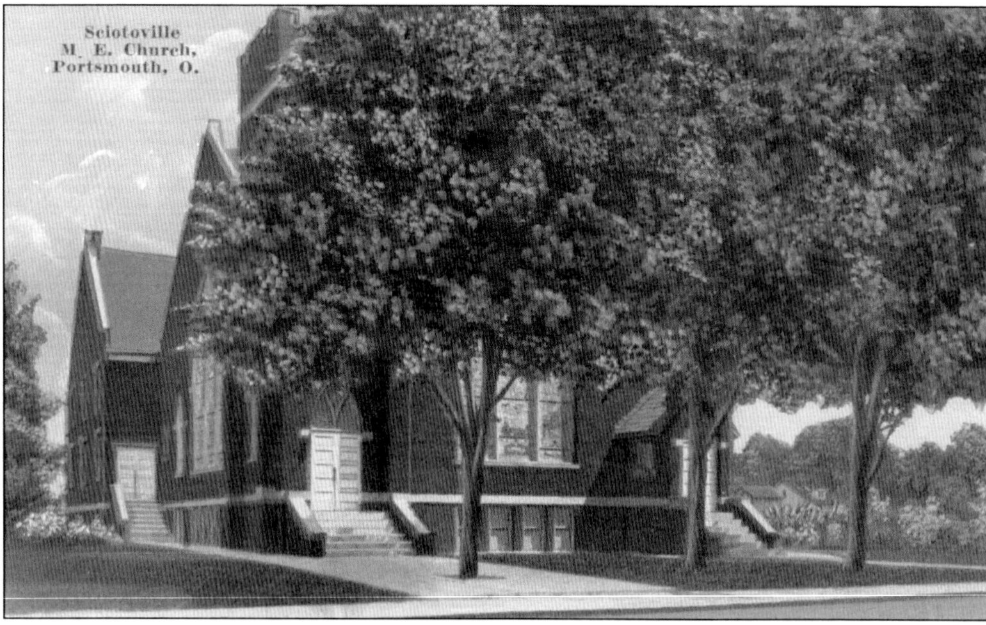

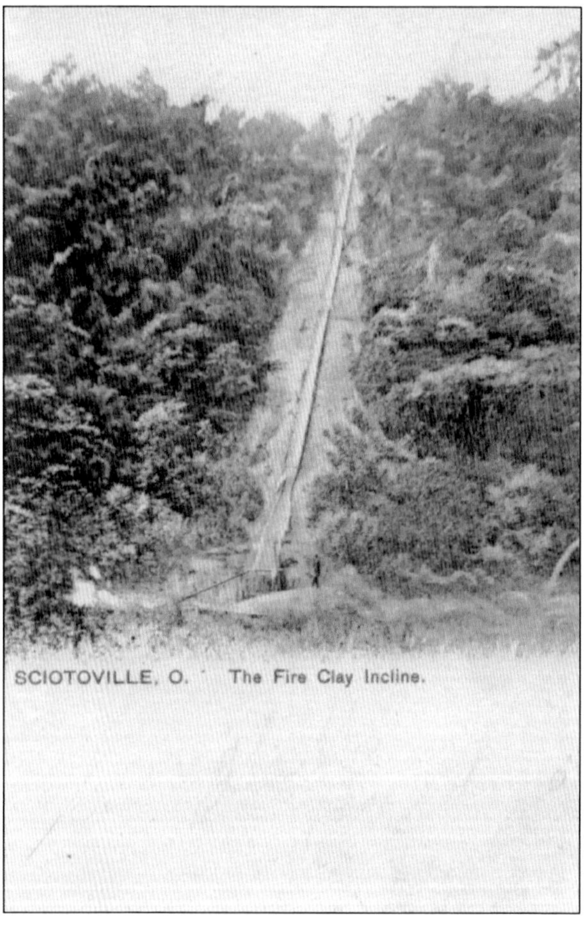

Sciotoville M.E. Church was built in June 1842 on land generously donated by Madison and Minerva Price. The building was used by Christian and Baptist churches after it was relocated to the back of the lot in 1866. A new church was built in December 1868 and greatly enlarged in 1916, as shown above. After the bank loan was paid off, a celebratory burning of the mortgage note occurred on Easter Sunday 1927. (Bill Glockner Collection.)

One method of transporting an important ingredient in the making of bricks is shown in this c. 1910 postcard. Clay mined from the top of the hill was transported to the brick plants at the bottom via dump cars, constructed of iron, that were hoisted up and down this steep incline near Sciotoville. Several incidents occurred in which men were seriously injured by runaway dump cars. (Paul O'Neill Collection.)

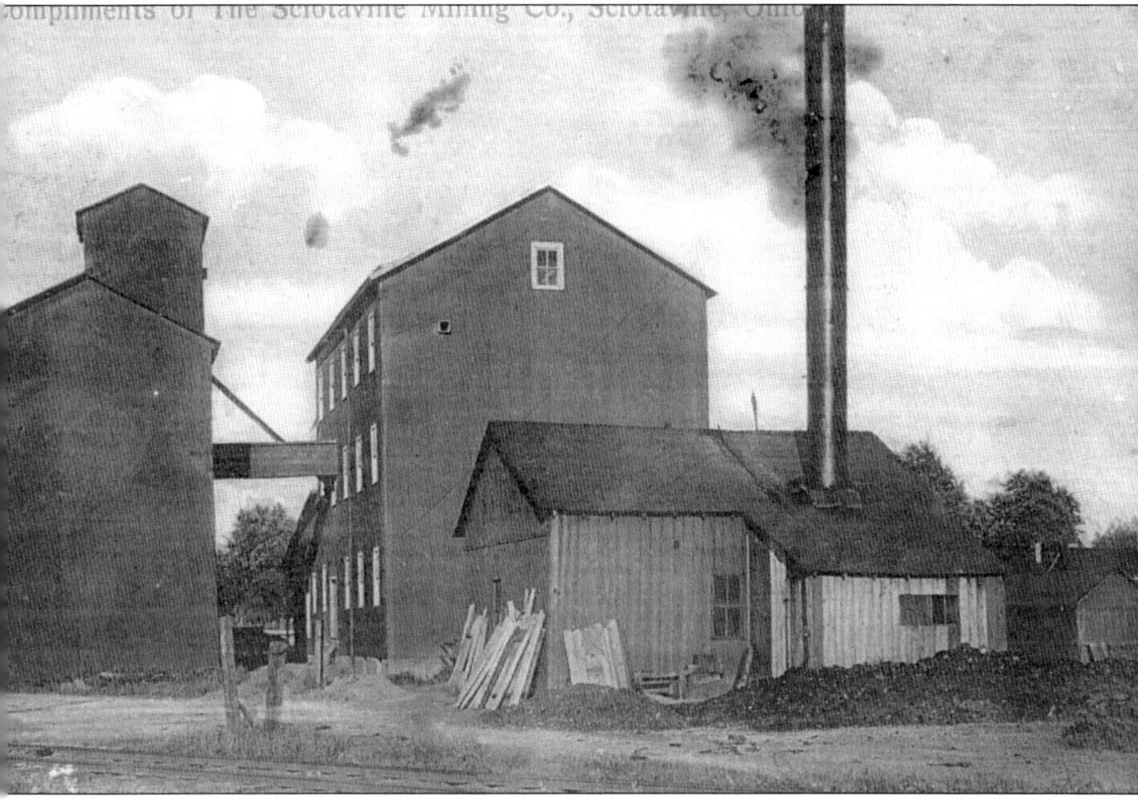

If there was ever a business that had misfortune, it was the Sciotoville Milling Company. Established in 1896 by Louis Marting and located near Fourth and Railroad Streets, it produced flour and cornmeal. Although it was originally successful, the company began to incur increased debts and lawsuits from creditors in 1914. On July 24, 1914, thieves broke into the business and stole cash and company checks. Tragically, three days later, the body of Marting was found in the Ohio River near his Ironton home in what was reported to be a suicide. In July 1915, foreclosure proceedings began with a public auction, but no bids were made. Local businessman Jackson Cropper finally purchased the company from the court in April 1916 for less than half of the appraised value. Unable to resell or restart the mill, he decided to raze the structures in late 1916. Cropper died only six months later—at age 55—from blood poisoning following a surgical procedure. (Bill Glockner Collection.)

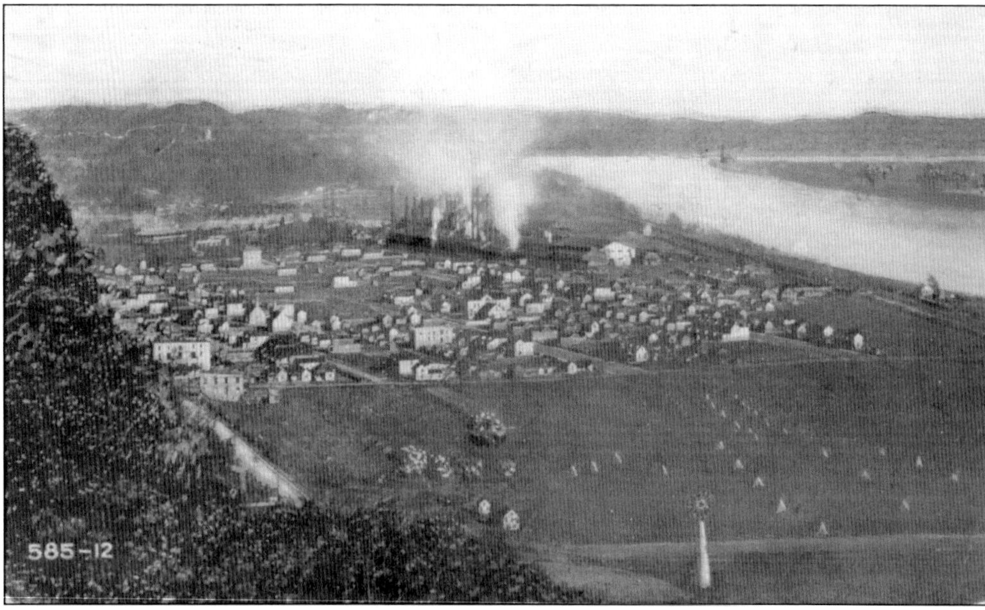

In 1887, entrepreneurs from Boston, Massachusetts, arrived in the area just east of Portsmouth to start and operate a lumber mill. They took advantage of the vast forests as a source for timber, and with railroads and waterways to transport it, the small settlement quickly grew to include more businesses and residents. Four years later, the community was officially platted and named New Boston in honor of the pioneers' home city. (Paul O'Neill Collection.)

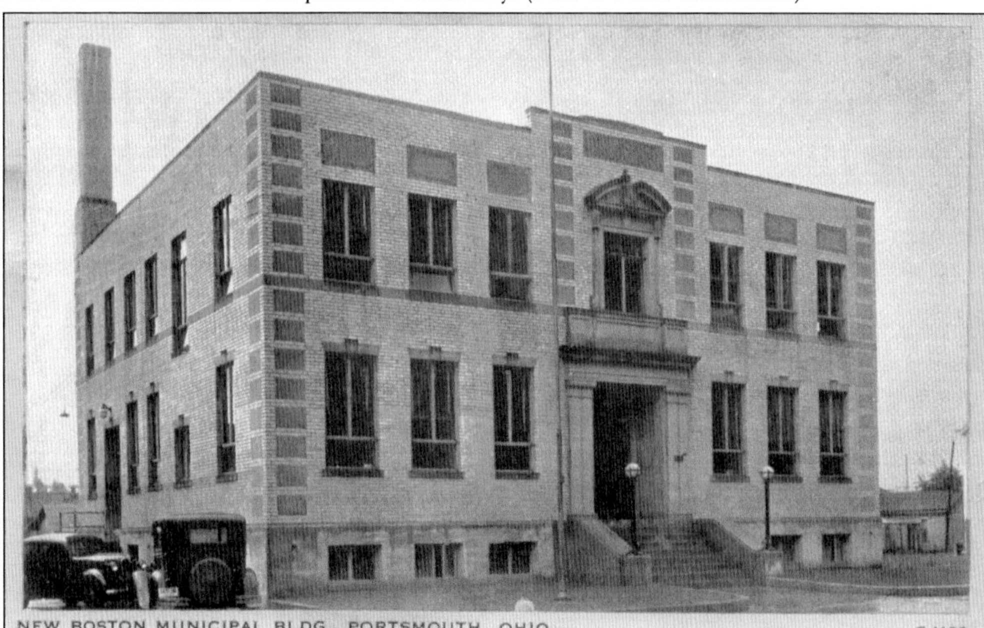

In 1936, New Boston began construction on their new municipal building thanks to a government grant that paid almost half of the $50,000 cost. It replaced the original building on Gallia Street and contained 18 rooms, including council chambers, the mayor's office, the police department, a courtroom, and the city jail. The library was located here before moving to Park Avenue. Scioto County Children's Services moved into the building in 1979. (Paul O'Neill Collection.)

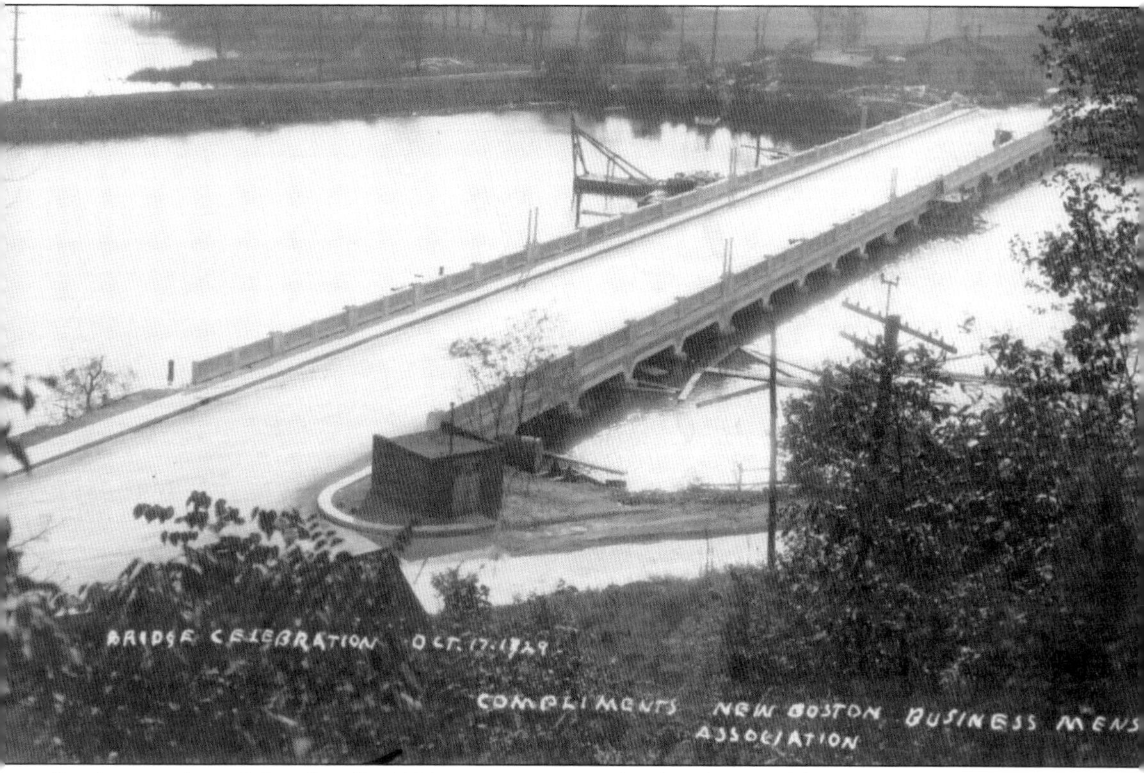

On the evening of October 17, 1929, New Boston schoolteacher Kathleen Adams and friend Hazel Adams distributed postcards, like the one shown above, to those attending the dedication ceremonies of the New Boston "Y Bridge." Built at a cost of $75,000 in less than one year, the bridge was financed by a special bond levy approved by village voters. The concrete bridge spanned Millbrook Lake and separated on the eastern end, with Rhodes Avenue going toward the left while Gallia Street diverted to the right. At 480 feet long, it featured boulevard lights for night illumination. Over 5,000 people attended the celebration, which featured a parade, guest speakers, a fireworks display, and dinner at nearby People's Corner Restaurant and culminated in a community outdoor square dance under the light of a full moon. One speaker proudly noted that the bridge "will stand for generations to come." It was replaced 32 years later. (Paul O'Neill Collection.)

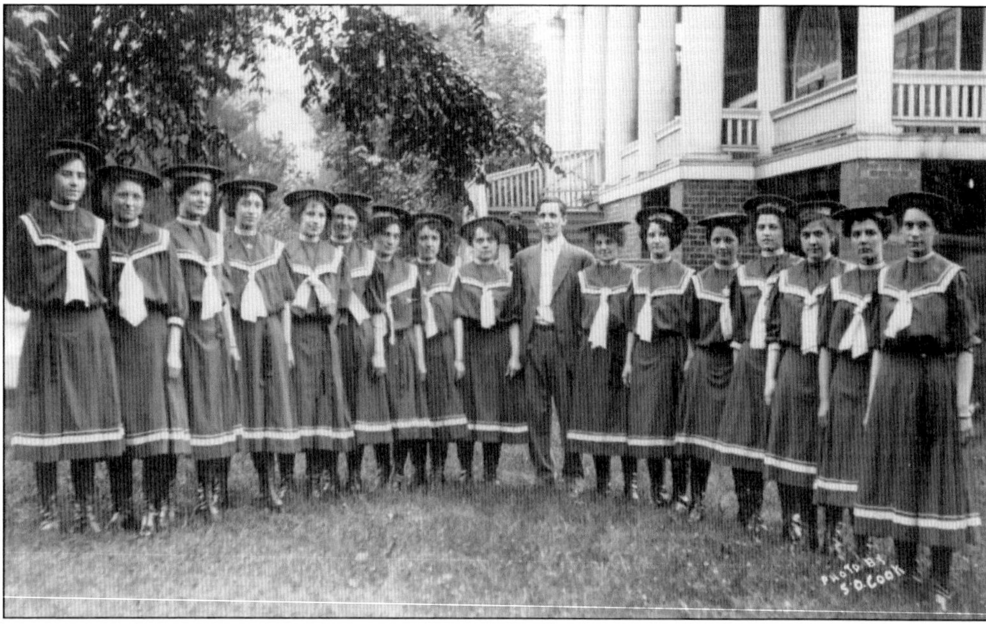

In the early 1900s, perhaps no place in Scioto County was more popular than Millbrook Park. The park's 85.4 acres boasted some of the most picturesque settings in the state of Ohio. Groups of people consistently assembled at the park for gatherings and festivities. A group of unidentified young ladies stands in front of the Millbrook Casino in this c. 1910 postcard. (Sharon Bender Collection.)

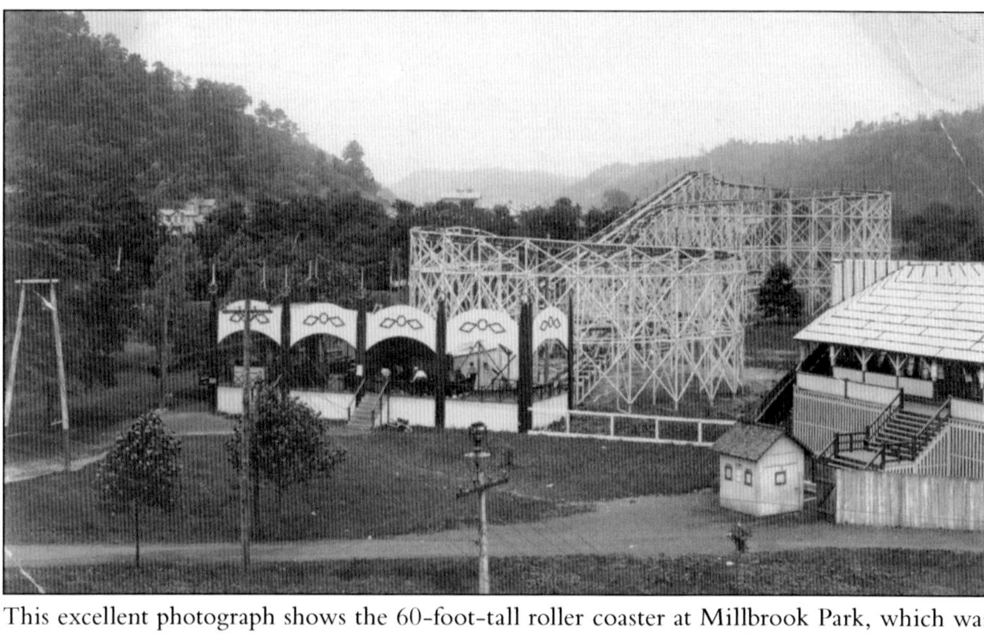

This excellent photograph shows the 60-foot-tall roller coaster at Millbrook Park, which was installed in April 1910 at a cost of $15,000. The 90-second thrill ride began and ended at the enclosed building to the left. A motorized hoist pulled the cars up the first incline, then gravity took over. Unfortunately, the roller coaster was short-lived—it was destroyed in the 1913 flood. (Sharon Bender Collection.)

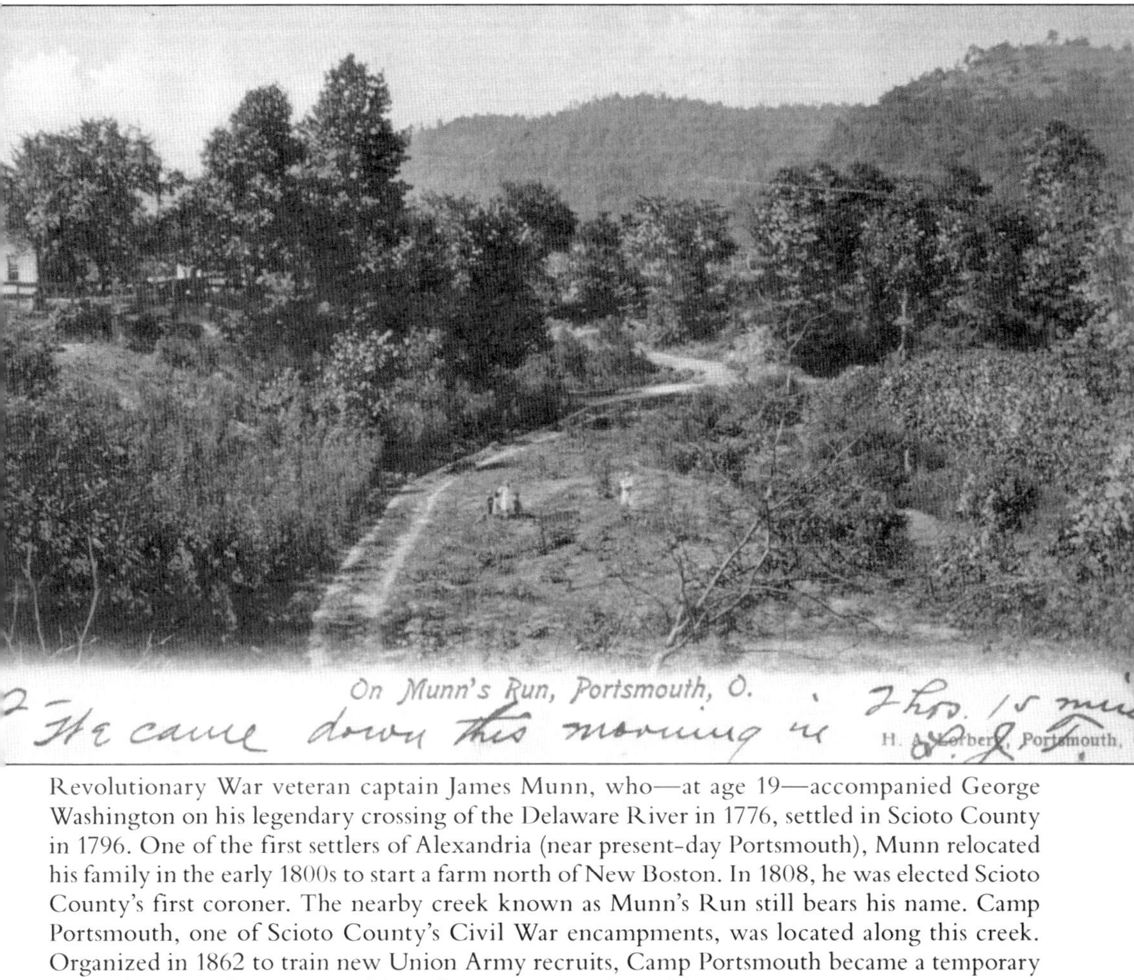

Revolutionary War veteran captain James Munn, who—at age 19—accompanied George Washington on his legendary crossing of the Delaware River in 1776, settled in Scioto County in 1796. One of the first settlers of Alexandria (near present-day Portsmouth), Munn relocated his family in the early 1800s to start a farm north of New Boston. In 1808, he was elected Scioto County's first coroner. The nearby creek known as Munn's Run still bears his name. Camp Portsmouth, one of Scioto County's Civil War encampments, was located along this creek. Organized in 1862 to train new Union Army recruits, Camp Portsmouth became a temporary home for more than 1,400 soldiers from Scioto and neighboring counties. Camp Morrow, located in Portsmouth, and Camp Portsmouth were vital to the preservation of the Union. By November 1862, the objective of Camp Portsmouth had been met, and thus the camp was no longer needed. (Bill Glockner Collection.)

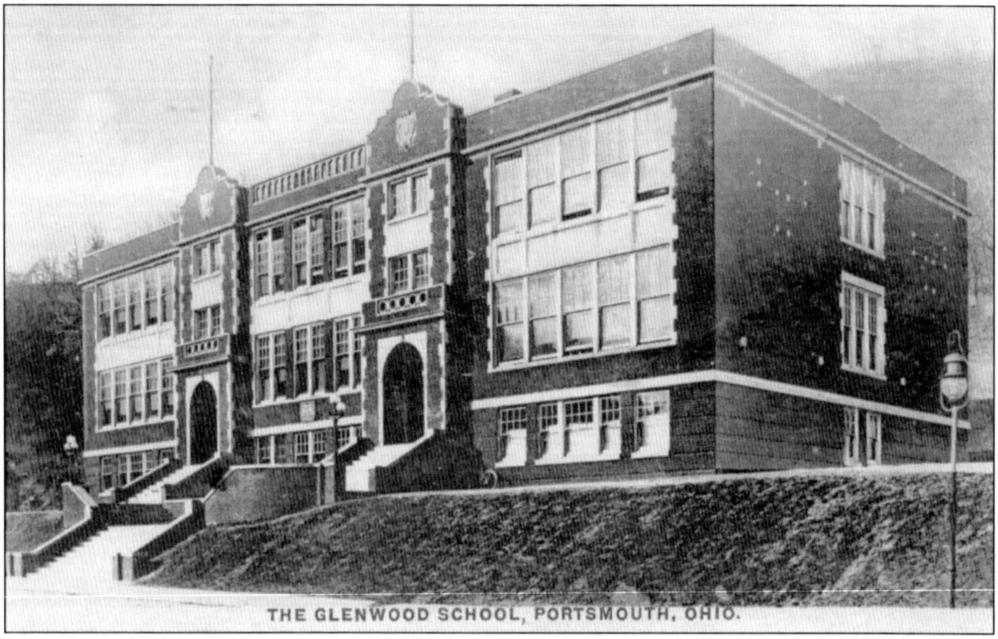

Completed in 1918, New Boston's Glenwood High School (pictured) graduated its first class, which consisted of six students, the following year. An addition to the school was completed in 1923, followed by the gymnasium (known as the smallest in the county) in 1927. In April 2011, ground was broken at No. 1 Glenwood Tiger Trail for a new $20-million building on the site of the former Sun and Funland Pool.

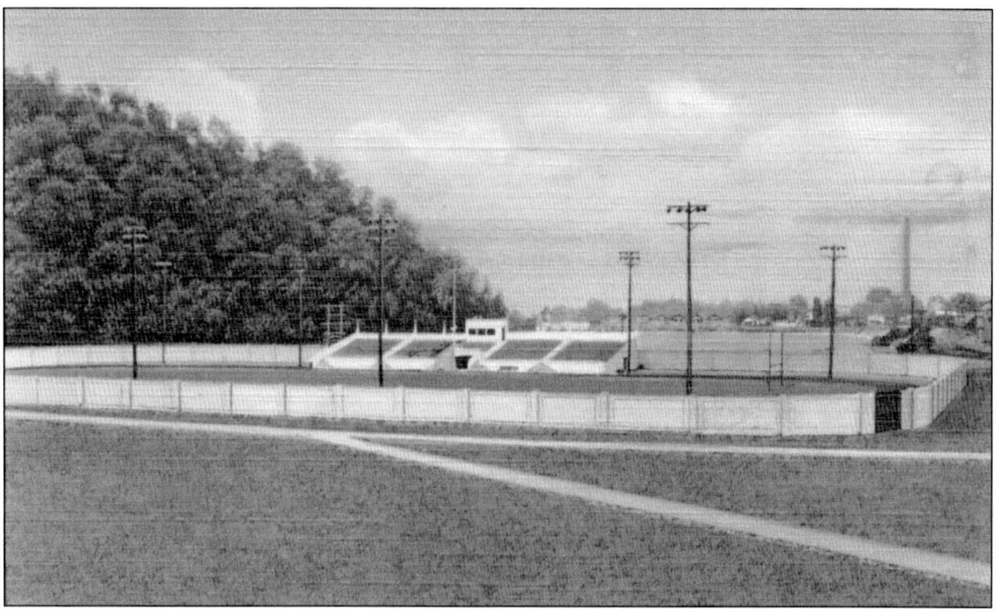

Built at a cost of $219,000, New Boston's municipal stadium was dedicated on September 27, 1940, when the New Boston Tigers faced their rival East Tartans in a high school football game. Over 2,000 people attended the sold-out game, which ended in a 0–0 tie. The stadium is still in use and has been the venue for many Glenwood High School graduations, as well as sporting events such as track meets and soccer tournaments. (Paul O'Neill Collection.)

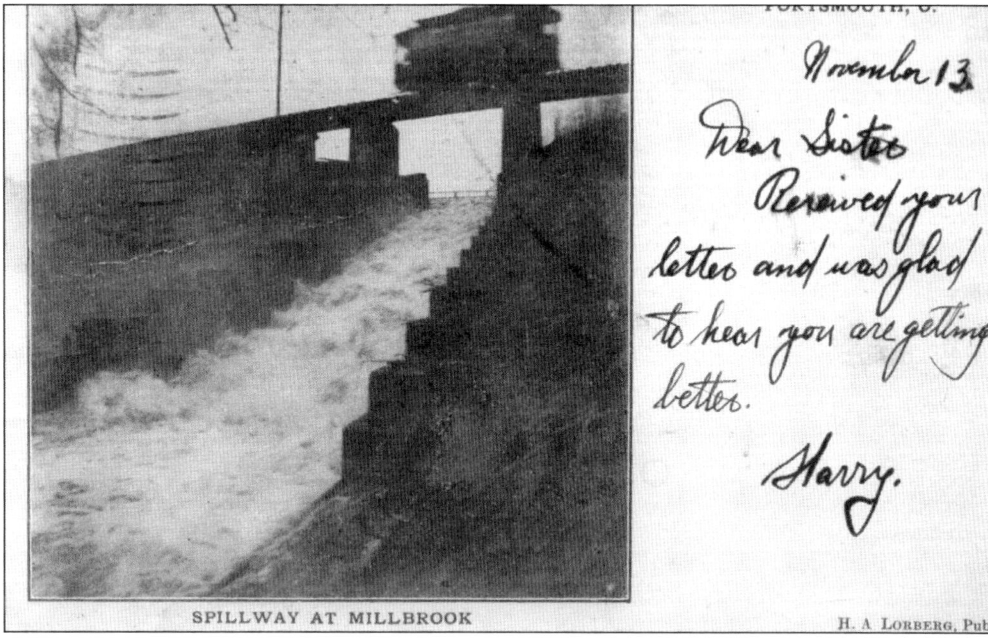

A Portsmouth Streetcar glides across a bridge and over a man-made spillway near New Boston's Millbrook Park in this c. 1903 postcard. The 150-foot waterway was constructed of concrete and directed any overflow of water from an adjacent 40-acre lake down to the Ohio River. Water cascading down the 10-inch-tall steps created a place of serenity and meditation. (Paul O'Neill Collection.)

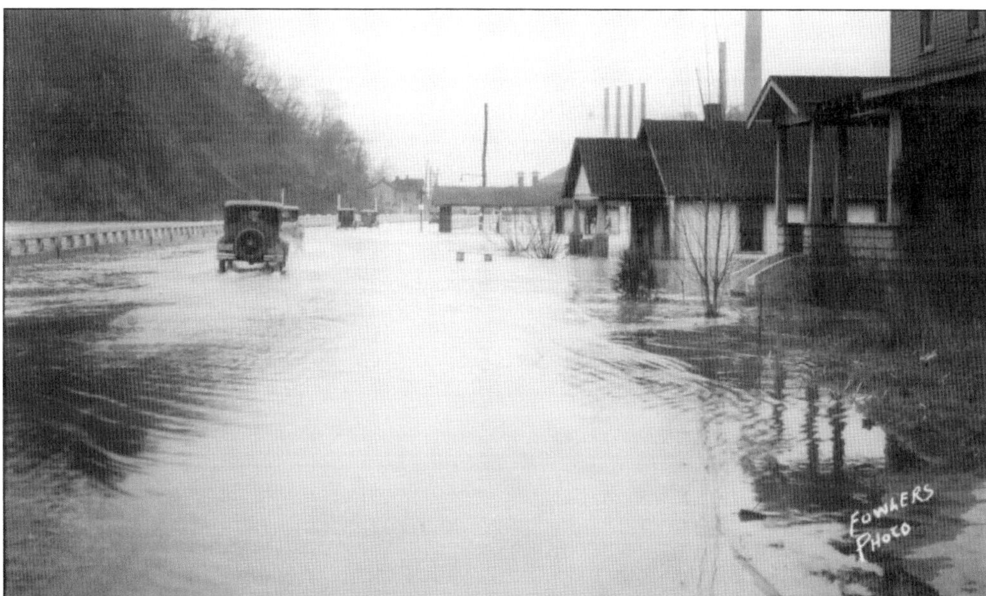

Motorists begin traveling eastbound on Route 52 through New Boston as waters recede from yet another flood in March 1933. This flood reached a crest of 60.5 feet and is listed as one of the highest Ohio River floods in Scioto County's history. With more advance warning than during previous floods, citizens were able to prepare for nature's wrath, and overall damage resulting from the flood was minimized. (Paul O'Neill Collection.)

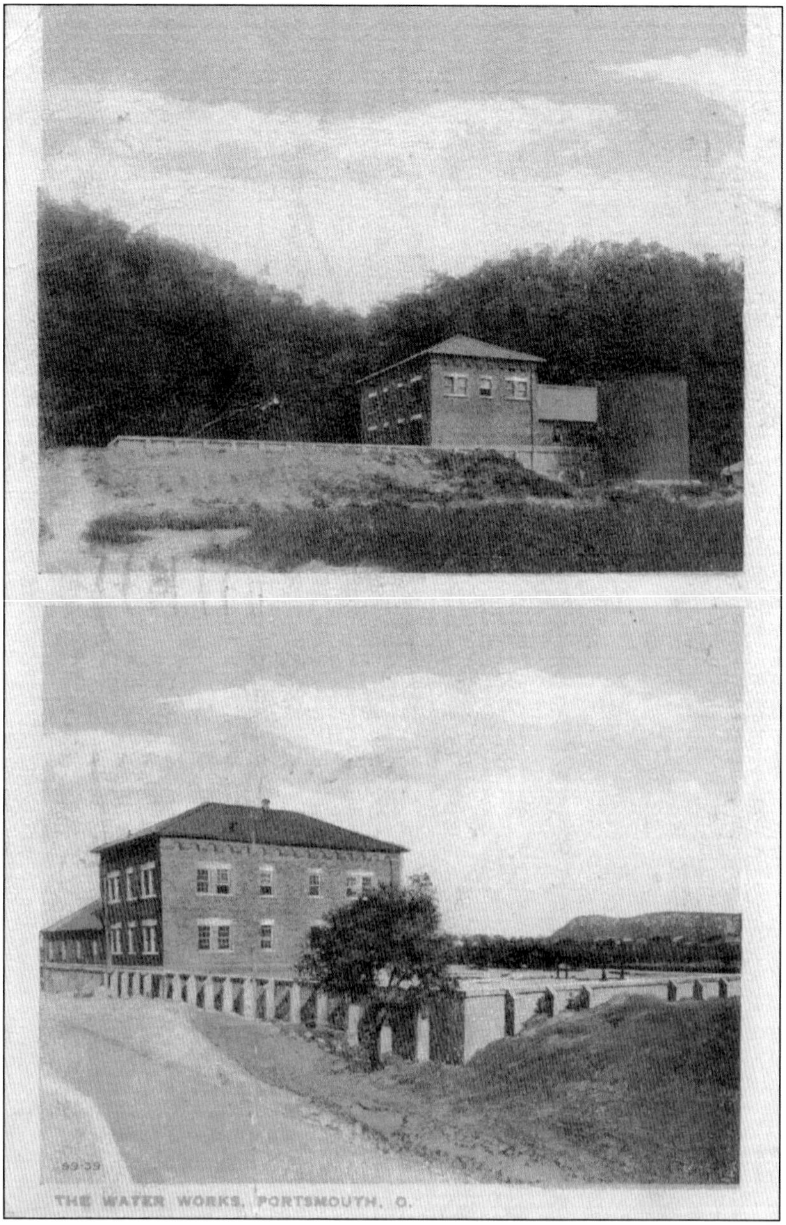

An increase in the Portsmouth area's population, a desire for safer drinking water, and outdated equipment necessitated the construction of a new water filtration plant on Gallia Street in New Boston. Financed by a special bond issue passed by voters in November 1910, the $500,000 water treatment plant opened on August 20, 1914. With a daily capacity of eight million gallons of water pumped from the Ohio River, it provided four times the volume the older facility on Mill Street could provide. An eight-million-gallon capacity concrete reservoir was also constructed on top of an adjacent hillside, parts of which are still visible today. Enough water was kept in reserve to supply the entire city for one week in case of emergencies. Built-in generators provided light or power for the facility, making it totally independent from the city's electrical system. In 1950, a major upgrade enlarged the facility, increased its water-purifying capabilities, and increased its daily capacity to 12 million gallons of water.

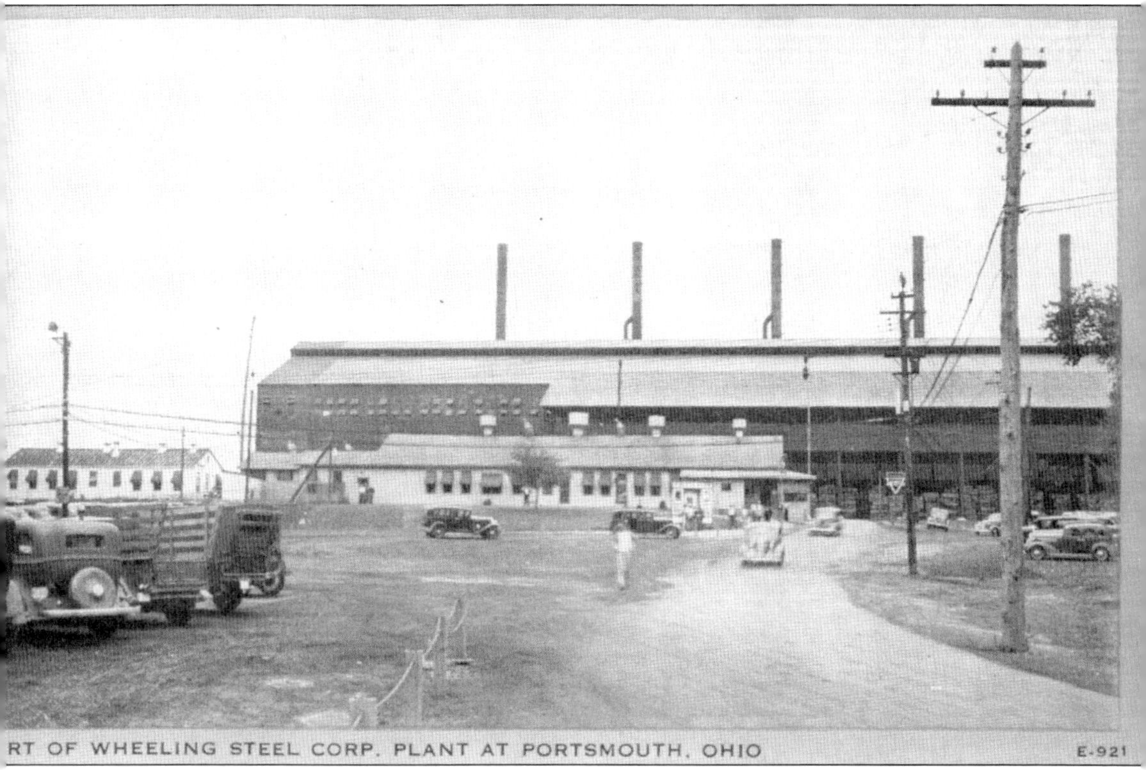

The Wheeling Steel Corporation was created on June 21, 1920, when companies Whitaker-Glessner, La Belle Iron, and Wheeling Steel united to create one enterprise. Major construction and renovations took place from 1920 to 1946. Rod and Wire Mill Divisions were added in 1921, with additional sheet mills added in 1924. The corporation provided employment for most New Boston residents by 1937; its monthly payroll was $500,250, and its annual output of steel was 500,000 tons. Employees decided to strike for better working conditions and recognition of a labor union in 1937. The company hired out-of-state workers to extinguish the strike, which proved disastrous. The outside workers arrived and lived in railroad cars while they worked the mill. The corporation completely underestimated the strong men of New Boston who were determined to succeed, and violence soon followed the arrival of the outside workers as destruction, ferocious fights, and even shootings became common. When an out-of-state worker was murdered, the others left in fear for their lives, finally ending the strike. After the strike ended, the workers formed a union and went back to work. The owners sold the company to Portsmouth Steel Corporation in 1946.

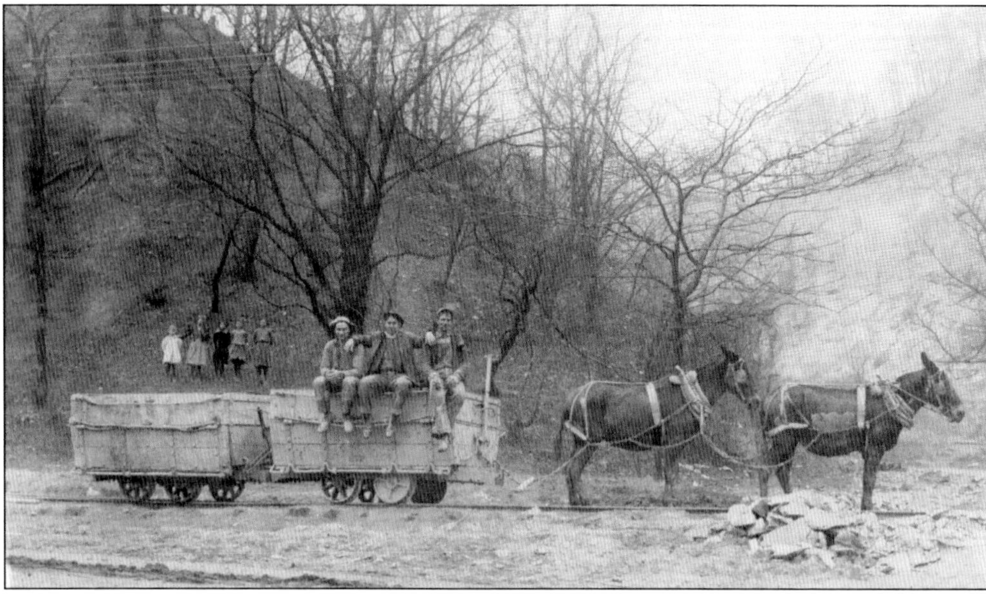

Workers and children pose in this 1906 postcard showing the Shale Bank Hollow entrance. Shale, an important component in producing brick at the nearby factories, was mined here and then transported to the neighboring Peebles Brick Plant, which was located between New Boston and Sciotoville on US Route 52. (Bill Glockner Collection.)

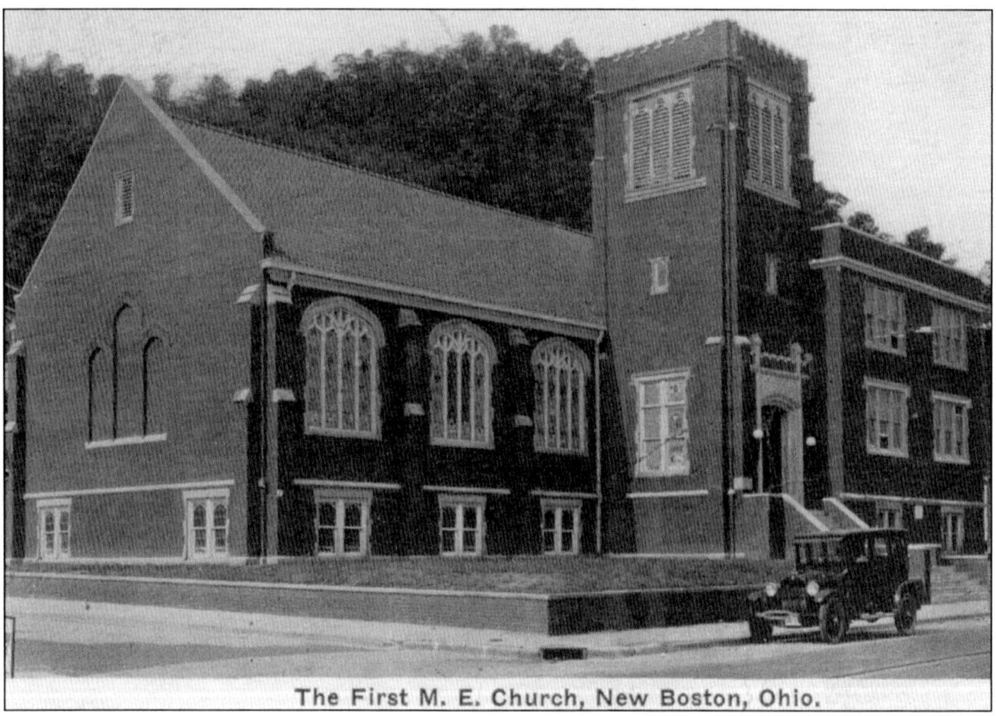

New Boston Methodist Church began with a pitched tent on the corners of Gallia Street and Glenwood Avenue in 1917. A tabernacle built in 1919 was used until 1923, when the cornerstone was laid for a new church. In 2001, the congregation merged with Sciotoville Methodist Church in a new building and was renamed Christ United Methodist Church. (Bill Glockner Collection.)

Five

Rarden and Otway

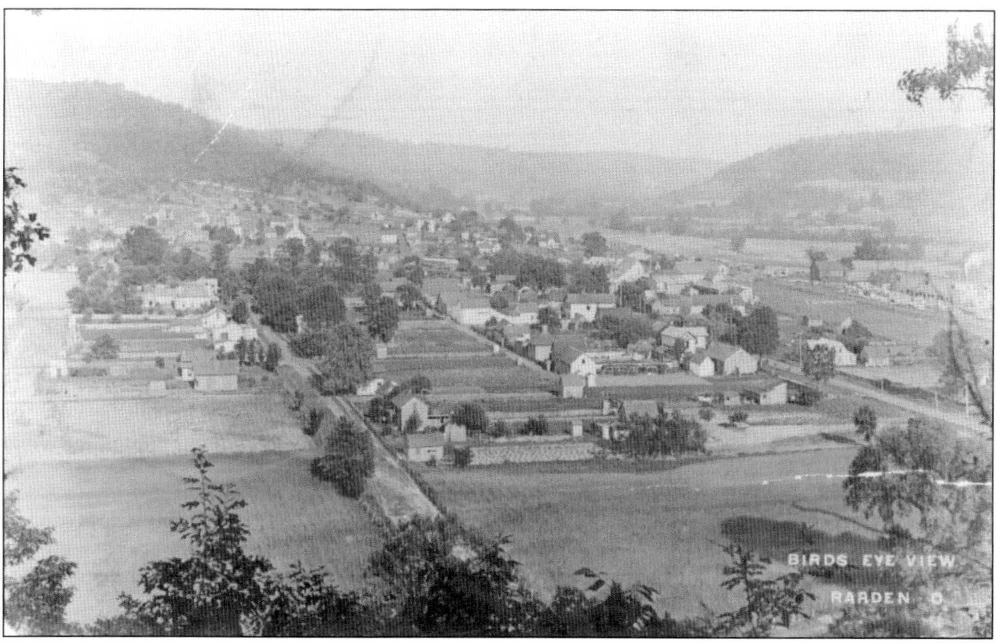

The town of Galena was originally named by early settler Orville Grant, brother of Gen. Ulysses S. Grant, to honor his hometown in Galena, Illinois. In 1883, it became the largest industrial center between Cincinnati and Portsmouth due to its access to the Cincinnati & Eastern Railroad. Galena was renamed Rarden when it was incorporated in 1886 to honor early settler Thomas Rarden. (Paul O'Neill Collection.)

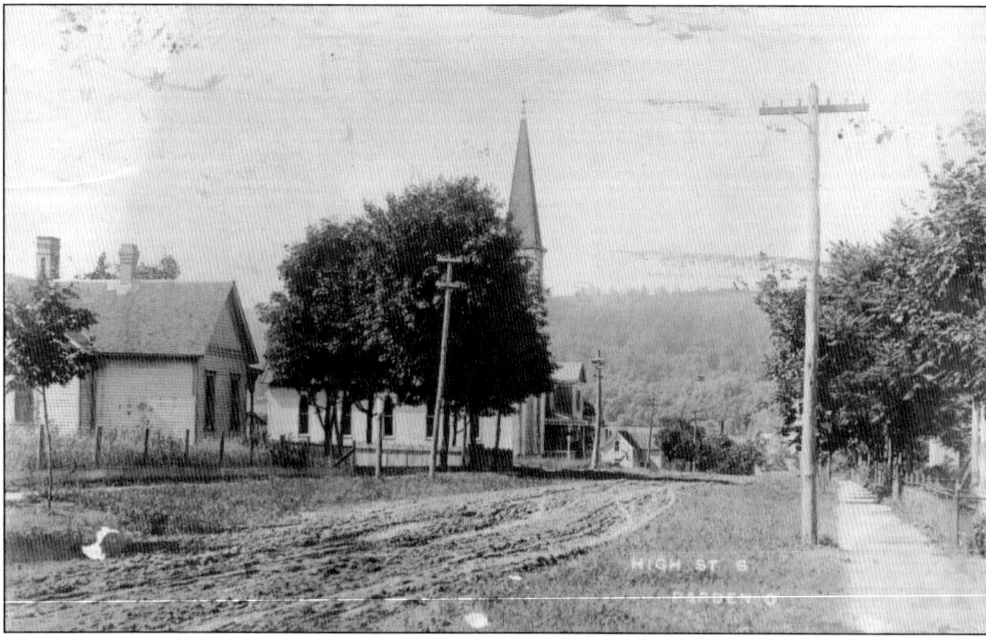

This photograph looking south on High Street in Rarden about 1920 offers a glimpse of an everyday scene in early Scioto County. During the following decade, the dirt road would become a portion of a lengthened and upgraded State Route 772. The house in the foreground has been removed, while the church and houses beyond it are still standing today. (Paul O'Neill Collection.)

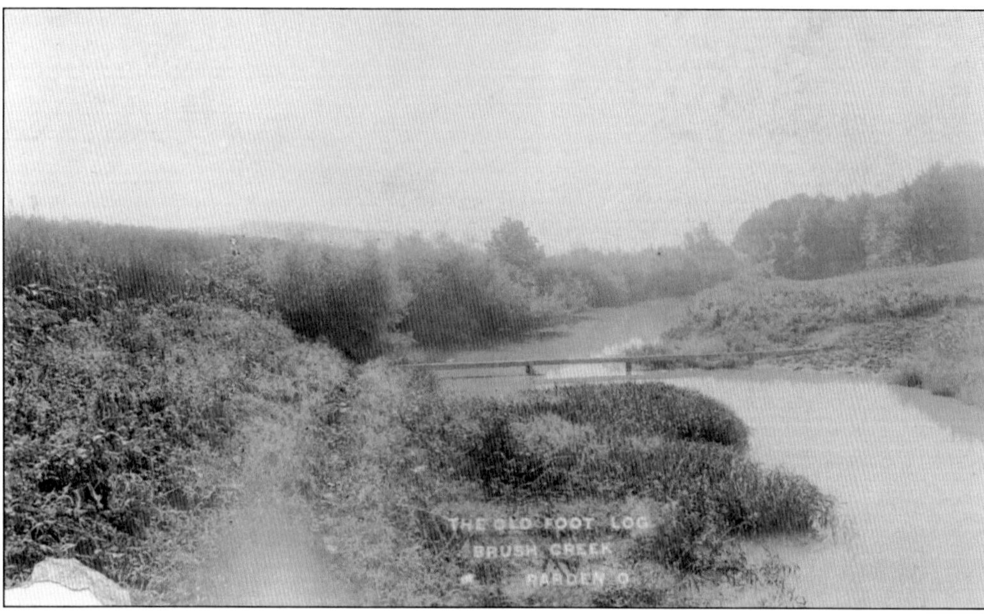

Scioto Brush Creek has long been a popular narrow stream for area fishermen. The tributary terminates at the Scioto River near McDermott and shares its name with Brush Creek Township, which was organized in 1820 in northwestern Scioto County. Depending on the height of the water, crossing could be treacherous with makeshift bridges like the one shown here, which was near Rarden. (Paul O'Neill Collection.)

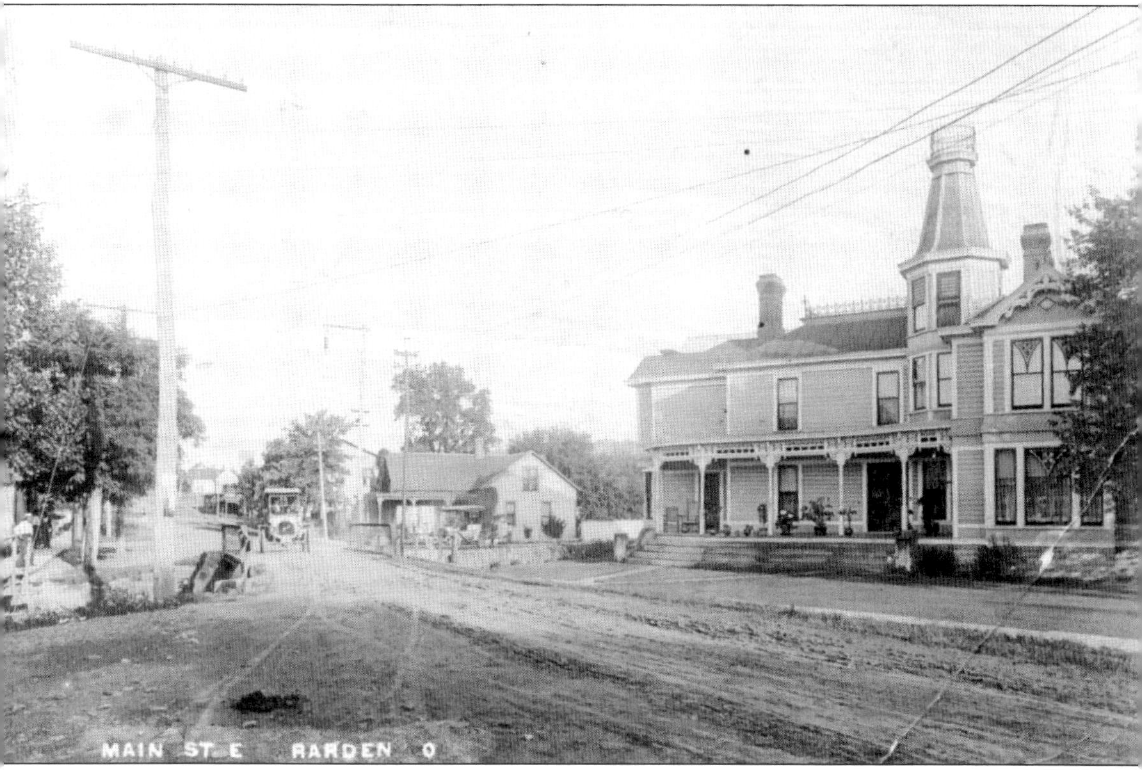

One of the most distinctive homes in Scioto County is shown on the right in this 1910 postcard featuring Main Street in Rarden. Constructed in 1899, the house was built by Lafe Taylor, who owned the nearby Taylor Stone Company. Taylor was a well-respected businessman who was also one of the political leaders who helped improve rural roads in the county. Taylor was also a big supporter and longtime president of the Scioto County Fair, often spending his own money to assist in the fair's operations when needed. Over the years, after Taylor moved his company to McDermott, the house changed ownership several times and was used as a hotel, a boardinghouse, and a nursing home. By the 1970s, the house had fallen into a state of disrepair and sat vacant for many years. In the early 1980s, a local businessman purchased the property and performed a complete restoration. Shortly thereafter, the Rarden Volunteer Fire Department used it as a haunted house to raise funds during the Halloween season. The structure remains standing and is now a residence. (Paul O'Neill Collection.)

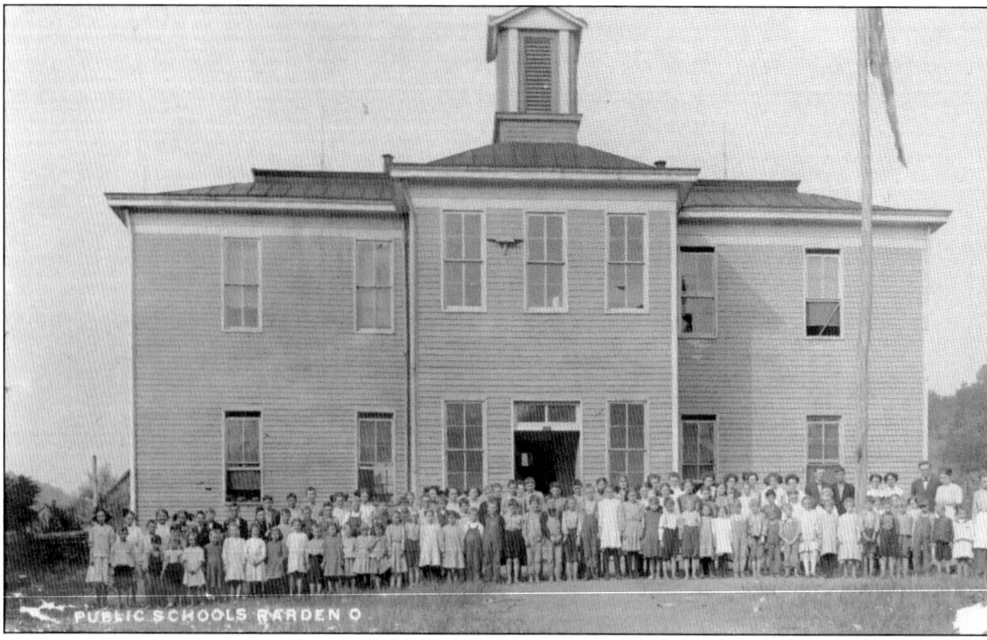

Constructed in 1900, this wood-frame building served as the grade school for much of the Rarden area for nearly 20 years. Although it appears large from the outside, the school only contained four large rooms for grades one through eight. As enrollment increased, voters passed a levy in 1918 to fund a larger brick structure, which included rooms for grades nine through twelve. (Bill Glockner Collection.)

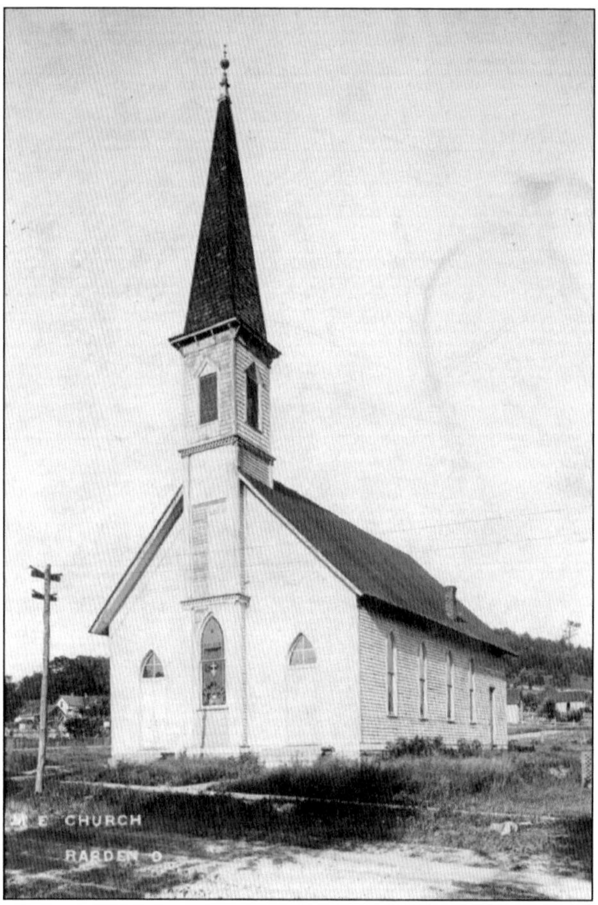

The organization of the Rarden Methodist Episcopal Church dates to 1820. In 1884, Evan Morgan deeded land to the church's trustees for $1 for a term of 99 years. The land was to be used for "just purposes," and if the agreement was broken, the land would revert back to Morgan. This church was constructed in 1887 on High Street and remains standing today. (Bill Glockner Collection.)

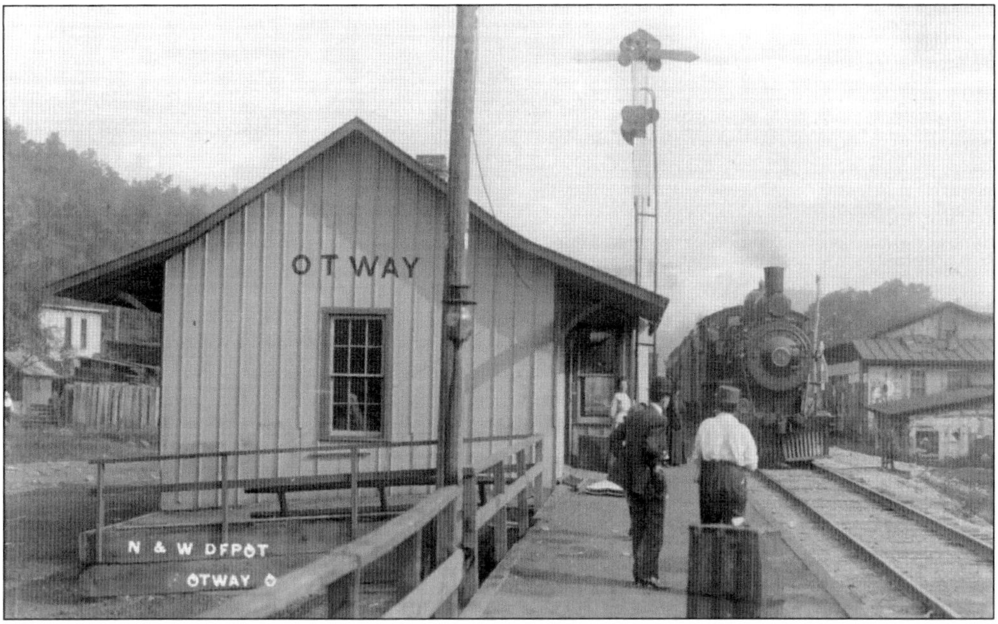

In this 1910 scene, a Norfolk & Western passenger train headed from Portsmouth to Cincinnati stops at the Otway depot. Train travel was the most efficient method of transportation for residents of rural northwestern Scioto County until the 1950s, when improved roadways became the preferred means of transportation for locals. In 1956, this depot building was relocated across the tracks along State Route 73; it then housed a convenience store until the late 1990s.

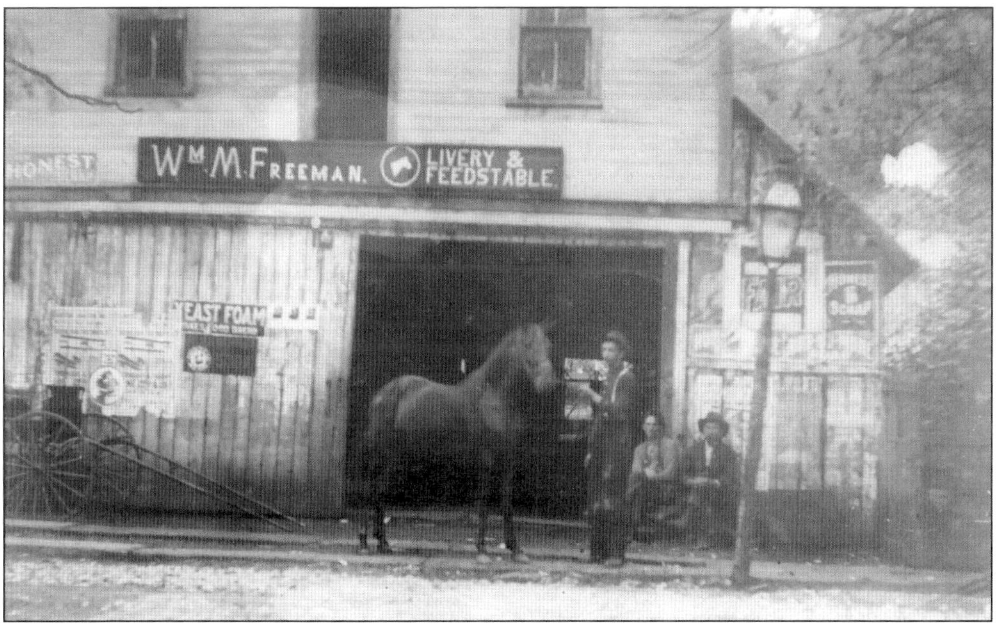

William Freeman operated a livery stable and feed store in Otway during the early 1900s. The building, was destroyed in 1916 by fire but was then rebuilt at nearly double its original size. Freeman was well respected within the community, and he and his wife were instrumental in raising funds to rebuild the heavily damaged Otway school and Christian Union Church following the historic fire. (Paul O'Neill Collection.)

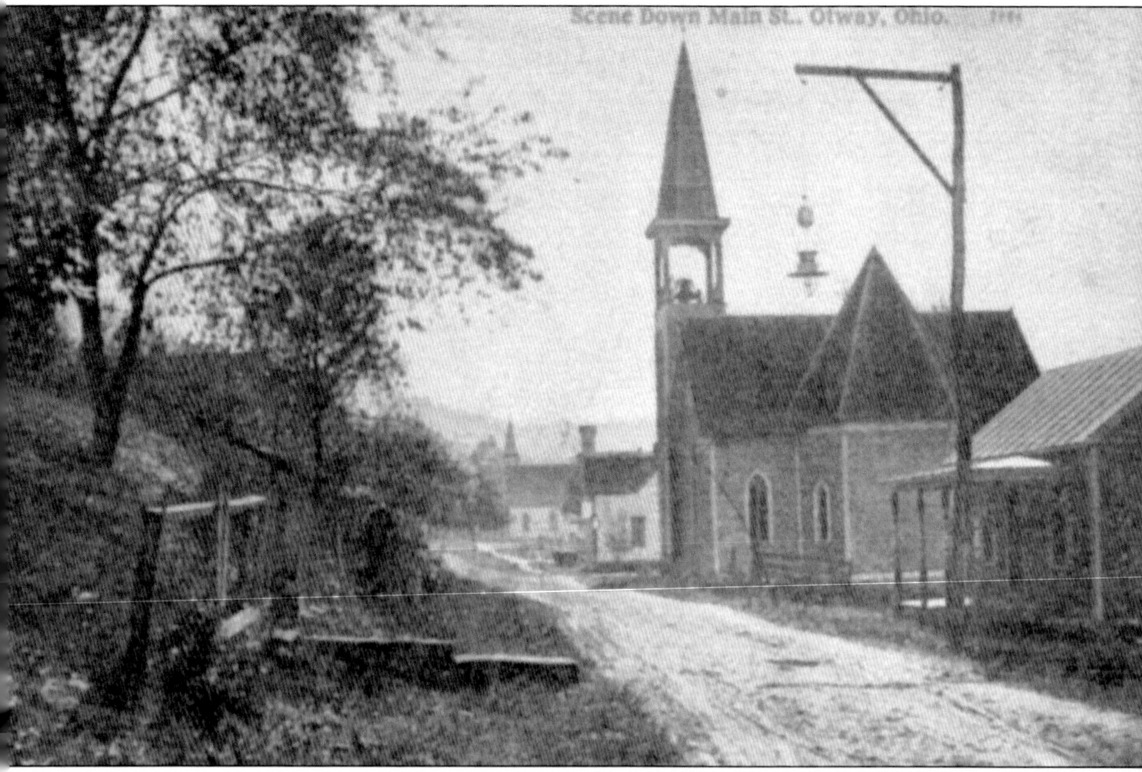

This image looking south on Main Street in Otway clearly shows the road conditions that were standard in 1908 but would be considered appalling today. This road, initially named Galena Pike, originated in West Portsmouth and terminated at Galena, which was later renamed Rarden. In the late 1920s, the State of Ohio took over ownership and maintenance of the roadway and designated it as State Route 73. Improvements consisted of converting the simple dirt path to gravel, which was replaced with a tar and gravel combination in the early 1930s. Now known as the Portsmouth and Hillsboro Road, it was advertised as one of the most scenic drives in Southern Ohio, causing an increase in traffic—and the complaints that followed. With other county lanes being upgraded, State Route 73 through Otway and Rarden was finally paved by the middle of 1940. (Bill Glockner Collection.)

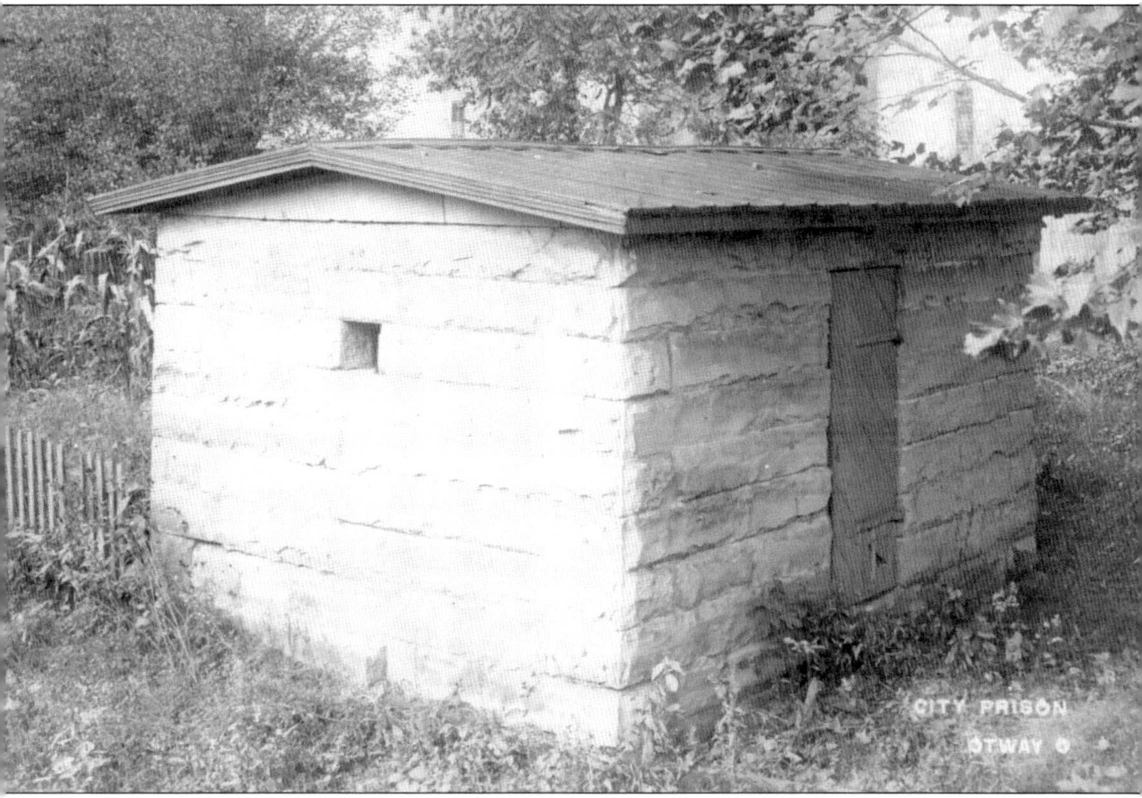

Some communities opted to construct their own village jails, as the nearest county jail could be located many miles away. Around 1910, the Otway jail, located—oddly enough—near a school and a church, temporarily housed those arrested by the town marshal or mayor. Drunken and disorderly conduct was the typical offense. The building was constructed of stone blocks and had one door and a few windows. The only way to access the jail was by wading through the nearby creek or walking down an embankment from the railroad tracks. In March 1932, two men charged with minor offenses escaped within 10 days of each other, and the *Portsmouth Daily Times* critically proclaimed the jail to be a "relic of the old saloon days." The escapees were later recaptured but left the impression that all a prisoner needed to make an escape was a friend with a large crowbar. The jail closed soon thereafter. (Paul O'Neill Collection.)

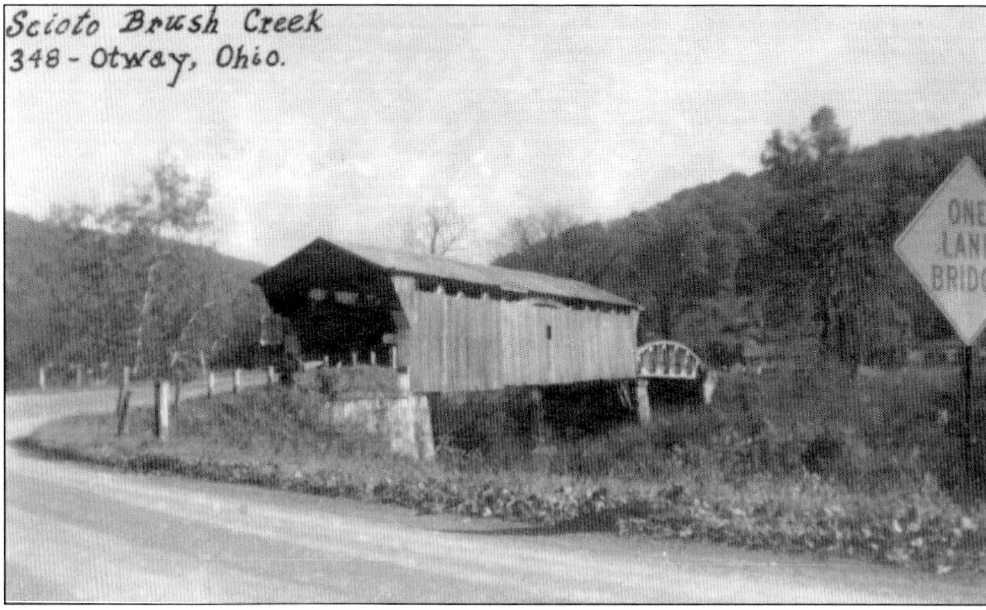

Built in 1874 by the Smith Bridge Company of Toledo, Ohio, the 127-foot-long Otway Covered Bridge was used by horse and buggies and automobiles until 1963, when it was closed to vehicular traffic. The bridge, which spans Scioto Brush Creek, remains standing today thanks to several preservation efforts and a major refurbishing in 2014. The bridge was listed in the National Register of Historic Places in 1974. (Sharon Bender Collection.)

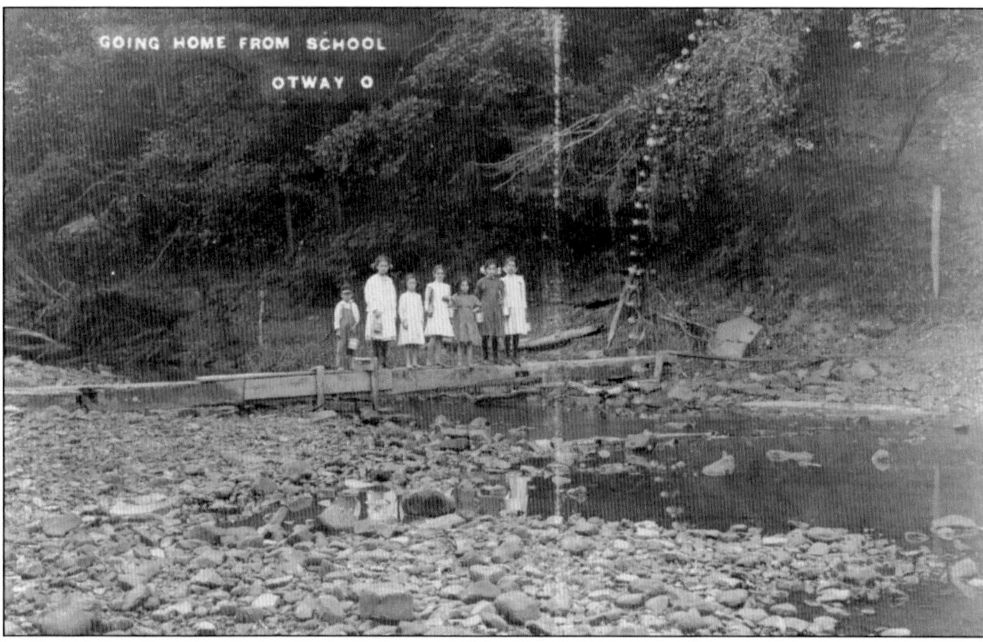

Children posed for this picture postcard while walking home from Otway School around 1910. Otway children attended school in a log cabin in the 1820s, then in one-room schoolhouses, and, eventually, in modern brick structures. After merging with other schools to form the Northwest School District a few miles away, Otway's final high school graduation was in 1958, while its last elementary school classes lasted until 1993. (Paul O'Neill Collection.)

Built in 1890 at a cost of $1,200, the Otway Public School employed one principal and two teachers. The wooden building contained three rooms—two upstairs and one downstairs. By 1916, due to increasing enrollment, the structure was scheduled to be razed and replaced with a modern brick facility. Fate intervened, as the school was destroyed during the Otway fire of April 21, 1916. (Bill Glockner Collection.)

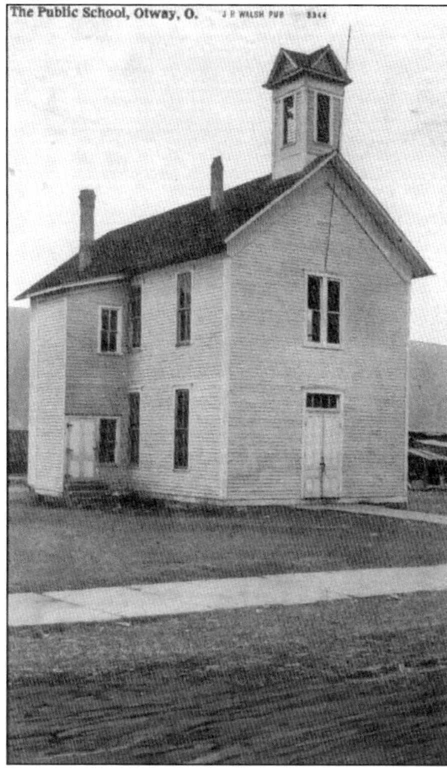

Elementary students from the one-room Mount Joy school posed for the photograph featured on this c. 1915 postcard. Mount Joy, one of 108 one-room schoolhouses listed in Scioto County at the time, and others were slowly reorganized into new school districts as ordered by state laws passed in 1914. By 1940, all of the one-room schools in Scioto County had closed. (Paul O'Neill Collection.)

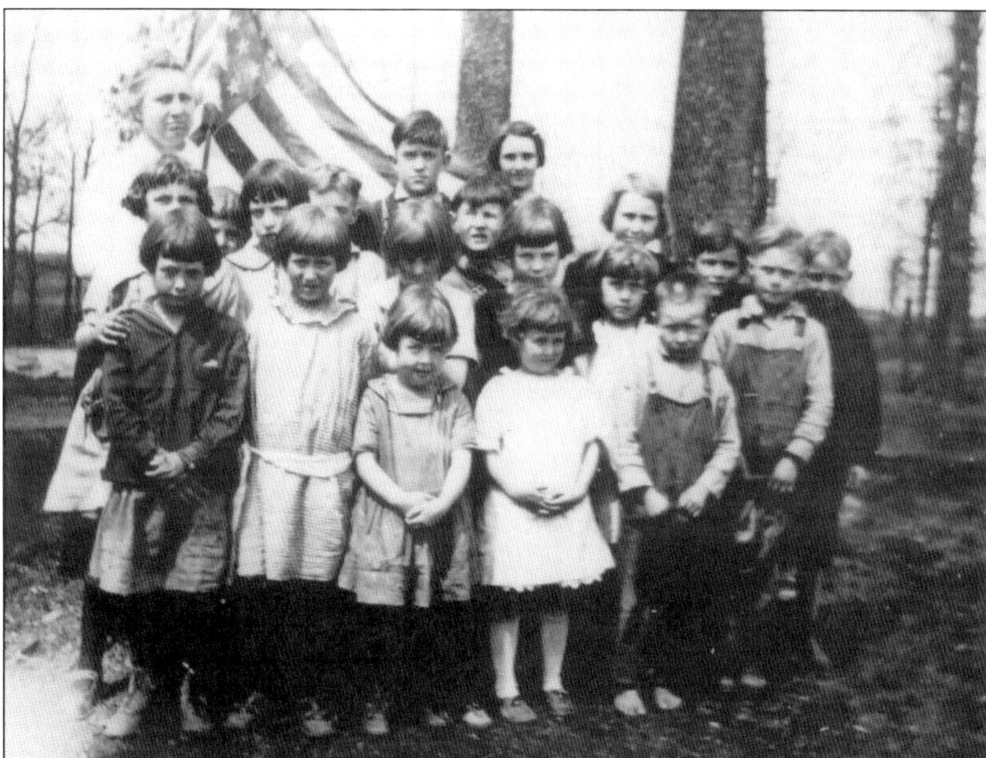

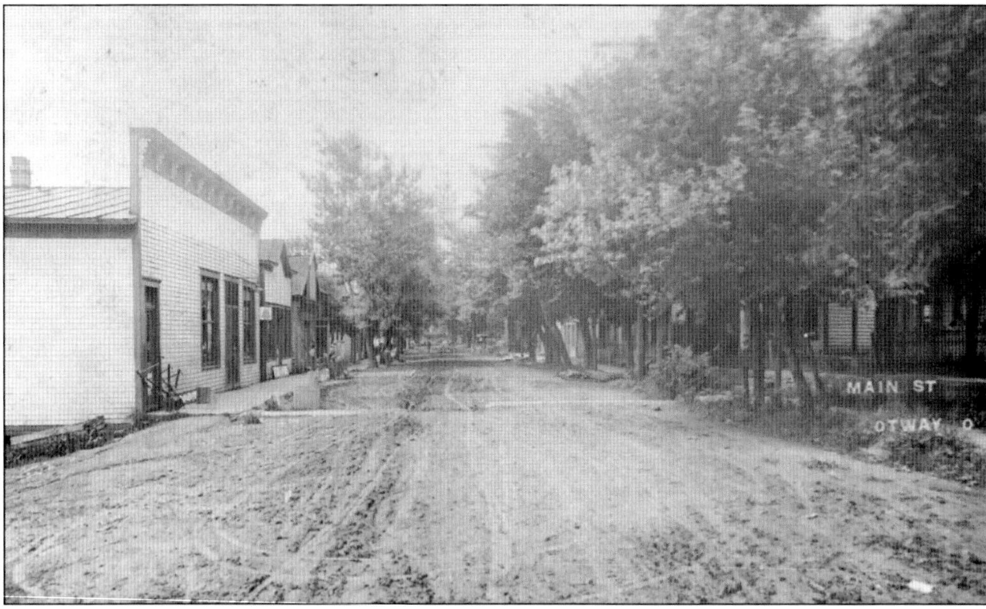

On April 21, 1916, an Otway man burning rubbish started one of the worst fires in Scioto County's history. High winds, closely spaced wooden structures, and inadequate firefighting equipment resulted in nearly the entire town being consumed by flames. In all, 31 buildings were lost or heavily damaged, including most of those shown in this 1908 view looking west on Main Street. (Paul O'Neill Collection.)

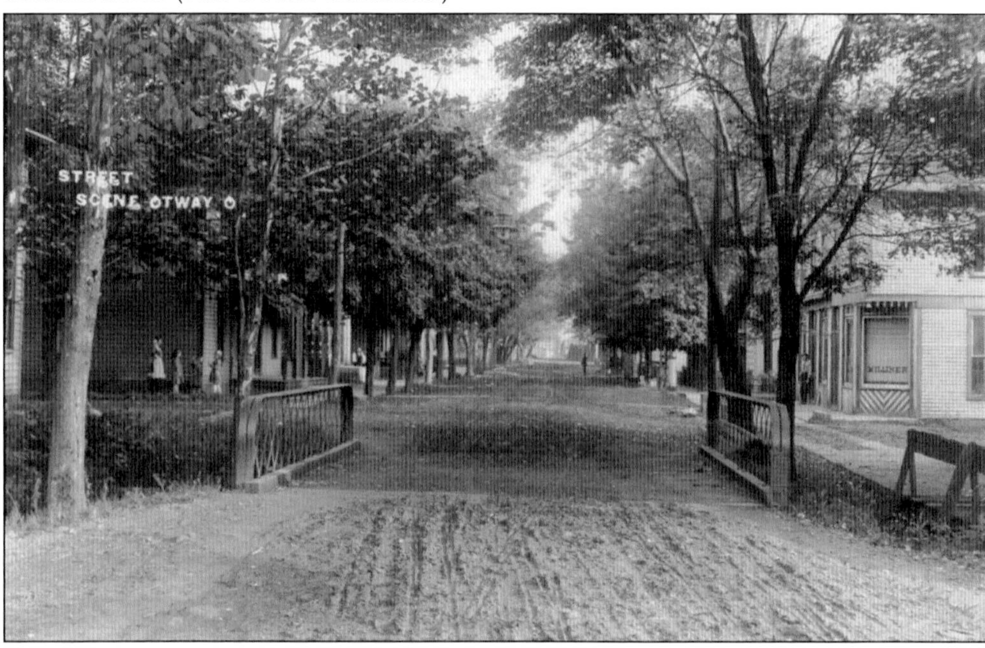

Otway, named after the 17th-century English poet Thomas Otway, was founded in the early 1800s but sprang to life with the arrival of the railroad in 1883. On October 31, 1890, it was incorporated as a village and contained many homes and businesses, as shown in this 1910 image. Among the village structures were a hotel, a livery stable, several stores, churches, and a school. (Bill Glockner Collection.)

In 1916, the brick church in Otway was dedicated and placed under the patronage of Our Lady of Lourdes. The archbishop of Cincinnati sent Father Richter to serve as the church's priest. The Our Lady of Lourdes church was remodeled in 1965 with improved lighting and new paneling, ceiling tiles, pews, and an altar; this was made possible from the bequest of Joseph Walsh. Fr. John Stattmiller currently serves as priest for the congregation. (Bill Glockner Collection.)

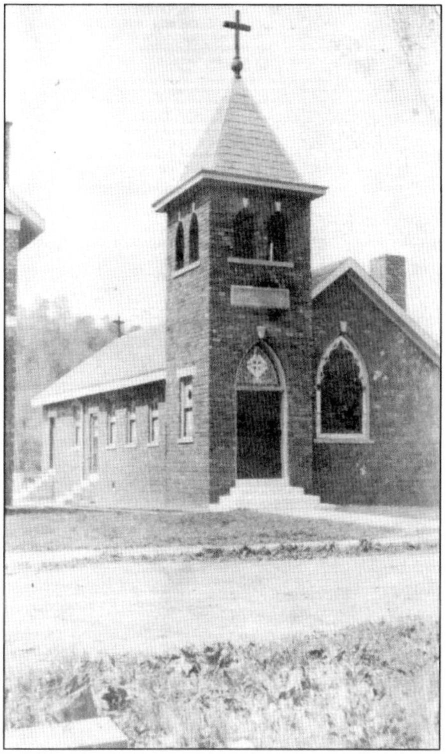

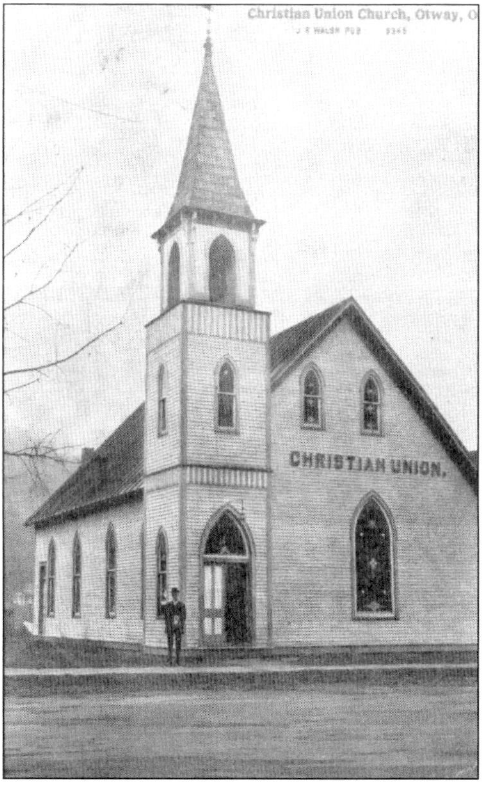

The Otway Christian Union Church was built in 1899 on Main Street near the center of the village. After it was destroyed by fire in April 1916, only a few pews and a bell—which was given to the village for the Town Hall—survived. Unfortunately, a replacement church built of bricks was also destroyed by fire in 1928. Another brick church, constructed after the second fire, remains standing. (Bill Glockner Collection.)

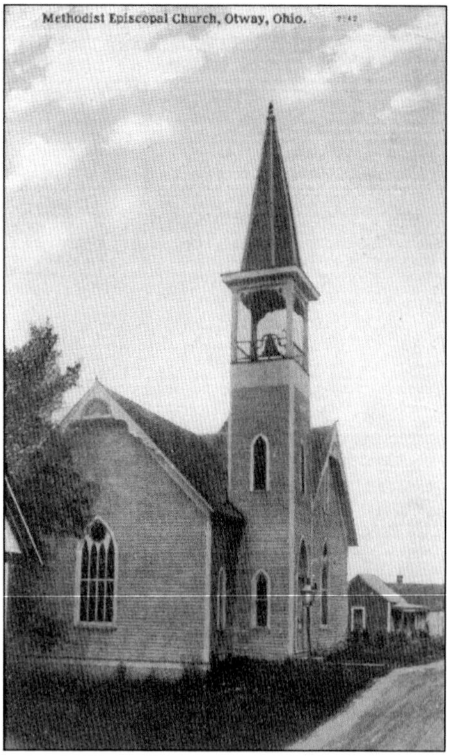

The horrific Otway fire of April 21, 1916, started only 100 feet away from the Otway Methodist Church. Built in 1898, the church escaped destruction due to the wind blowing the opposite direction. Odella Upton, wife of the pastor at the time, was credited with helping families save their belongings before the fire reached their homes. The church later housed those left homeless, along with their belongings, while they made other living arrangements. (Paul O'Neill Collection.)

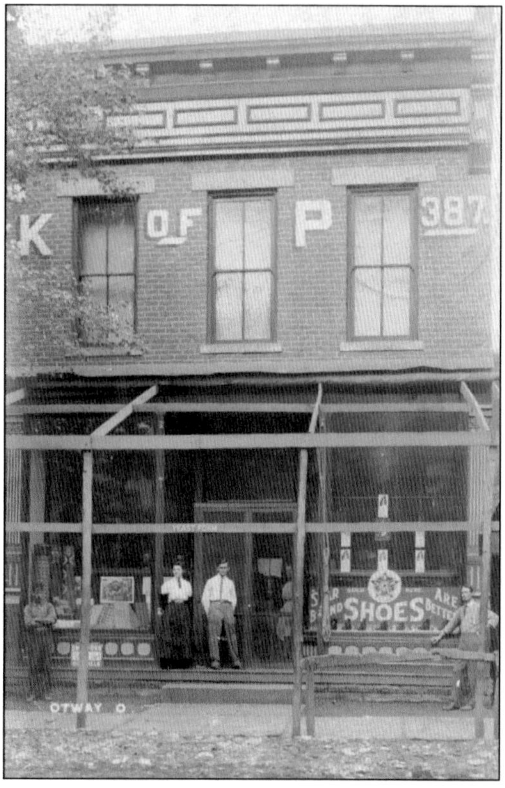

The fraternal and secret society of the Knights of Pythias was founded in Washington, DC, in 1864. In 1904, the Knights leased the upper story of a brick building in Otway owned by George Chabot. The ideals of loyalty, honor, and friendship were at the center of the order. Jim Blackburn operated a grocery store on the ground floor of the building until the disastrous April 1916 Otway fire. (Paul O'Neill Collection.)

Six

South Webster and Minford

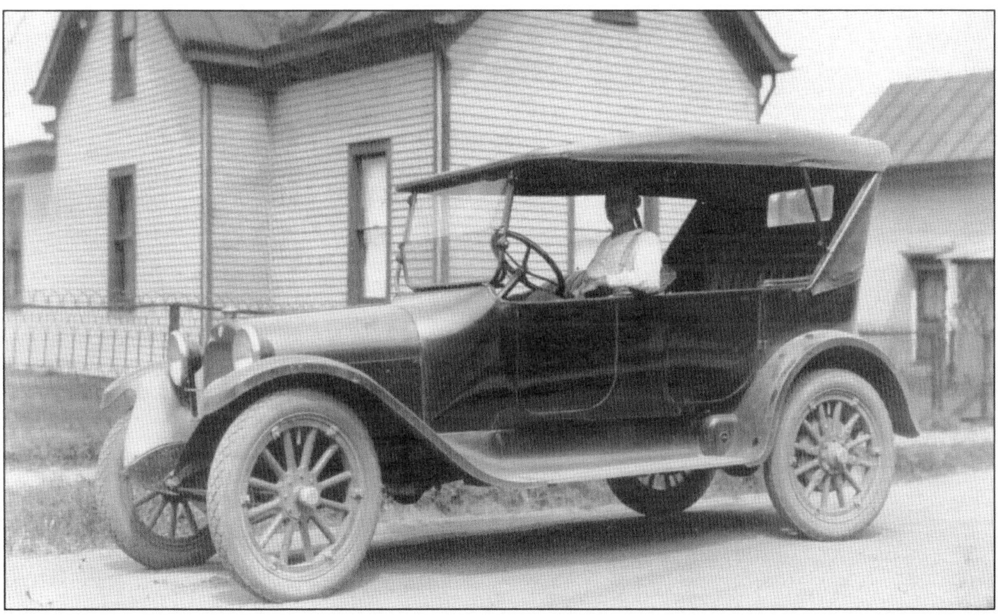

Harmon Simmering was a well-known businessman in the South Webster area during the early 20th century. In March 1921, he opened the first movie theater in the village. One year later, he and his brother Fred founded the Simmering Motor Company. Harmon is shown here in the mid-1920s proudly displaying the latest Ford Model T. The Simmering siblings installed the first electric streetlights in South Webster in January 1924. (Susie Beaumont Collection.)

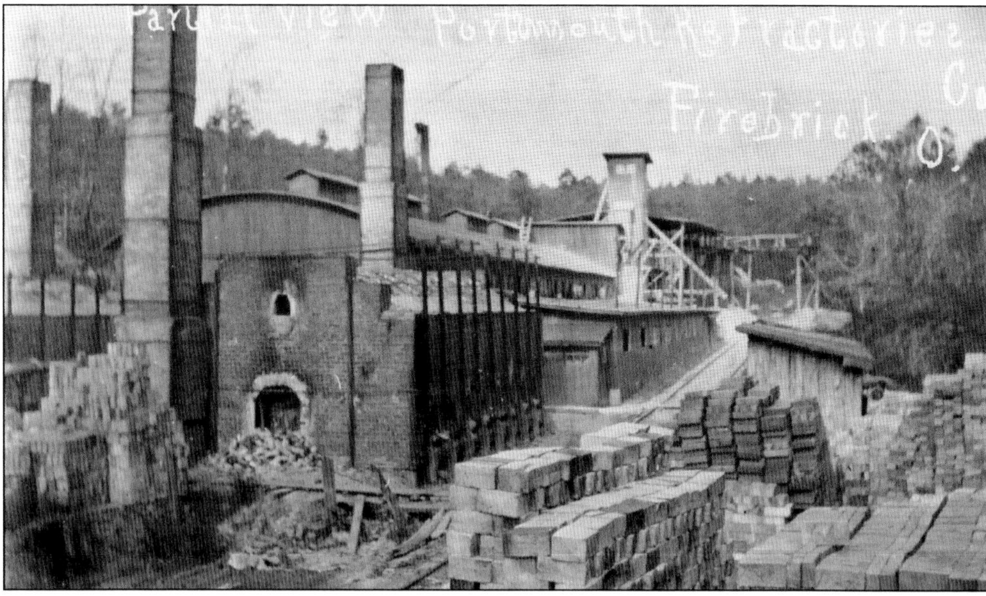

Portsmouth Refractories opened in 1907 and was located just a few miles east of South Webster. Shown here in two photographs from the 1920s, it provided many jobs for northeastern Scioto County residents during the 20th century. The facility produced thousands of bricks each day using the abundant and exceptionally quality material from nearby clay mines, and the bricks were highly sought after for their strength at very high temperatures, making them ideal for use in industries such as steel mills and railroads. Bricks manufactured at Portsmouth Refractories can still be found throughout the world. The owners opened a similar operation in Portsmouth in 1917. The business was sold in June 1929 to Plibrico Jointless Firebrick of Chicago and remains in operation today. (Susie Beaumont Collection.)

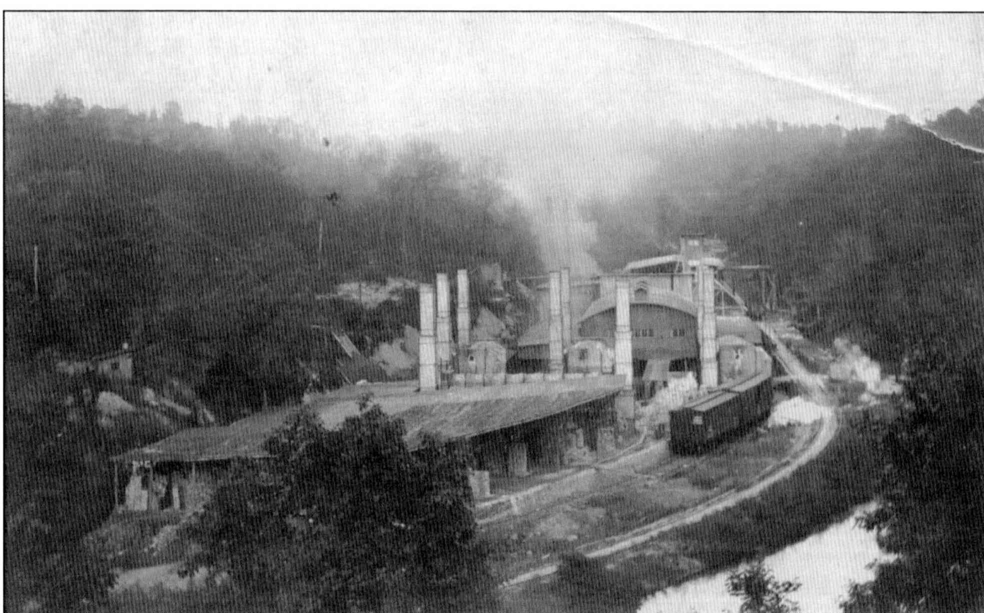

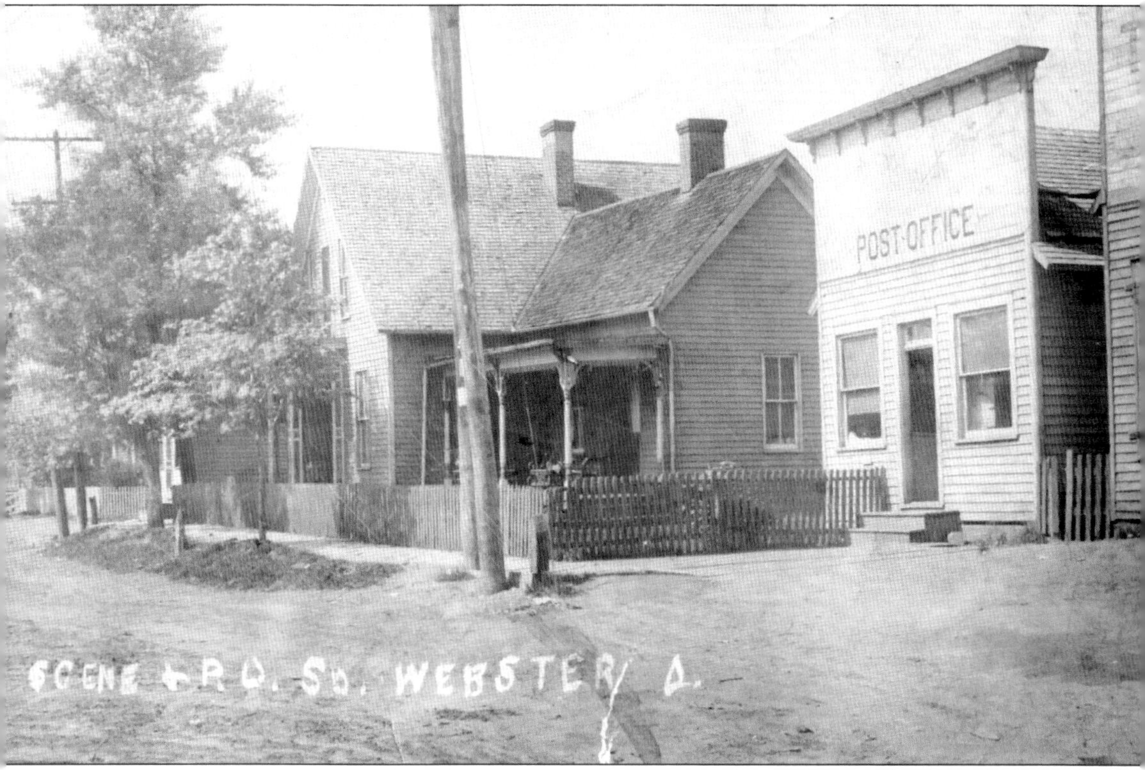

The village officially named South Webster was in its youth when this early 1900 view of a residence and post office was caught on film. The area was first settled in 1837 as the community of Bloomfield, and settlements named Webster and Bennett were formed nearby in the following years. In December 1887, these small hamlets combined and were renamed South Webster. Prior to the arrival of white settlers, the entire area was covered with virgin forest and inhabited by groups of Indians, primarily the Shawnee. An Indian trail leading north toward valuable salt deposits in Jackson County went through South Webster. After being captured in Kentucky in 1778, famed frontiersman Daniel Boone and two dozen men were marched along this trail by Shawnee Indians. Boone escaped and continued the adventures that crafted his larger-than-life image. (Susie Beaumont Collection.)

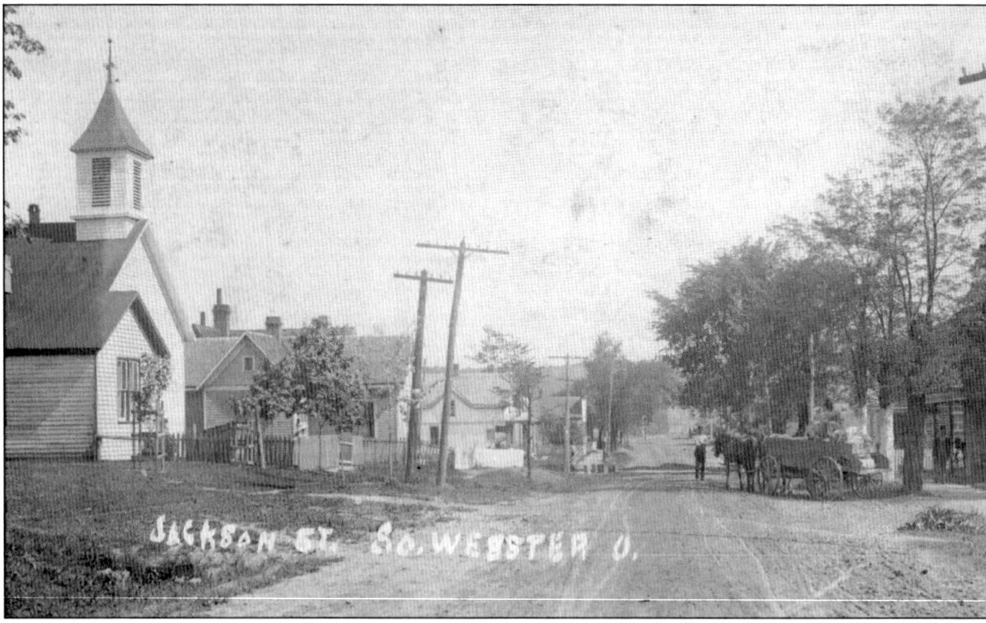

The United Brethren Church is shown in the 1910 postcard above. It was organized in 1879 as the South Webster German Lutheran Church, and early services were conducted in both German and English. Children who attended Sunday school classes were taught in both languages. The historic building was destroyed by fire on June 11, 1932. While the organ and pews were saved by nearby residents, the building was a total loss. On June 11, 1944, the congregation posed for the below photograph, which was taken in front of the rebuilt church. (Both, Susie Beaumont Collection.)

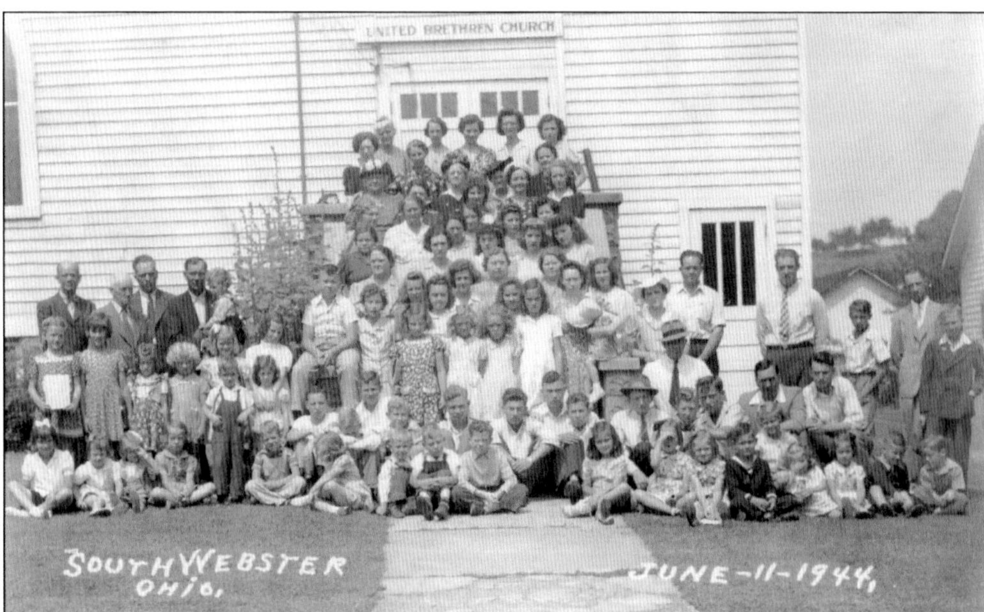

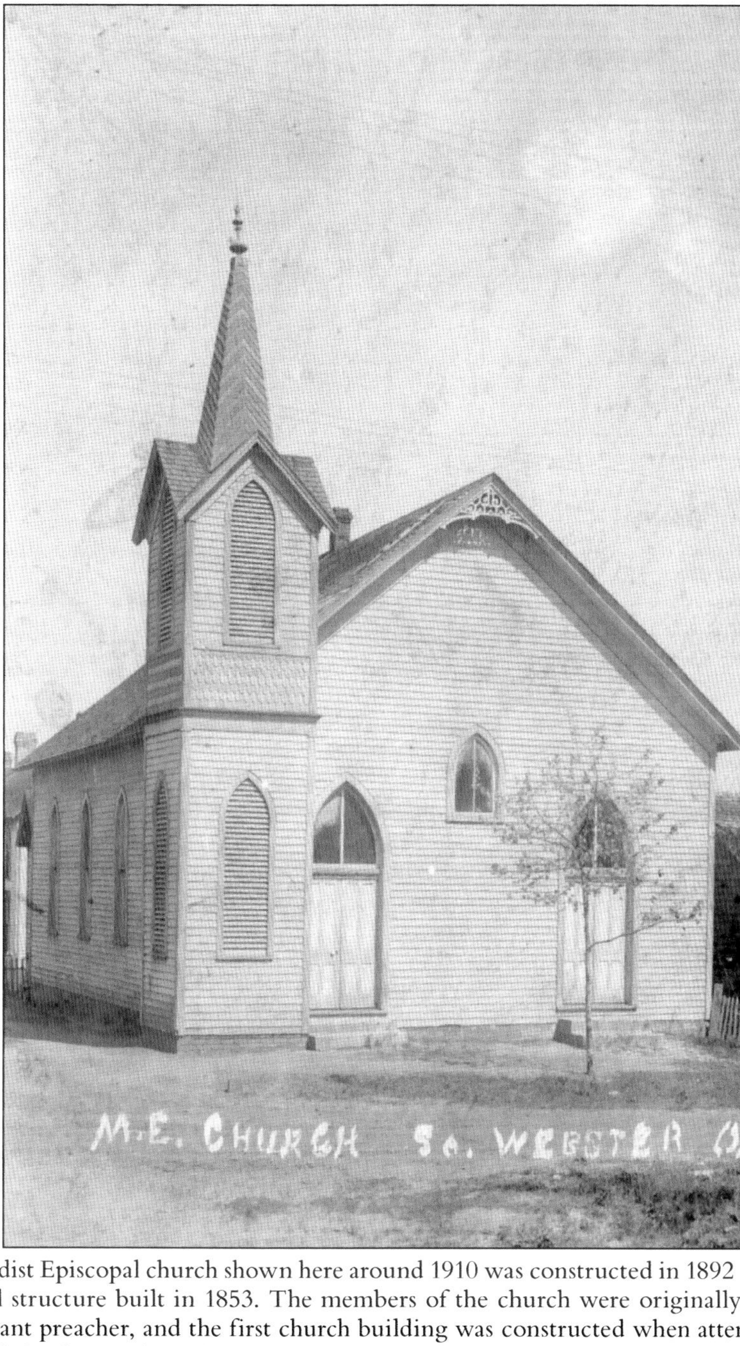

The Methodist Episcopal church shown here around 1910 was constructed in 1892 and replaced the original structure built in 1853. The members of the church were originally attended to by an itinerant preacher, and the first church building was constructed when attendance grew large enough for them to have their own dedicated pastor. On Saturday, June 11, 1932, two men were burning discarded cement sacks in the church's furnace. A defective chimney flue directed several burning pieces of the bags onto the roof, which caught on fire. As winds increased, flying embers rapidly spread to a nearby residence and to the adjacent United Brethren Church, both of which were soon in flames. By the time area fire departments and citizens had the blaze under control, the house and both churches had been completely destroyed. They were all swiftly rebuilt stronger than before. (Susie Beaumont Collection.)

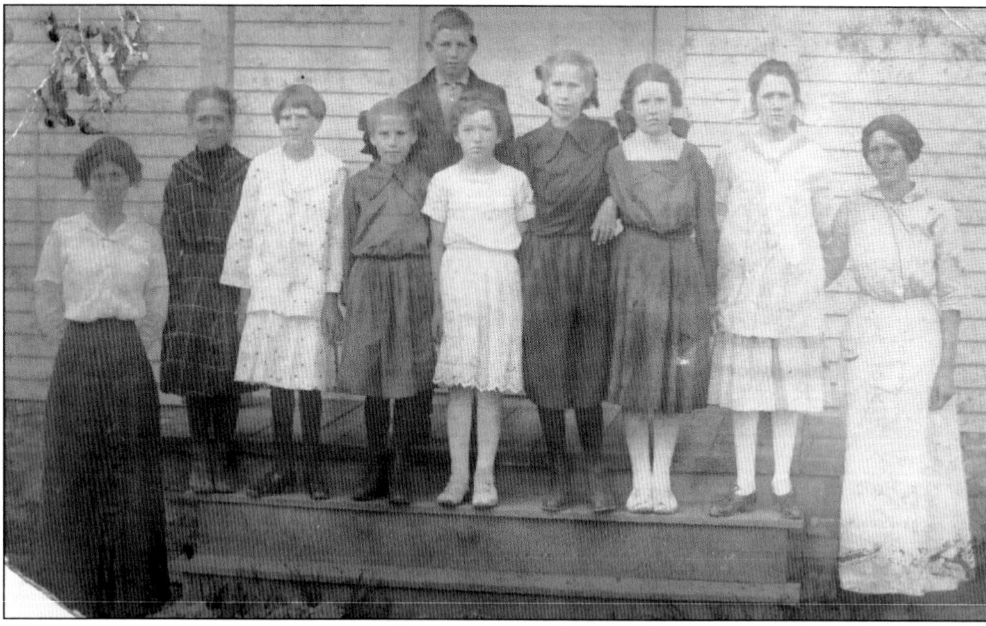

By the early 1900s, dozens of one-room schoolhouses were scattered throughout rural Scioto County. Shown in 1914 in front of their new school building at Bloom Furnace are, from left to right, students Georgia Townsend, Myrta Crabtree, Ethel Queen, Earl Crabtree, Della Crabtree, Isabell Queen, Bessie Townsend, and Zella Crabtree. The teachers (at far left and right) are unidentified. The previous structure was destroyed by a tornado in 1912. (Susie Beaumont Collection.)

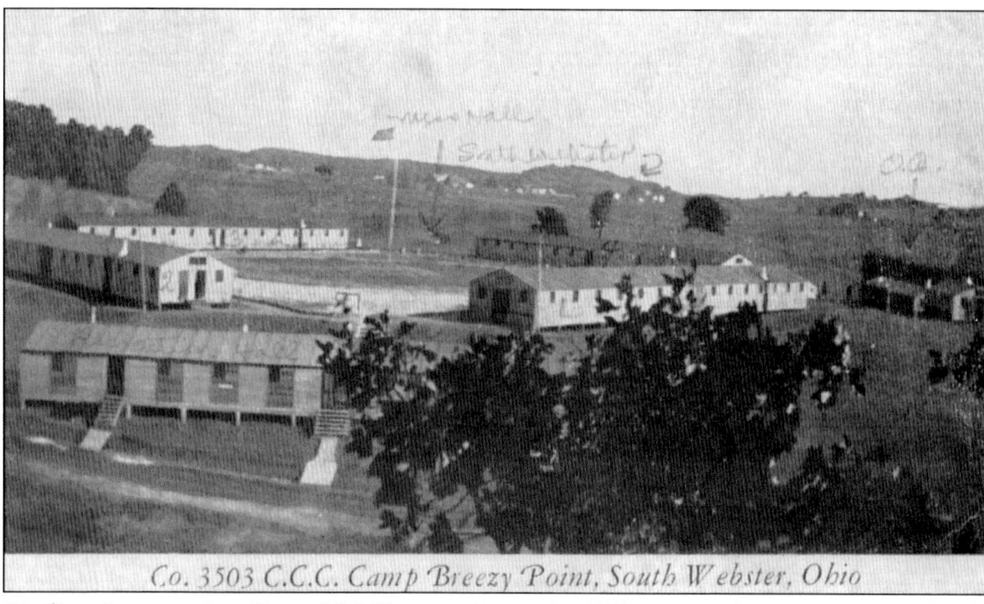

Civilian Conservation Corps (CCC) camps began in 1933 to provide young men with jobs during the Great Depression. Camp Breezy Point, located near South Webster, was one of several such facilities in Scioto County. Under the direction of US Army officers, men were paid $30 monthly and given food, clothing, and shelter in exchange for manual labor. The program ended in 1942 amidst the draft and World War II. (Bill Glockner Collection.)

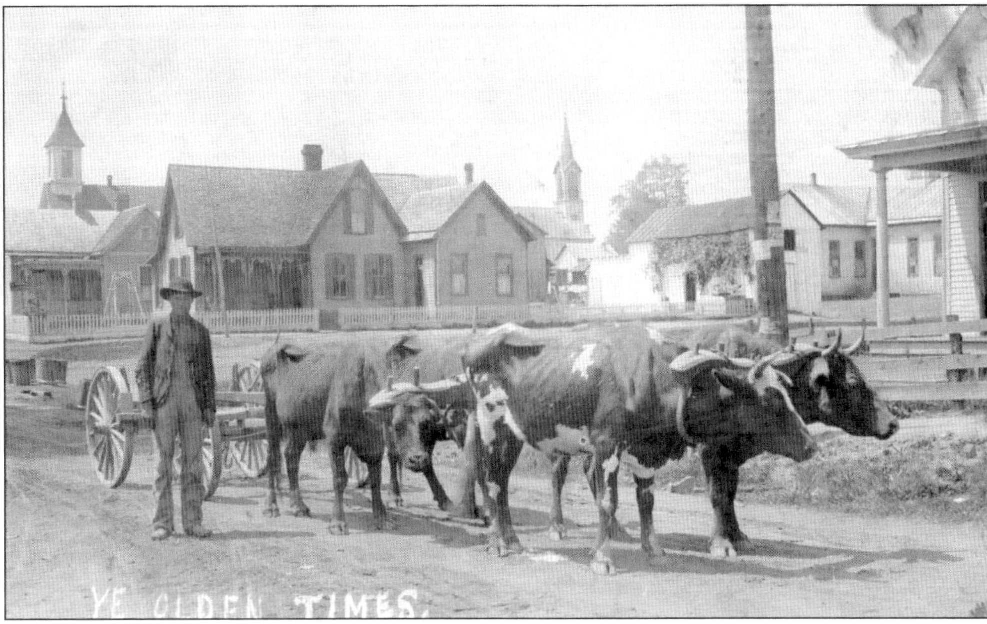

It may be hard for some to imagine, but before the days of paved roads, automobiles, and trucks, it was not uncommon to see a team of horses or oxen delivering goods to businesses and households. In this c. 1900 photograph, an oxen team pulls an empty wagon along the dirt streets of South Webster. (Susie Beaumont Collection.)

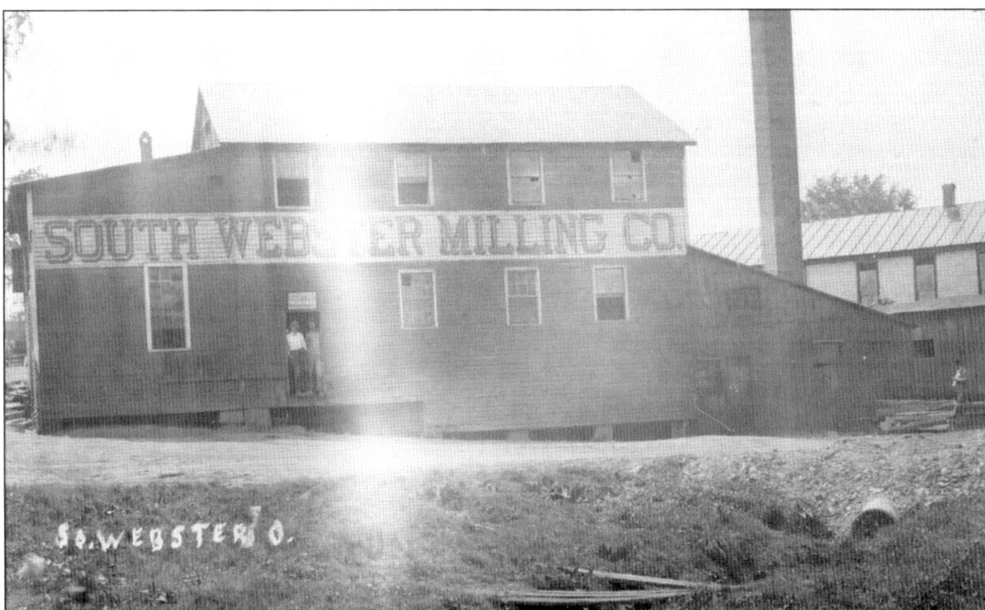

The Tisen and Bennett Company, named after the owners, began producing cornmeal, flour, and animal feed on Clingman Street near the Baltimore & Ohio Railroad in 1857. After changing owners several times, with the last being H.H. Mittendorf (in 1909), it became the South Webster Milling Company. The mill closed in the early 1920s and was demolished in 1936. (Susie Beaumont Collection.)

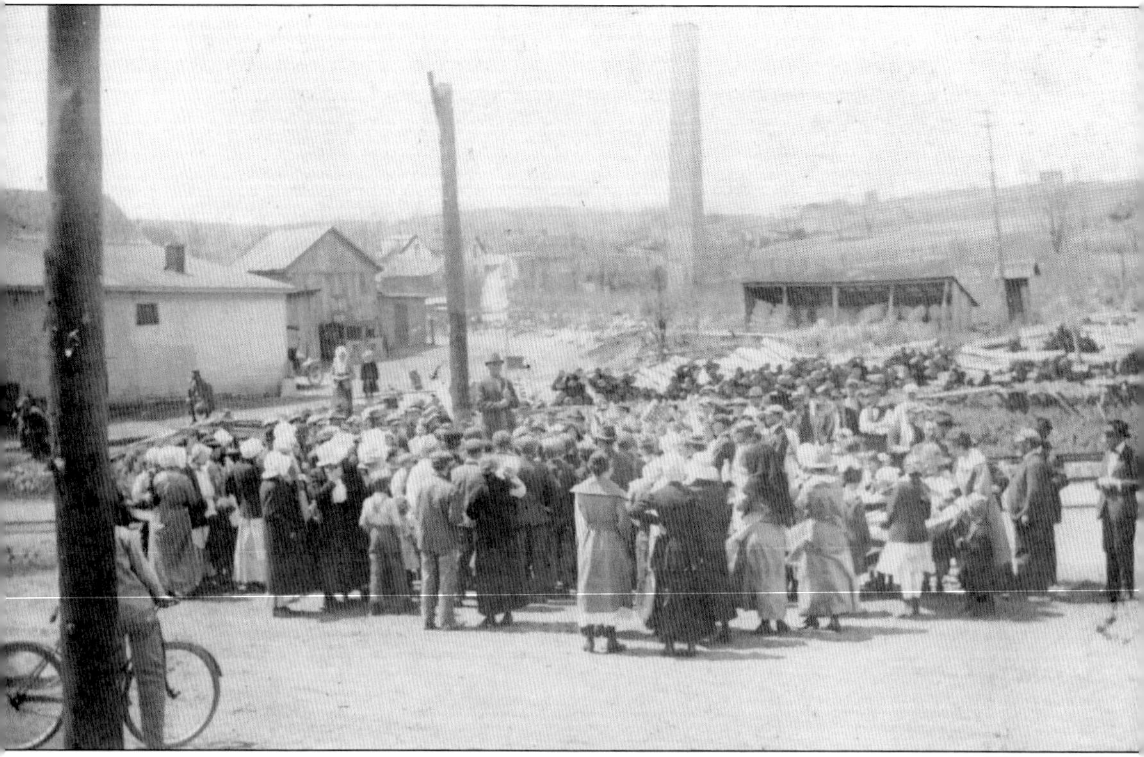

In May 1918, Congress passed the Sedition Act, making it illegal to act or speak against the government in any way. Primarily intended to weaken critics of the war against Germany during World War I, the law carried stiff penalties, including fines and possible imprisonment. The local press reported approximately six cases of citizens violating the rule; many were of German descent. No doubt many more cases were not reported. Several local historians believe this 1918 view of downtown South Webster shows a punishment being administered to one of its residents. While the details of the charge have been lost to history, a local farmer whose parents were from Germany was publicly forgiven for his act. After giving a public apology and kissing the American flag, he pledged his support to the cause and led one of many local patriotic parades held during the era. The Sedition Act was repealed by Congress in 1920. (Susie Beaumont Collection.)

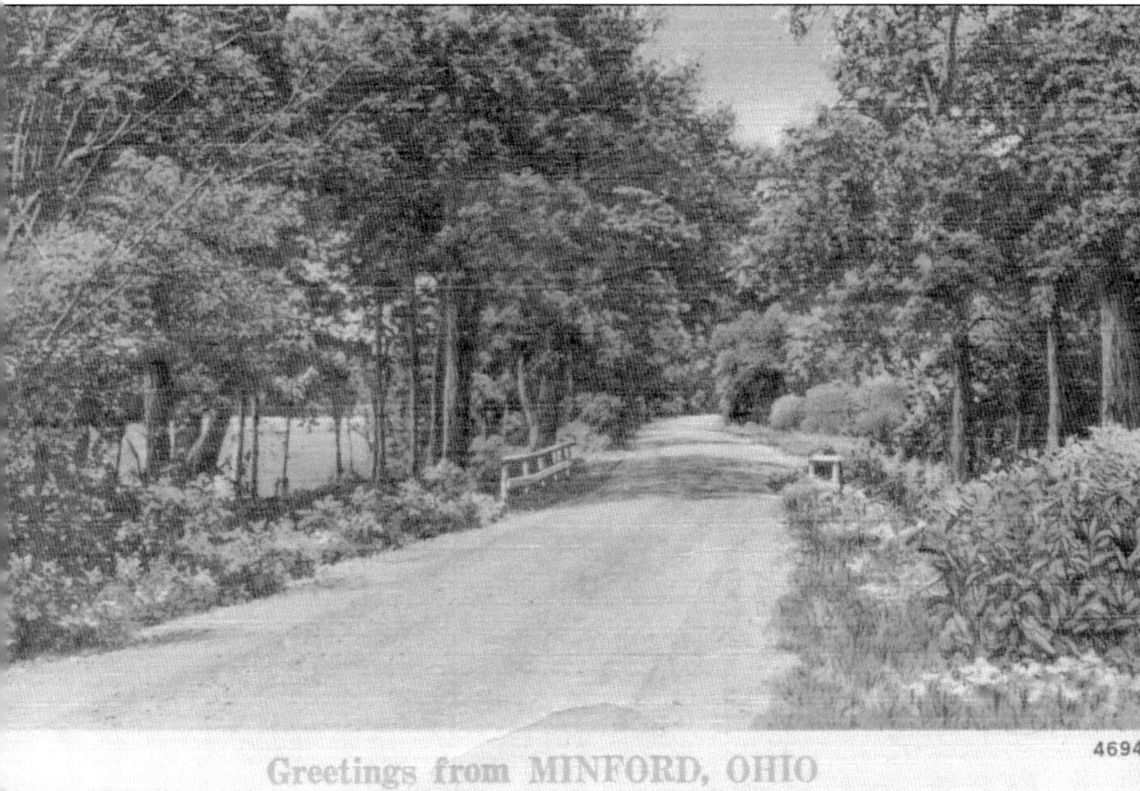

The community of Harrisonville was settled around 1823 by Peter Laforgy, owner and operator of the area store. Named after Army general and future president William Henry Harrison, the town was officially surveyed on May 24, 1859. The early village consisted of three general stores, a blacksmith shop, a funeral home, and a harness shop. When the Chesapeake & Ohio Railroad constructed a major rail line in 1917, it was discovered that a town named Harrisonville already existed along the line. Knowing the importance of what the railroad could mean for the area, citizens happily obliged in choosing a new name. Minford was chosen in honor of the oldest (and longest-residing) resident of the town, 51-year-old blacksmith Frank R. Minford. Many businesses, countless homes, schools, churches, and the Greater Portsmouth Regional Airport are now located in the Minford area. (Bill Glockner Collection.)

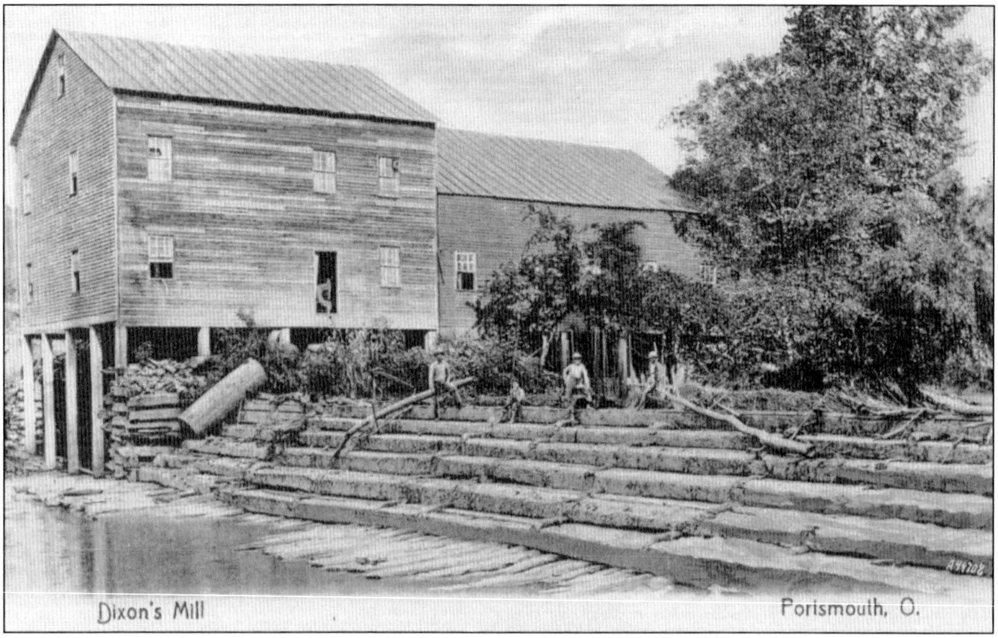

Constructed in 1804 by Emmanuel Traxler, Dixon's Mill was located along the Little Scioto River south of Minford. Purchased by Silas Dixon in 1866, the mill was later owned by his son Noah Dixon. The younger Dixon added a large sawmill and flour mill, which had a daily capacity of 30 barrels of flour. This c. 1908 postcard shows the facility in its prime. (Bill Glockner Collection.)

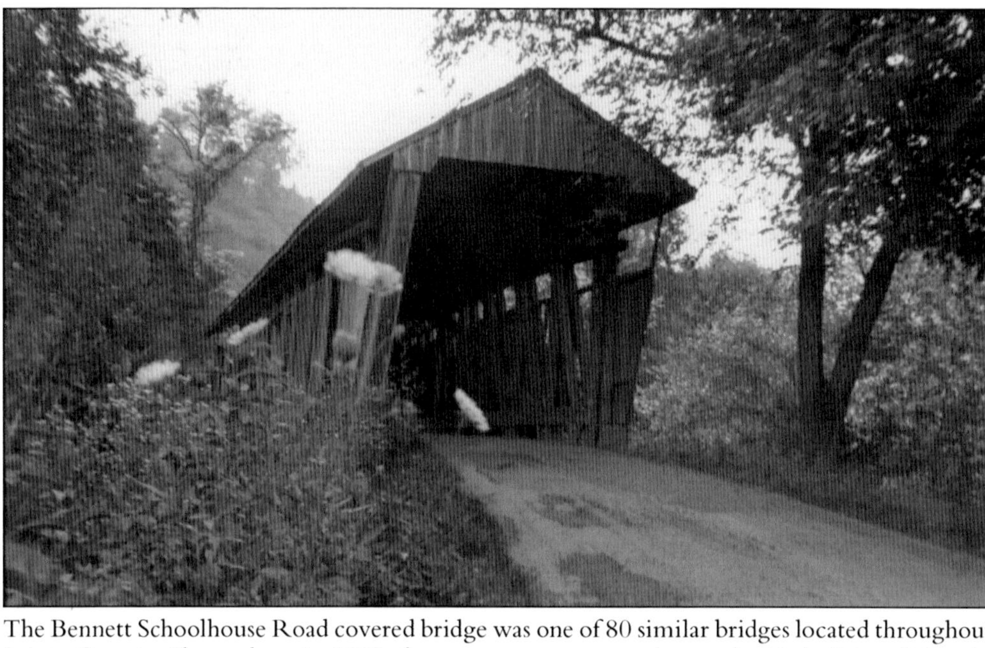

The Bennett Schoolhouse Road covered bridge was one of 80 similar bridges located throughout Scioto County. Shown here in 1963, the span was constructed over the Little Scioto River in 1867. The 112-foot-long bridge was listed in the National Register of Historic Places in October 1978; however, the distinction did not last long, as six years later, it collapsed into the river. (Bill Glockner Collection.)

Seven

Rosemount and Portsmouth

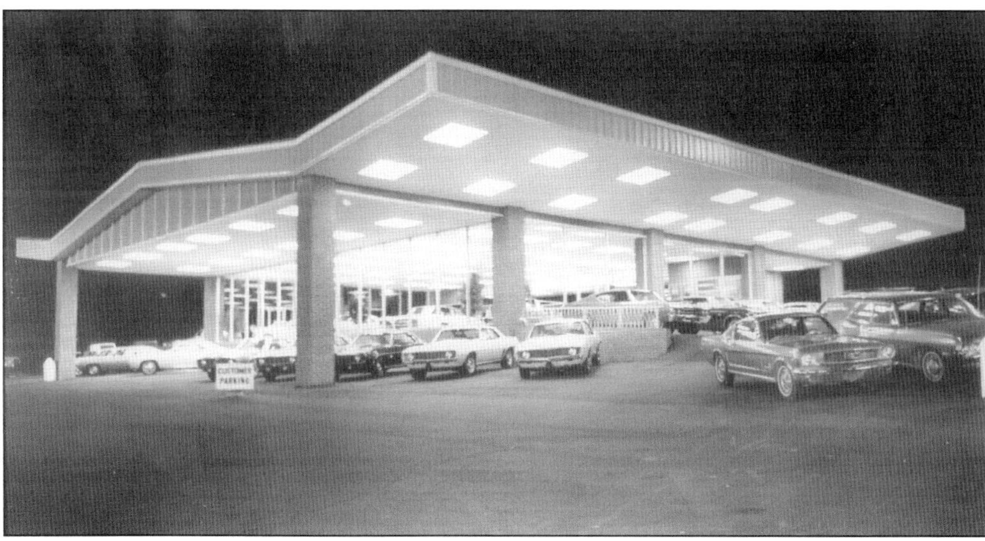

Glockner, the oldest Chevy dealership in Ohio, sold the first Chevrolet in the state in 1912. Originally located at Gallia and Gay Streets, the business moved to Second and Chillicothe Streets in 1919. After relocating to Route 23 in Rosemount in 1969 with an attractively expanded showroom (pictured), Glockner continued to grow, with several additional dealerships now located throughout Southern Ohio and Northern Kentucky. (Glockner Family of Dealerships.)

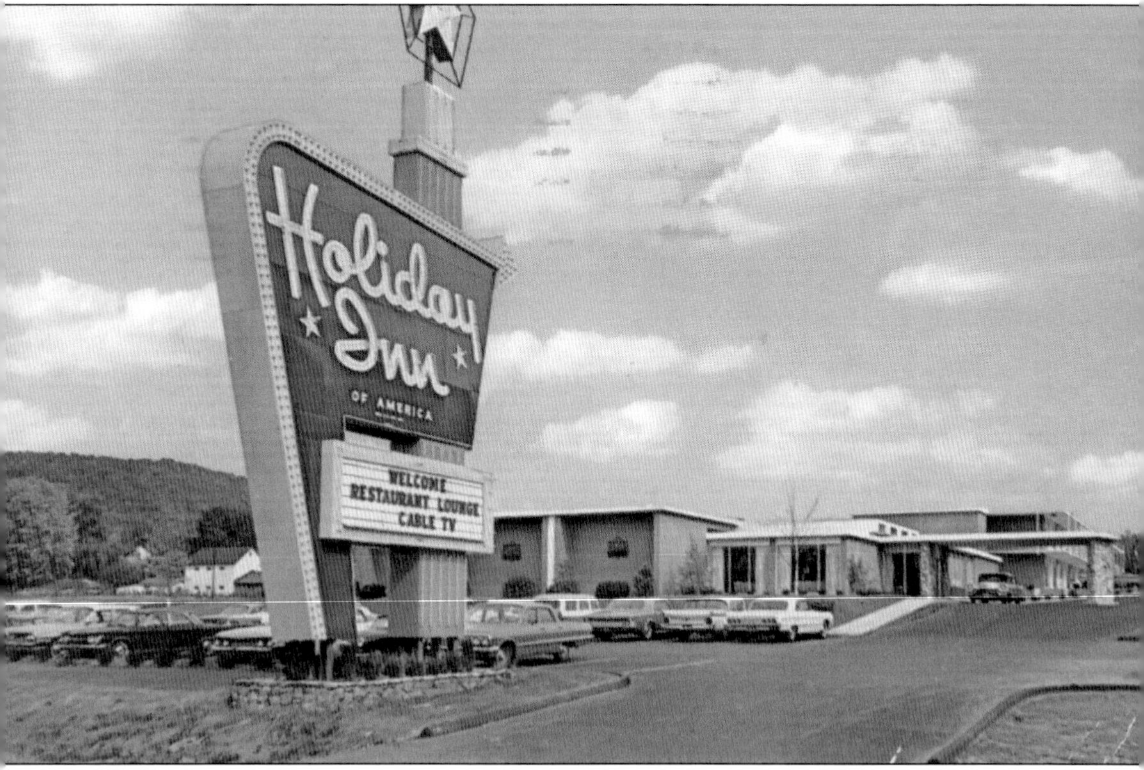

This Holiday Inn opened in early September 1964 and was located on US Route 23 in Rosemount. One of the first 500 Holiday Inns operating in the United States, it included 100 guest rooms, an indoor swimming pool, conference rooms, a bar area with a capacity of 80 people, a banquet room that could seat 200, and an all-you-can-eat buffet (priced at $2.50) at the "Southern Lounge." Ameristay Inn and Suites now occupies the building. When this Holiday Inn was in its construction phase, a major natural gas line was extended from Portsmouth to reach the new motel. Additional utility lines were also installed or upgraded, leading to an economic boom for the Rosemount area. Within two years, Harts Family Center department store, the Shake Shoppe, and several other new businesses opened along Route 23. In 1969, Glockner Chevrolet opened a spacious new showroom in the vicinity and later moved its operations to Rosemount from their Second Street location in Portsmouth.

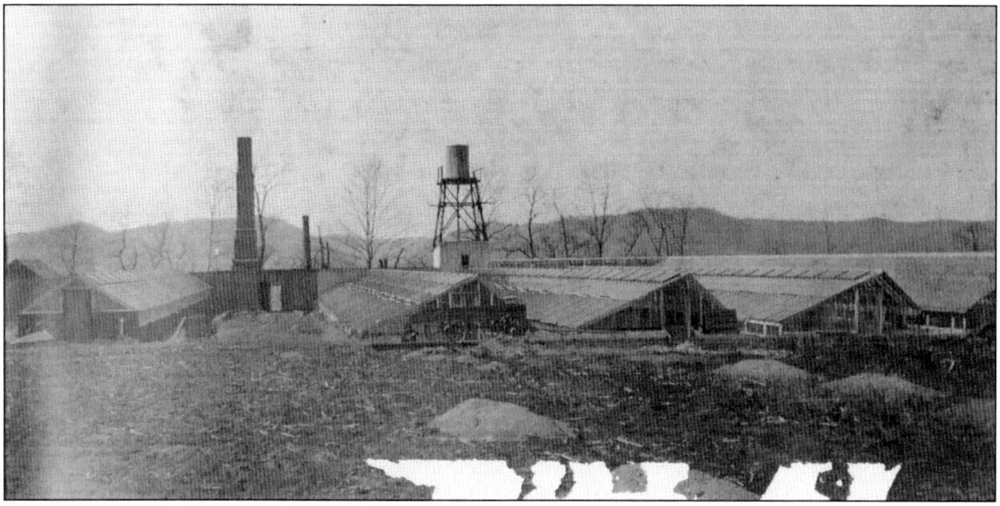

Founded in 1894, Herm's Florist in Portsmouth was one of the largest floral companies in Southern Ohio. Offering fresh-cut flower arrangements year-round, the company included a massive network of greenhouses on Scioto Trail near Rosemount that consisted of several buildings and more than 65,000 feet of glass. The climate-controlled buildings remained in place for nearly 70 years, until they were sold and razed to make way for a Volkswagen dealership. Glockner Toyota has occupied this property since 1975.

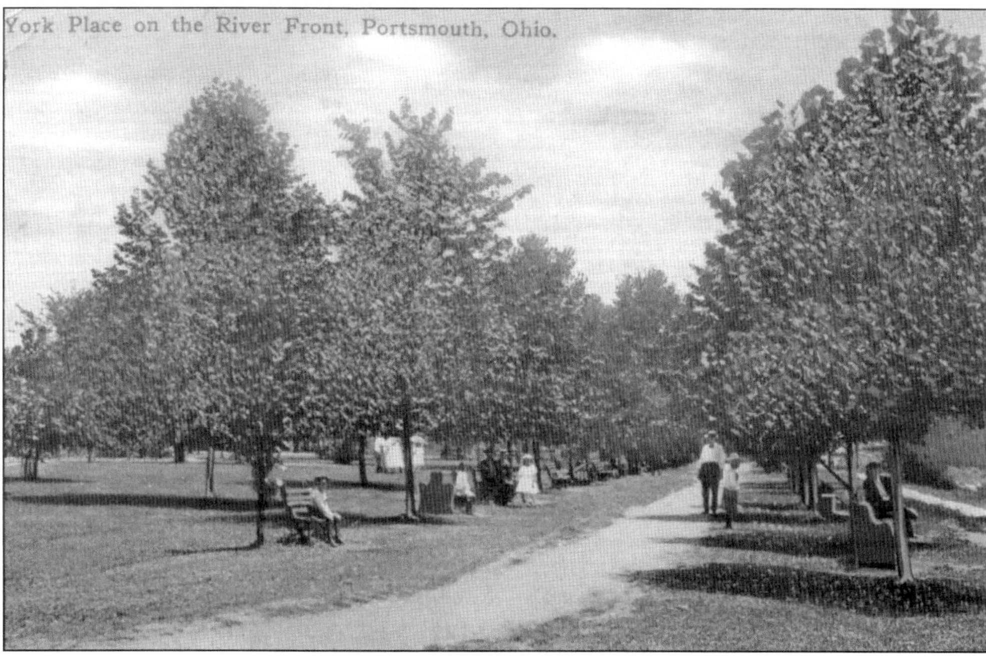

Created in the early 1900s, York Park (also known as York Place) was located along the Ohio River southwest of Front and Chillicothe Streets. Named after Levi York, who donated the property, the park had a playground that consisted of a giant slide, swings, teeter-totters, and a shelter house. A wading pool, which was divided in the middle to allow boys and girls to play at the same time, was a popular feature. (Paul O'Neill Collection.)

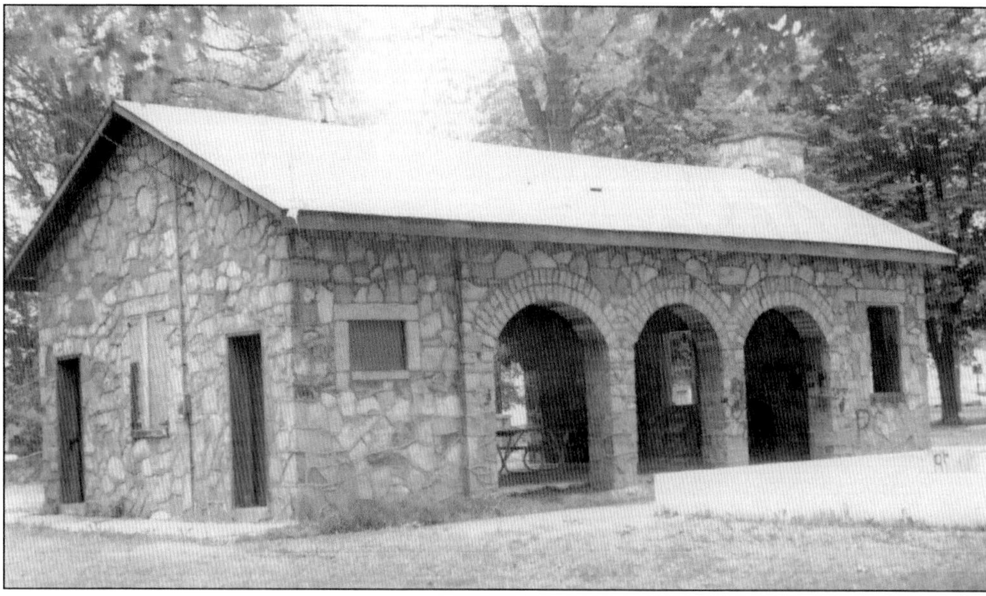

Tracy Park was donated to the city in 1853 by Chillicothe resident Francis Campbell to honor his friend, attorney Samuel Tracy, a Scioto County prosecuting attorney from 1821 to 1850. The park, located between Ninth and Tenth Streets, was bounded by Chillicothe and Gay Streets. A public shelter house (above) and a covered wooden bandstand for concerts were constructed in the 1940s and stood for several years. The centerpiece of Tracy Park is the monument honoring Portsmouth area soldiers who sacrificed their lives during the Civil War. It took 12 years to raise the $7,500 needed to build the 40-foot-tall memorial, and it was dedicated on May 30, 1879. The first Scioto County soldier to die in the Civil War was John Barnes, who is honored on top of the monument. Tracy Park remains a gathering place for community events such as concerts, symphonies, rallies, parades, Easter egg hunts, and the yearly Tour of the Scioto River Valley bicycle event, which brings hundreds of visitors to the city. (Both, Sharon Bender Collection.)

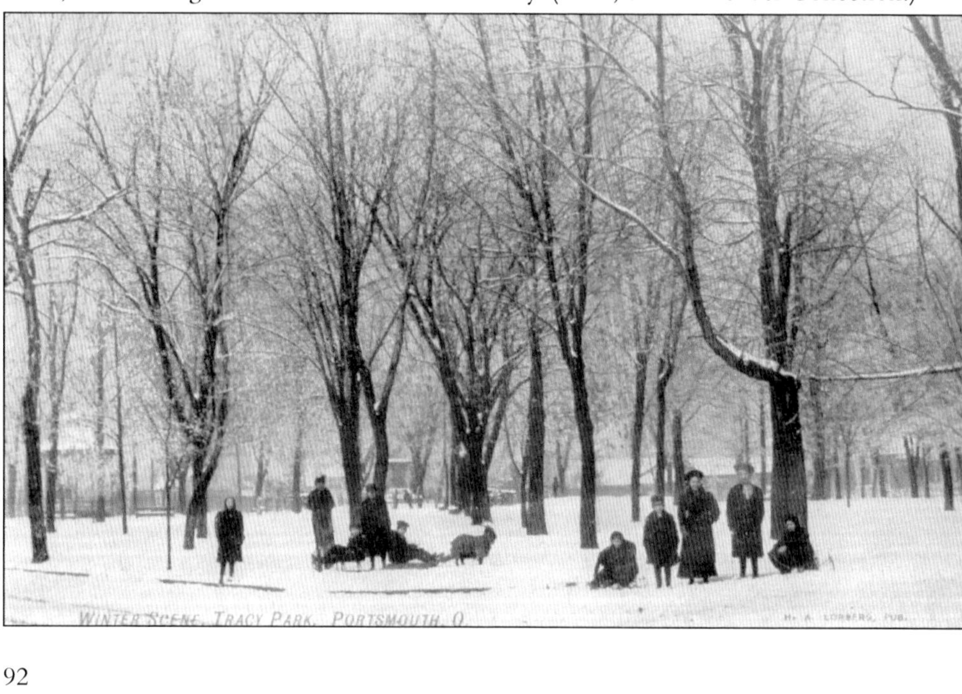

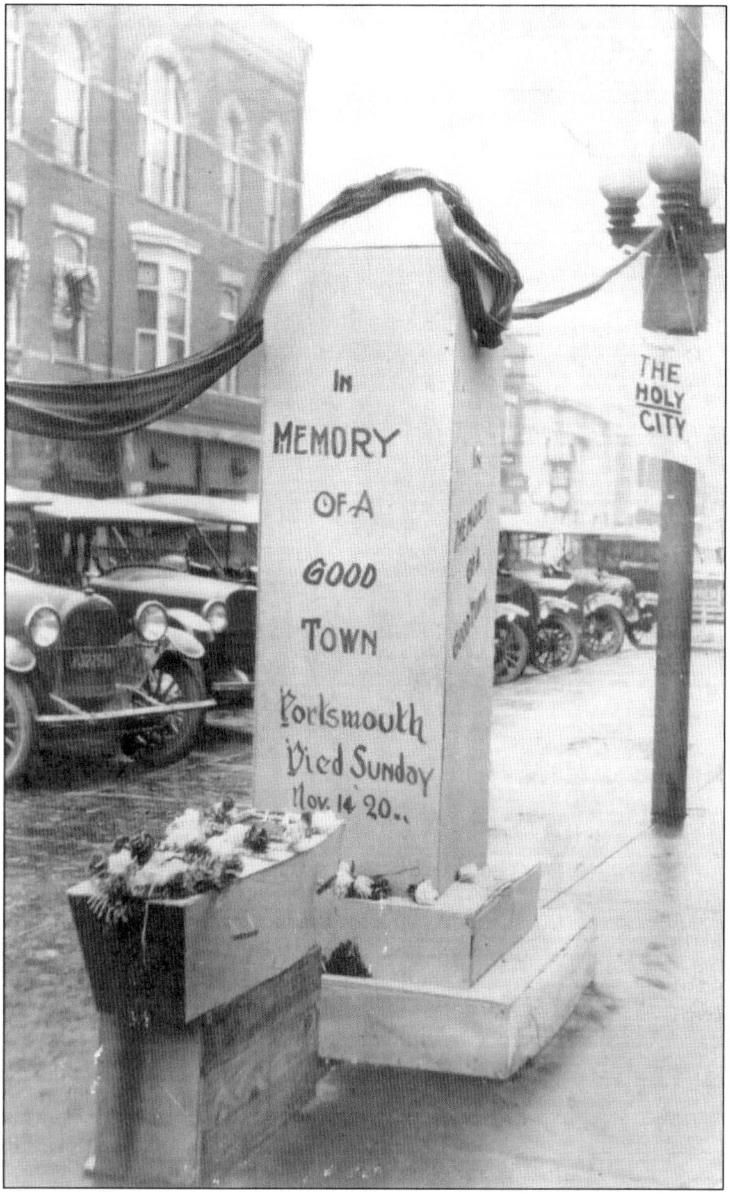

One of the most unusual chapters in Scioto County's history began on November 14, 1920, when Portsmouth mayor William Gableman, in an effort to restore goodness and decency to the city, unexpectedly ordered the closing of practically every Portsmouth retail business on Sundays so citizens could focus their attention on church. Known as Blue Sunday, it gained popularity throughout the region and was thought to lower drunkenness and crime for at least one day per week. Although the rule was supported by most churches and local press, not all were in favor of it. While Sciotoville complied with the rule, New Boston and the remainder of Scioto County refused to even consider such a law. The night before it went into effect, protesting citizens erected this makeshift tombstone and coffin on Gallia Street and placed flowers on the grave; it was quickly removed and destroyed by police. After meeting with local businessmen, and despite a loud outcry from ministers, Mayor Gableman claimed the brief program a success and rescinded the controversial rule on March 31, 1921. (Sharon Bender Collection.)

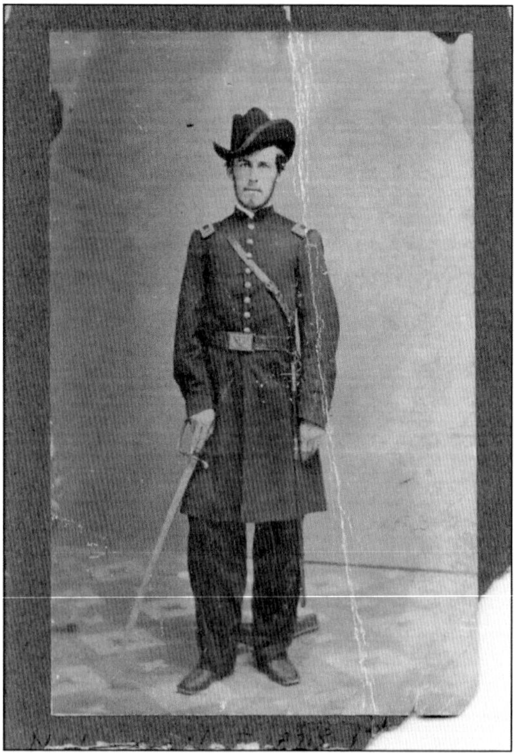

Nelson Evans was born in 1842, raised in Adams County, and graduated from Miami University in Oxford, Ohio, in 1864. After serving as a Union army captain during the Civil War, he received his law degree in Cincinnati in 1866 before moving to Portsmouth. A highly respected gentleman and local historian, he authored the thorough *The History of Scioto County* in 1903. (Bill Glockner Collection.)

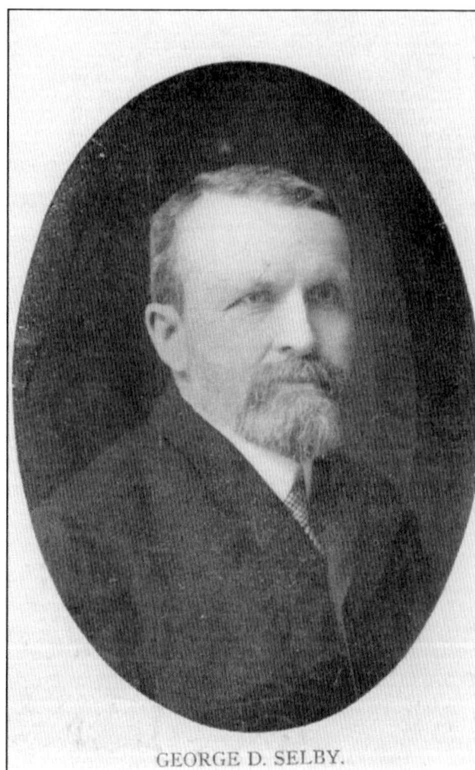

Born in Athens County, Ohio, in 1846, George Selby, a Union corporal during the Civil War, later became a salesman for Singer Sewing Machines. After arriving in Portsmouth in 1867, he became interested in the emerging shoe industry. By the late 19th century, he became the owner of Selby Shoes, the world's largest manufacturer of women's shoes. (Paul O'Neill Collection.)

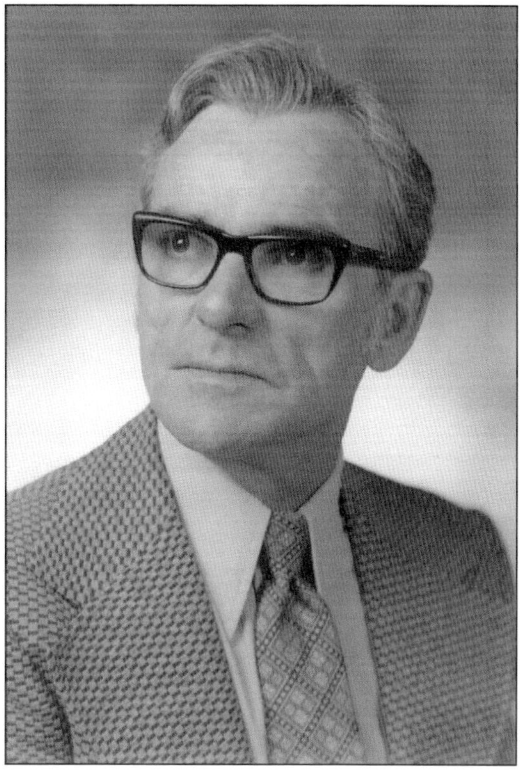

The name Carl Ackerman may come to mind when one thinks of influential and successful people who have preserved Scioto County's history. A World War II veteran captured in Normandy and taken as a prisoner of war, Ackerman returned to Portsmouth following the war and began compiling a massive collection of county memorabilia. The collection was initially stored at his home, which he shared with his wife, Dorothy, but was later displayed in the lobby of the Washington House. Ackerman was always eager to show his collection and wrote the popular "Those Were the Days" feature in the *Portsmouth Daily Times* from the mid-1970s through the mid-1990s. Blessed with a green thumb, Ackerman kept busy after retirement by enhancing the Market Street area (below) with beautiful plant and flower displays. Shortly before his death in 1997, he donated his photograph collection to the Southern Ohio Museum.

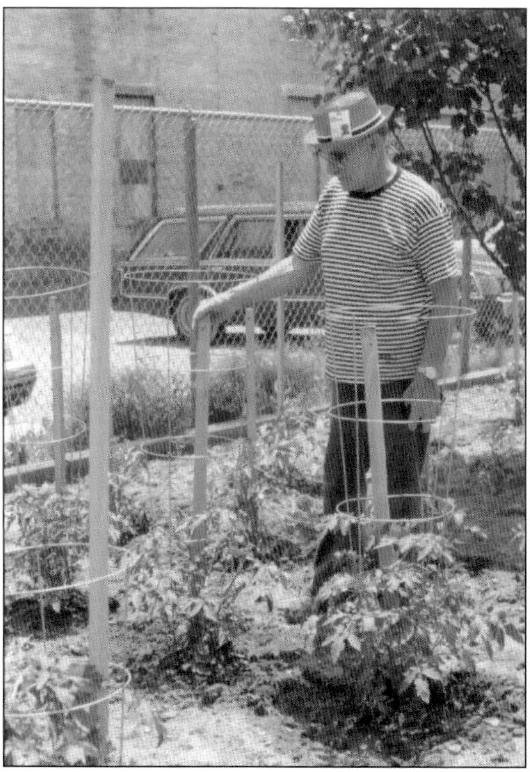

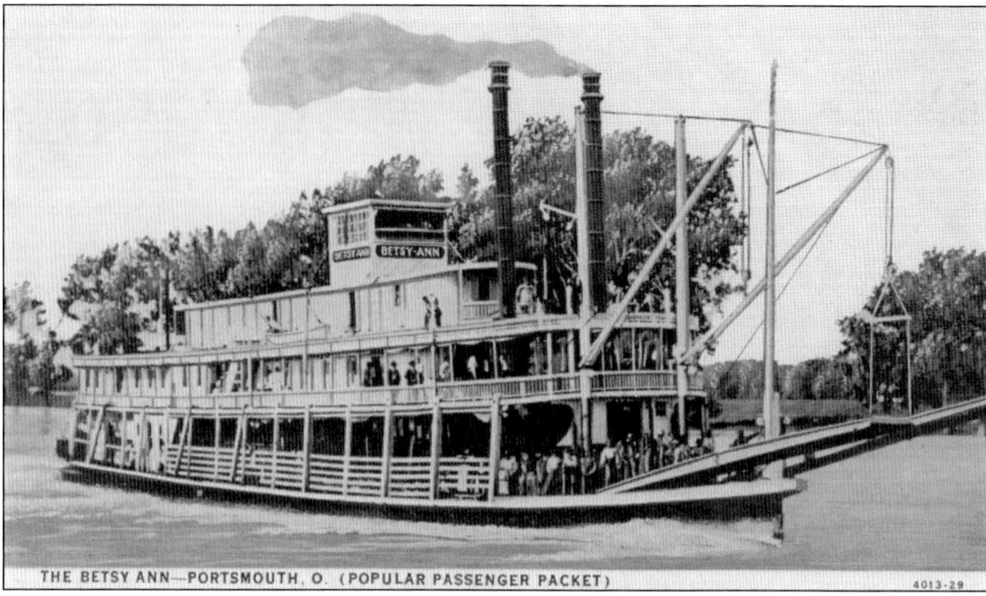

Built in Iowa in 1899, the steamer *Betsy Ann* was considered one of the fastest boats of its era. In addition to working the mail and passenger route between Portsmouth and Pittsburgh during its long history, it also held the Mississippi River speed record in the early 1900s. When racing other steamships on the Ohio River, it always brought excitement along the riverbanks wherever it competed. (Bill Glockner Collection.)

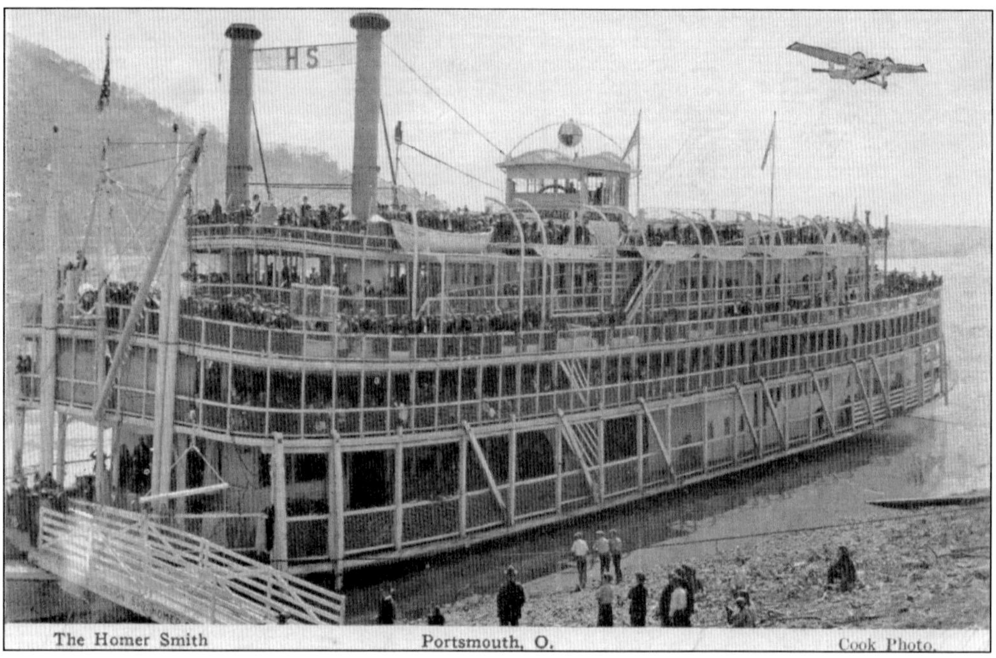

The *Homer Smith*, the longest excursion boat on the Ohio River, could accommodate 125 overnight guests and 2,000 for day or night excursions. Built in 1914 for the Security Steamboat Company of Point Pleasant, it was the first boat to have her decks outlined with electric lights. The ship was later sold to Pittsburgh Amusement Company and burned in April 1931 while moored on the Allegheny River. (Bill Glockner Collection.)

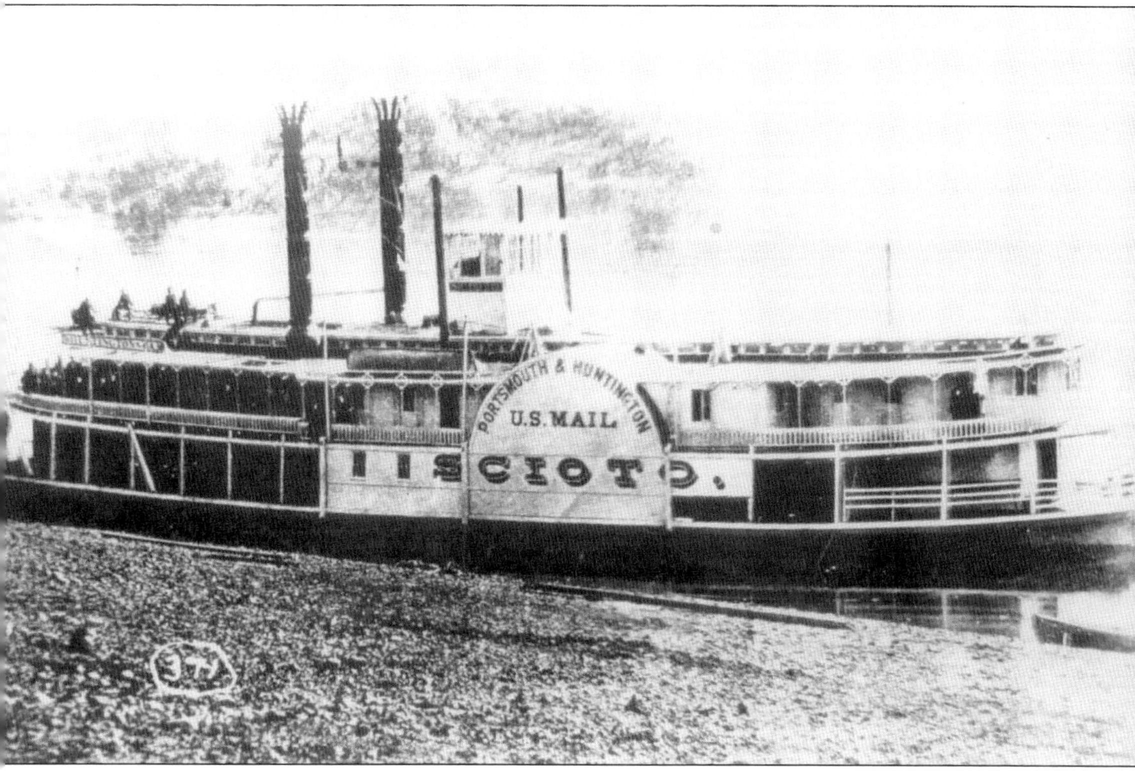

The *Scioto* was built in 1875 to carry mail between Portsmouth and Huntington, West Virginia, and was later purchased by the Parkersburg Transportation Company and converted into an excursion boat. On July 4, 1882, the Wellsville Coronet Band chartered the *Scioto* for a holiday pleasure trip on the Ohio River with approximately 500 people on board. Under the command of Capt. Thad Thomas, the *Scioto* departed Wellsville, Ohio. Near Cross Creek, West Virginia, they met the equally crowded steamer *John Lomas* coming down the river. Due to confusion stemming from recent changes in the law regarding whistle signals, the two boats collided, which caused the sinking of the *Scioto*. Although the boat was only 200 feet from the Ohio River shore, she sank in less than three minutes in 15 feet of water. Seventy people perished in the incident, and *Scioto* pilot David Keller was put on trial for manslaughter. After the first trial ended with a hung jury, Keller was convicted in his second trial and sentenced to two years in jail plus a $500 fine. He was pardoned one year later by Pres. Grover Cleveland. (Bill Glockner Collection.)

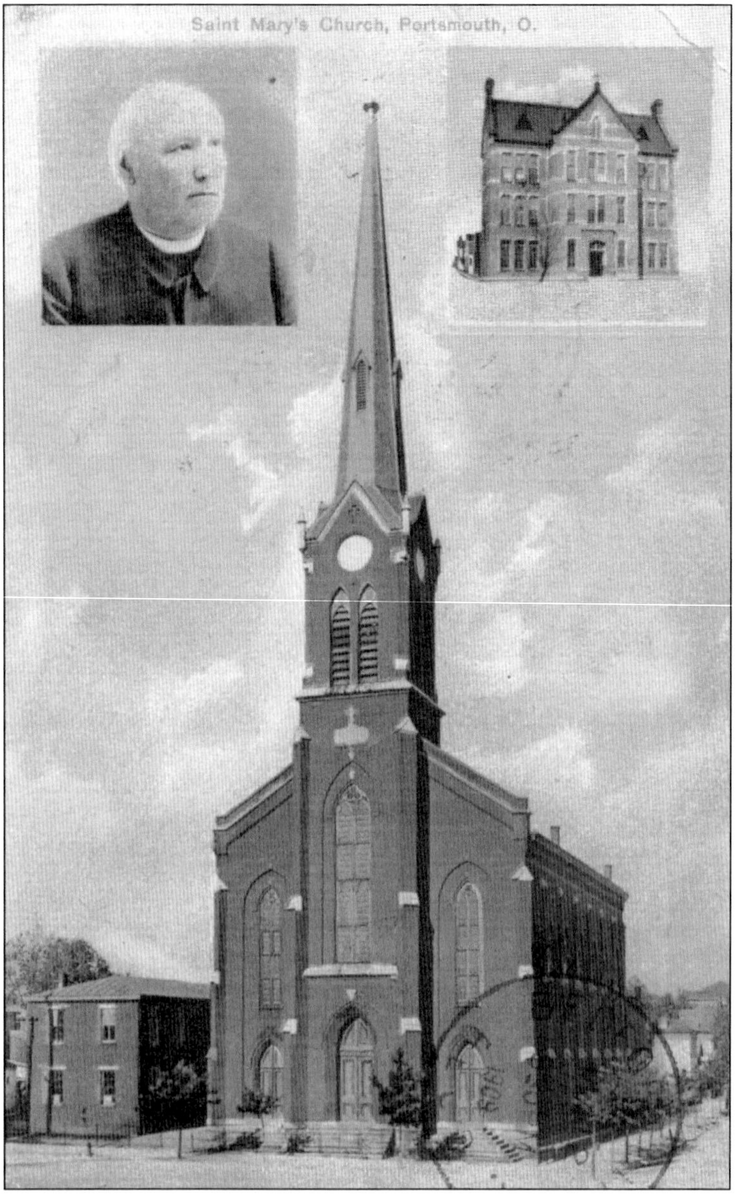

The earliest written records of St. Mary's Church date to April 20, 1841, when religious services were held in homes or rented buildings. In 1844, Father O'Mealy purchased a site on the northwest corner of Third and Madison Streets on which a brick church and parish house were constructed and dedicated on Christmas Day as Church of the Nativity. The congregation was composed of Irish and German immigrants. Conflict erupted when the German-speaking members could not understand the English sermons, causing a split within the congregation. A German-speaking priest was requested, and Bishop Purcell of Cincinnati appointed Father Karge. The German immigrants remained in the St. Mary's congregation, while the Irish immigrants departed and formed Holy Redeemer Church. In 1859, property was purchased on the corner of Fifth and Market Streets for $2,520 for a new church. After nearly six years of construction and at a cost of $50,000, the beautiful and iconic St. Mary's Church was dedicated on July 31, 1870. This stunning church remains standing today. (Sharon Bender Collection.)

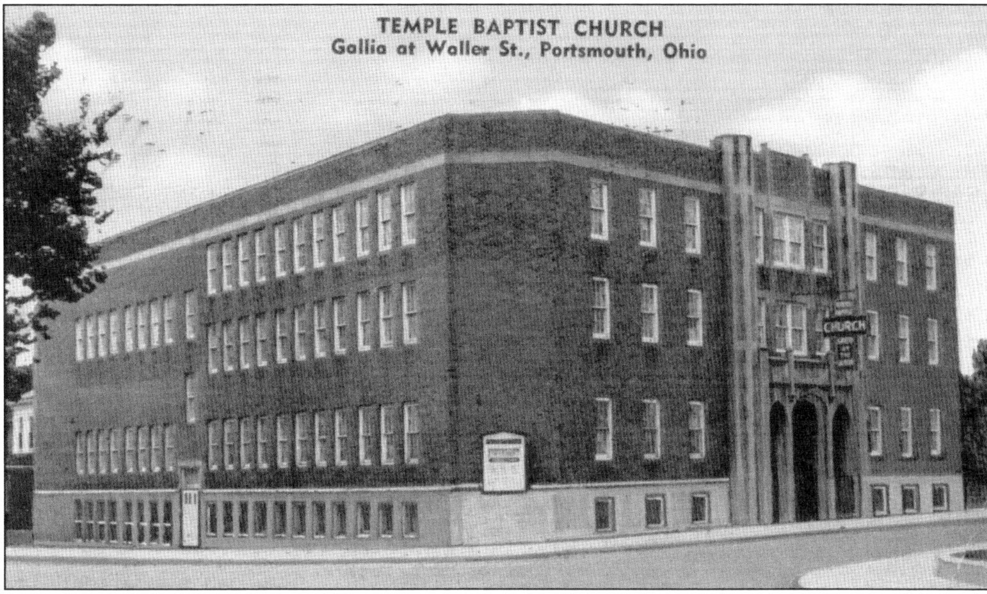

The congregation of First Baptist Church, constructed in 1916, experienced its share of triumph over tragedies. The church, located on Gallia and Waller Streets, was destroyed by fire in 1925—one year after the mortgage had been paid off. Services resumed in 1928 after the church was rebuilt. After defaulting on its bank loan in 1936, the church was forced to dissolve. It was reorganized as Temple Baptist Church in 1939, and worshipers still attend the beautiful church.

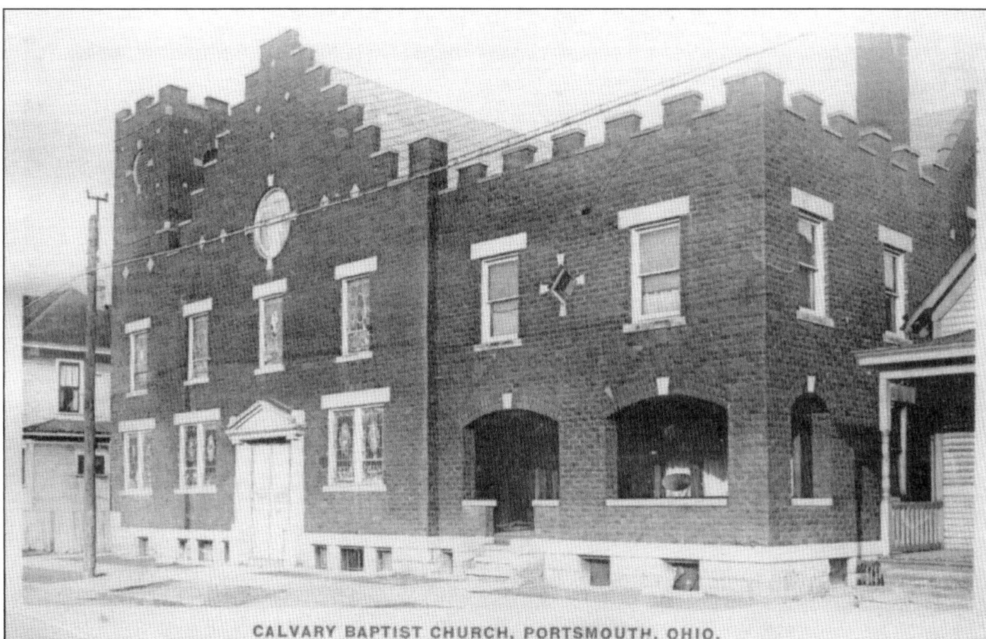

The Calvary Baptist Church, located at 1118 Hutchins Street, began in 1895. Proclaiming itself the "singing church" in the 1920s, it served its members well for over 118 years. In 2012, Calvary acquired the former Central Presbyterian Church at 2306 Waller Street and, after extensive remodeling, held the first services there the following year. The original church building (pictured) remains standing today. (Sharon Bender Collection.)

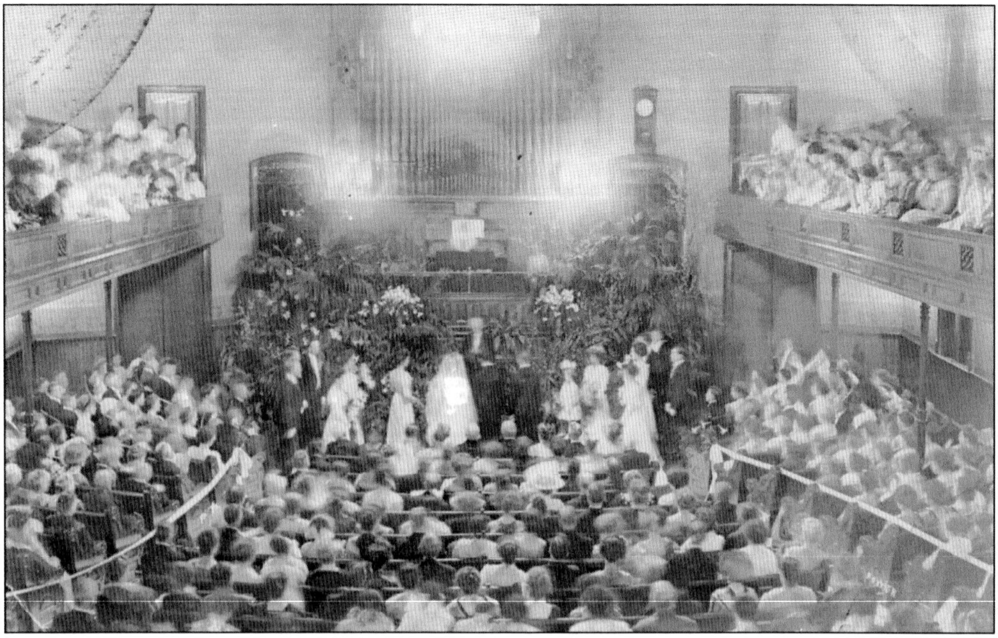

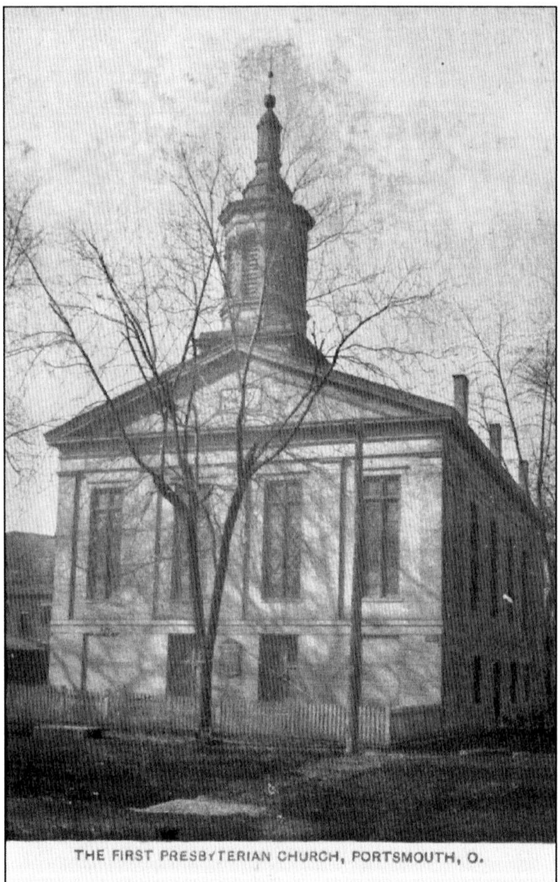

A large crowd of family and friends gather for a wedding at Bigelow Church in this c. 1920 postcard. Constructed in 1858 at Fifth and Washington Streets, it survived two fires (1859 and 1867) and four floods (1889, 1913, 1921, and 1937). The last Methodist service was held at this church on the last Sunday in December 1982. It is now known as the Grace Community Church. (Sharon Bender Collection.)

First Presbyterian Church was designed and constructed in 1850 on the southeast corner of Third and Court Streets by local builder William Newman. The Greek Revival church features handmade native brick and local sandstone. Listed in the National Register of Historic Places since 1973, it is the oldest church still in use in the city. (Sharon Bender Collection.)

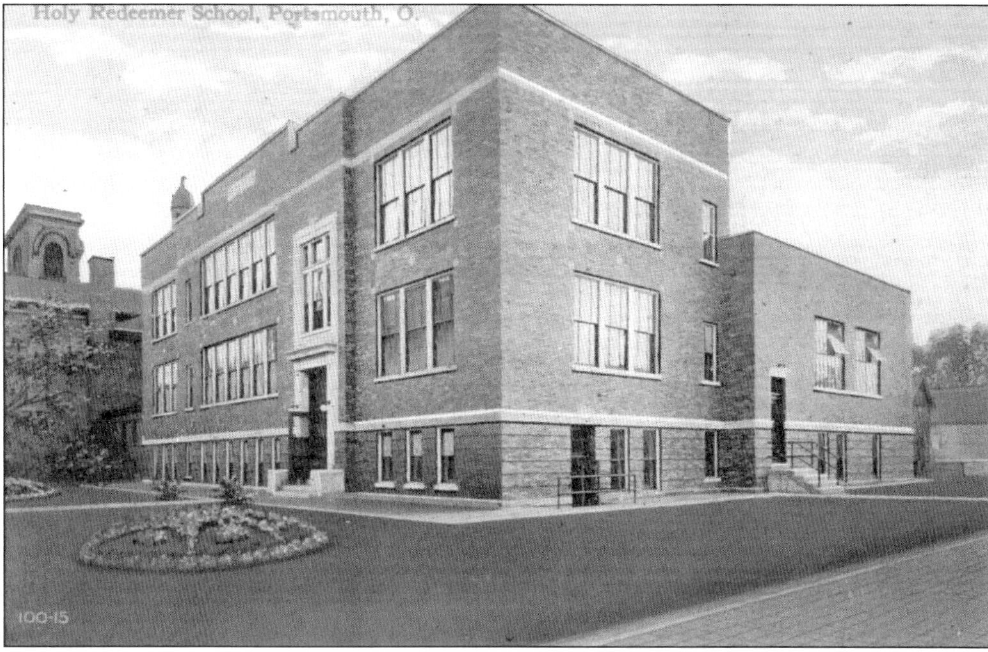

Construction of Holy Redeemer School (above) began in 1916; it was dedicated on October 23, 1917. Conveniently located behind Holy Redeemer Church and adjacent to the priest's residence (below), it operated as a four-year high school from 1922 to 1953. In 1953, Holy Redeemer merged with St. Mary's High School, and students began attending the newly built Notre Dame High School. In an effort to decrease overcrowding, the church began renovations in 1959, with a gymnasium being converted to four large classrooms, offices, and faculty rooms. In 1970, the churches' elementary schools merged; the school's name was changed to Portsmouth Catholic Elementary in 1972 and to Notre Dame Elementary on January 20, 1984. (Bill Glockner Collection.)

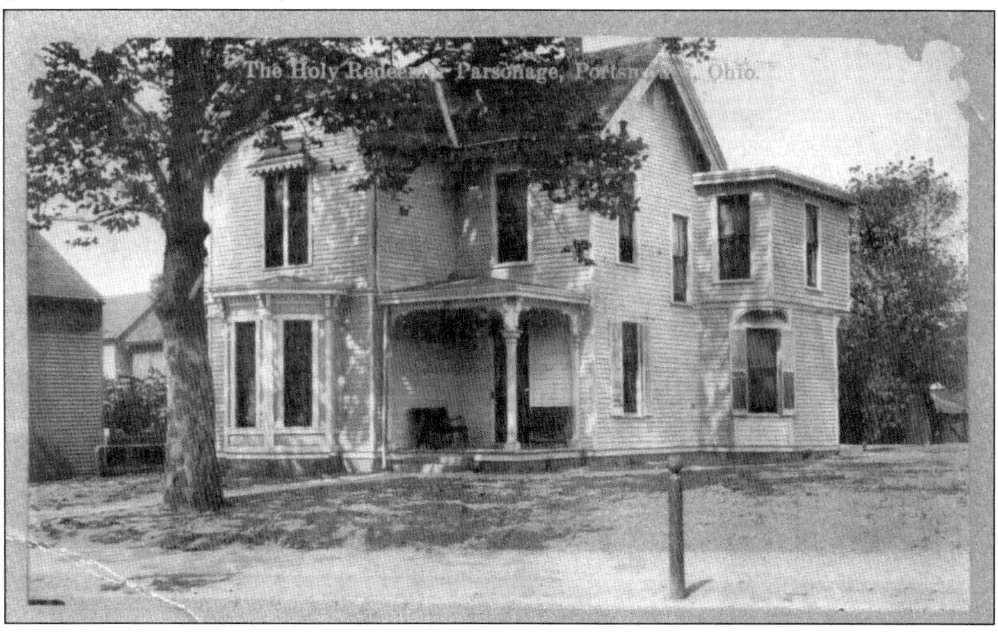

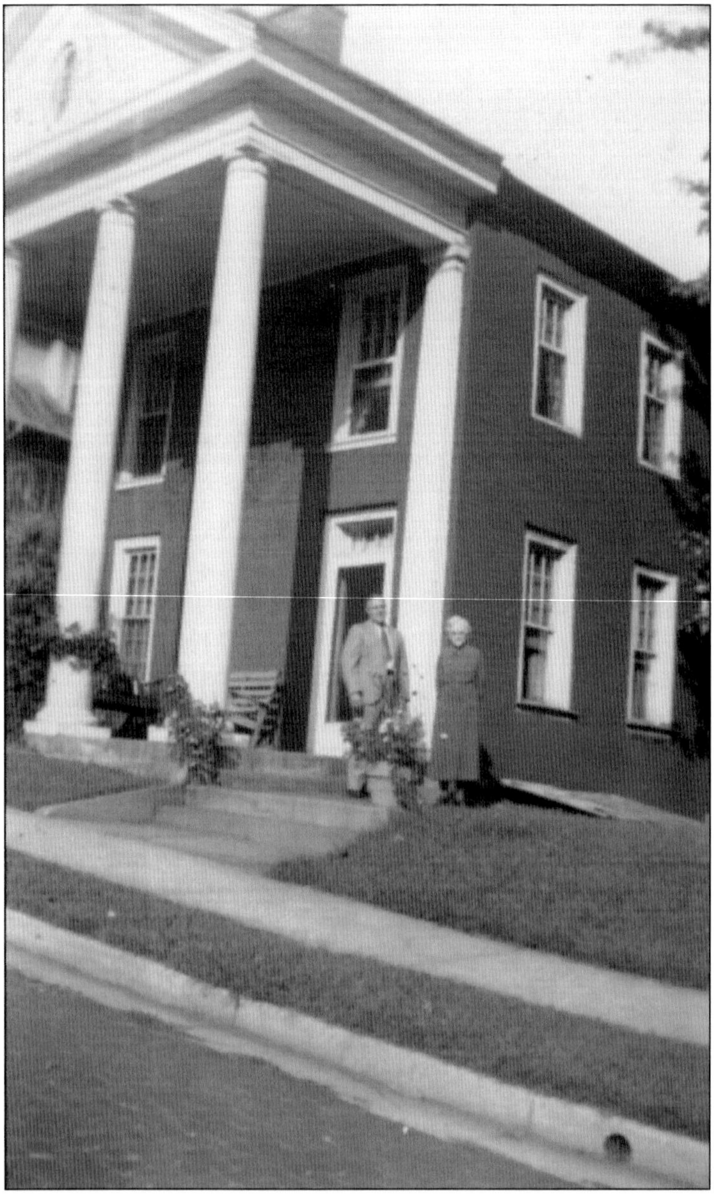

One of Portsmouth's most interesting attractions is the 1810 House located at 1926 Waller Street. Hand-built by Aaron and Mary Kinney in 1810, the house, which faces Kinney's Lane, had four large rooms and a spiral staircase. Four more rooms were added in 1812. Aaron and Mary had 12 children, who helped with farming and tanning work. In 1913, a tall porch and columns were added to make the residence look less like a farmhouse. A new front door and windows were cut on the west side, allowing the front door to face Waller Street. Three generations of the Kinney family lived here. Isabel Kinney, granddaughter of Aaron and Mary (pictured above with her cousin), was the last person to live in the house; she died in 1946. The vacant house deteriorated and became a target for vandals. It was slated to be demolished, but local residents came to the aid of the Scioto County Historical Society in efforts to preserve it. The house, run by volunteers, was fully restored and stocked with pioneer artifacts; it opened as a museum on August 25, 1979. (Scioto County Historical Society.)

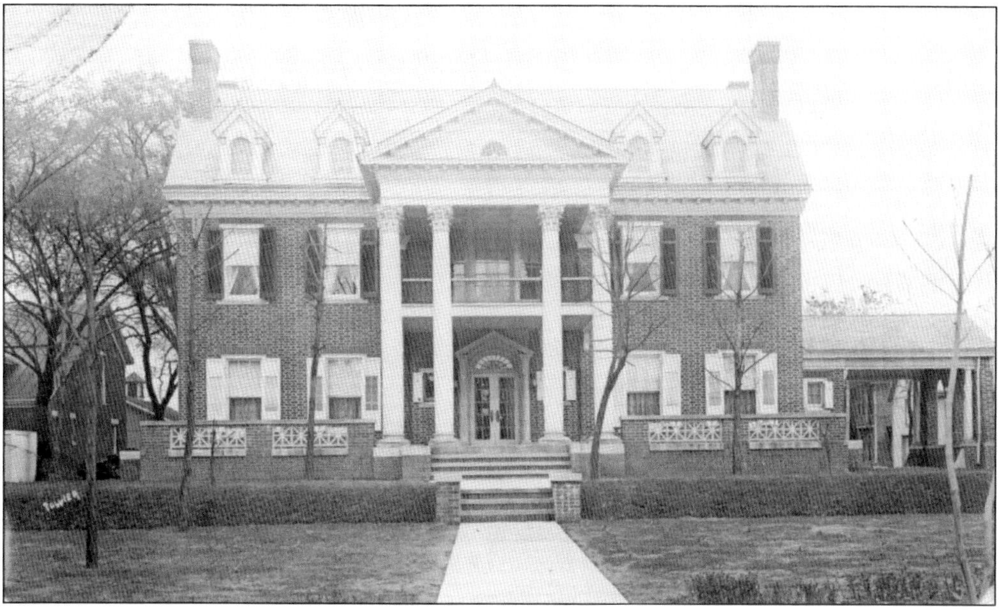

When George Appel, president of the Gilbert Grocery Company, and his family moved into their new home at 1223 Gallia Street in 1909, the local press called it one of the finest homes in Ohio. It was owned by the Appel family until 1947 and was later converted into apartments. The house was razed in the early 1990s, when it barely reflected its original elegance, to make way for the new Portsmouth High School. (Sharon Bender Collection.)

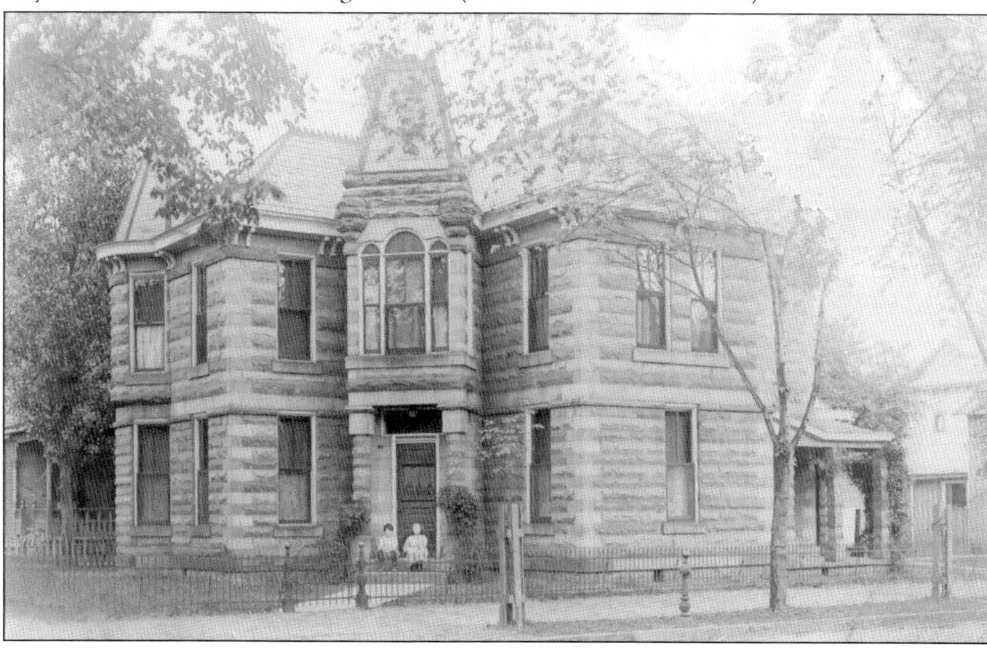

This beautiful stone house was constructed in the 1890s on the southeast corner of Third and Waller Streets. Owned in the early 1900s by newspaperman and insurance executive Gus Barlow, it was known as the Barlow Mansion even after his death. Occupied by several families over the following decades, the handsome structure was purchased by Shawnee State University in 1989 and was razed shortly thereafter.

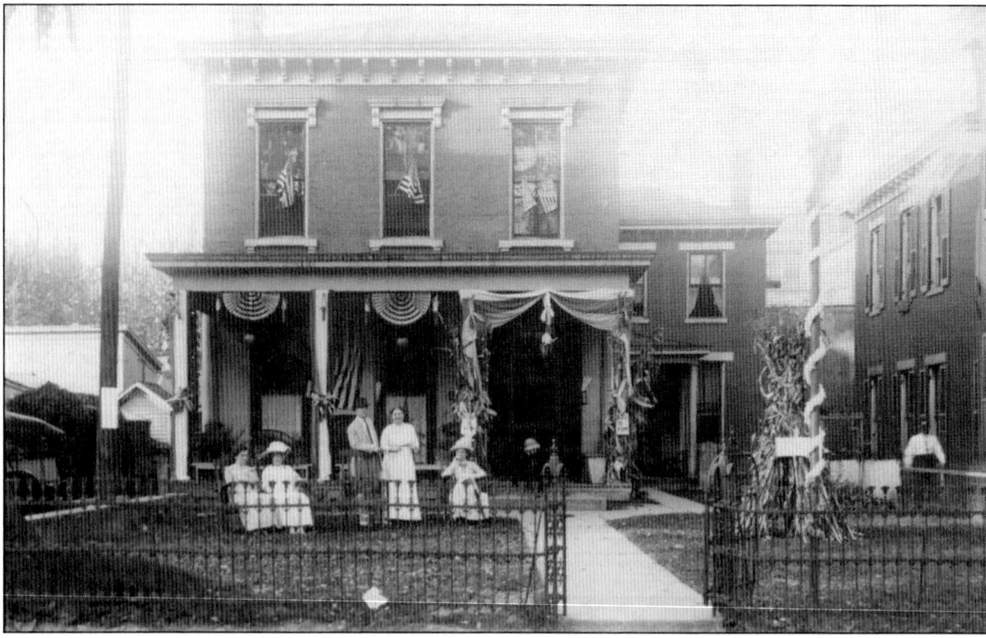

Dr. William Gault and family are pictured at their 733 Second Street residence, which is decorated for the 1914 Kum Korn Karnival. Dr. Gault died in January 1942 at his home, which was located in the present-day vicinity of Smith's Drugs. He served his community for over four decades.

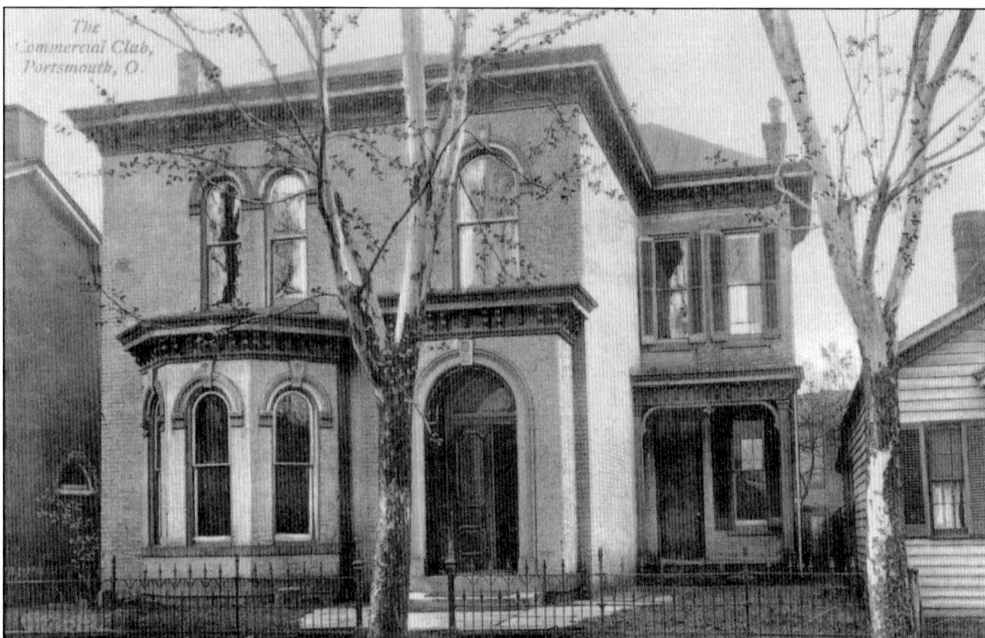

The Commercial Club, founded in August 1899, was located at 17 West Second Street on property currently owned by Shawnee State University. It was initially a political club for local Republican businessmen who met to discuss and establish improvements to the city but soon became more bipartisan and expanded to over 250 members. While the club accomplished much good, infighting among the members led to its disbanding in March 1911. (Paul O'Neill Collection.)

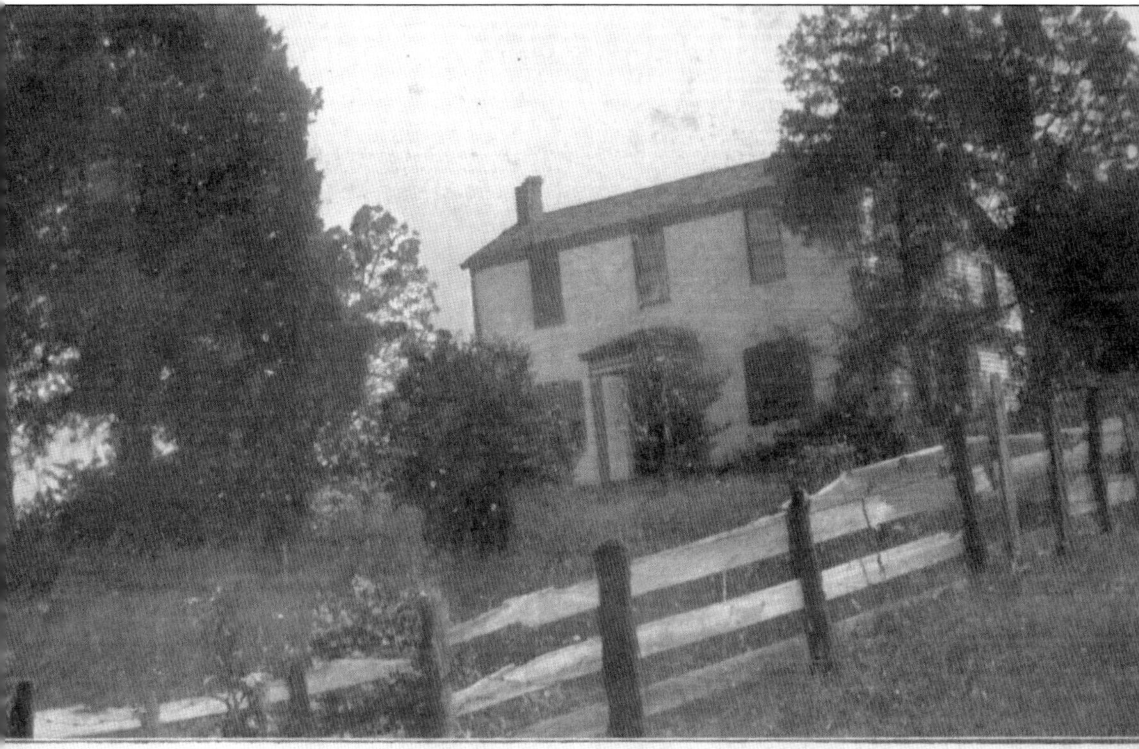

The Old Dugan Homestead, Portsmouth, O.
(H. A. Lorberg, Publ.)

Thomas Dugan was born in Pittsburgh, Pennsylvania, on Christmas Day in 1824. As a teenager, he moved to Portsmouth and began selling apples to passengers and crews of steamboats that stopped in Portsmouth. While delivering milk, Dugan was hired by a local banker who noticed his intelligence and financial knowledge. Working his way up through the ranks, Dugan soon became a successful and well-liked banker, eventually becoming the president of the Farmers National Bank in 1865. In addition to being a popular member of city council, Dugan also owned considerable property in Scioto County, including what later became the Scioto County Fairgrounds. Known for his generosity and kindness toward children, he often sponsored and funded school picnics and sporting events at his many properties. His residence (pictured), located on the northwest corner of Eighth and Chillicothe Streets, was one of the most elaborate homes in Portsmouth. Dugan passed away at home on November 18, 1873. (Bill Glockner Collection.)

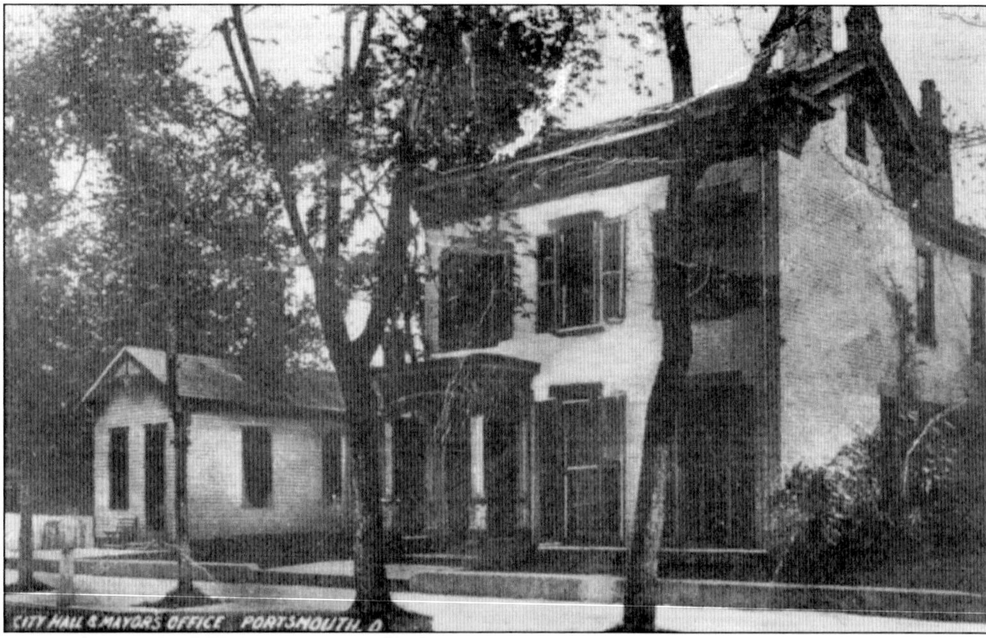

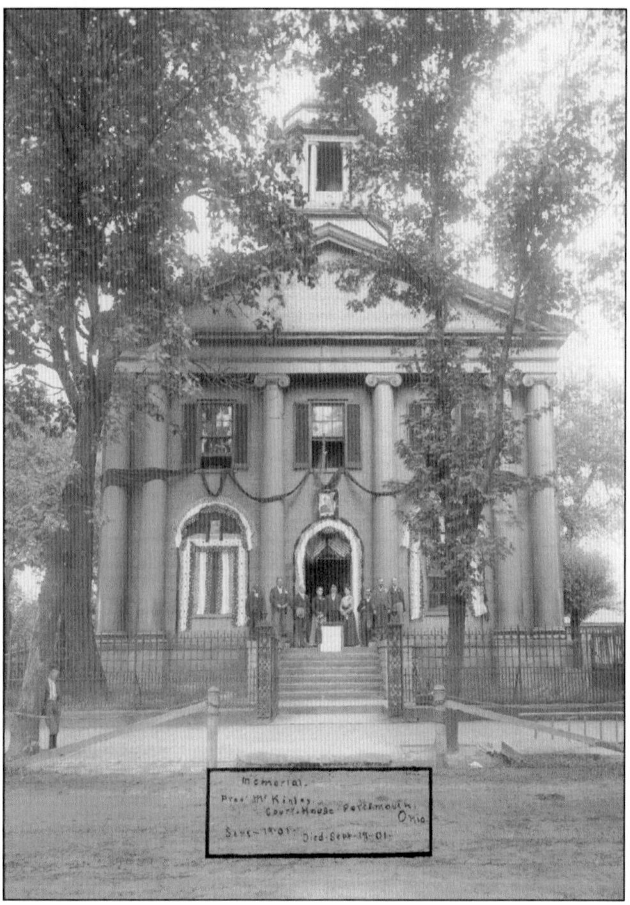

City hall (at right in the above image) served Portsmouth for three decades beginning in 1904. Located on Second Street, it housed several offices, the city jail, and a courtroom. The mayor's office was next door, allowing the city's chief executive to conduct daily business while also serving as judge for minor offenses. These buildings were razed in 1934 for construction of a new municipal building, which remains in use on the property.

On September 6, 1901, the nation was stunned to learn that Pres. William McKinley had been shot twice while in Buffalo, New York. McKinley was an Ohio native and former governor, and the entire state followed his condition closely. On September 14, the 25th US president died of complications from the wounds. The Scioto County Courthouse was draped in black bunting to mourn the slain president. (Stephen C. Rodeheffer.)

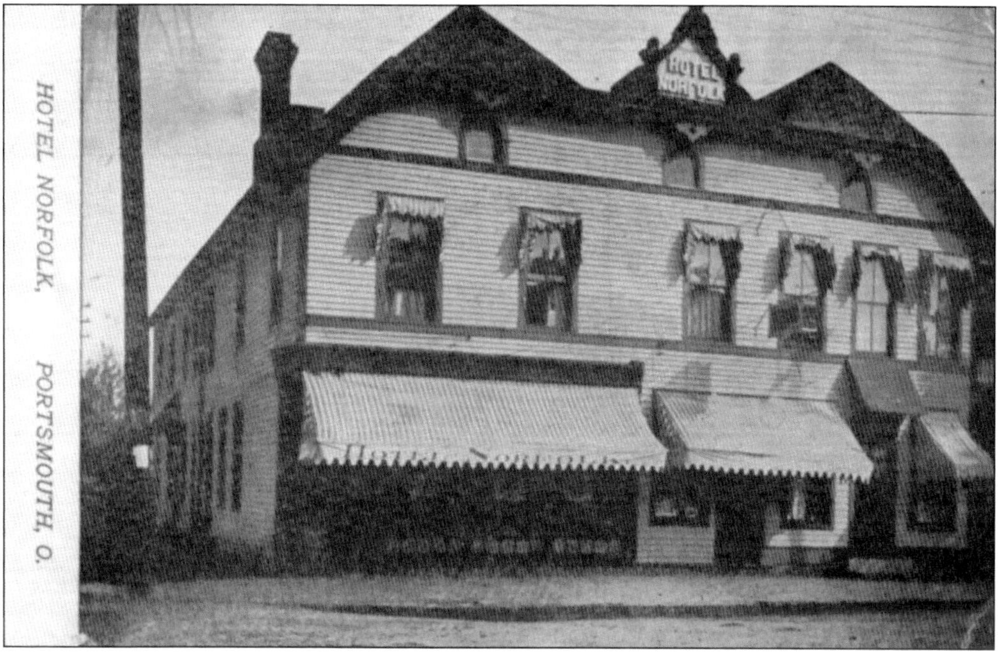

Constructed in 1886 as the Junction Hotel, this 30-room structure was situated directly across from the railroad depot at Tenth and Waller Streets. The hotel changed owners several times, and its name was changed to the Hotel Norfolk in 1908. Once considered one of the finest hotels in the city, it deteriorated over the years and eventually became an apartment building. It was razed in 2012. (Bill Glockner Collection.)

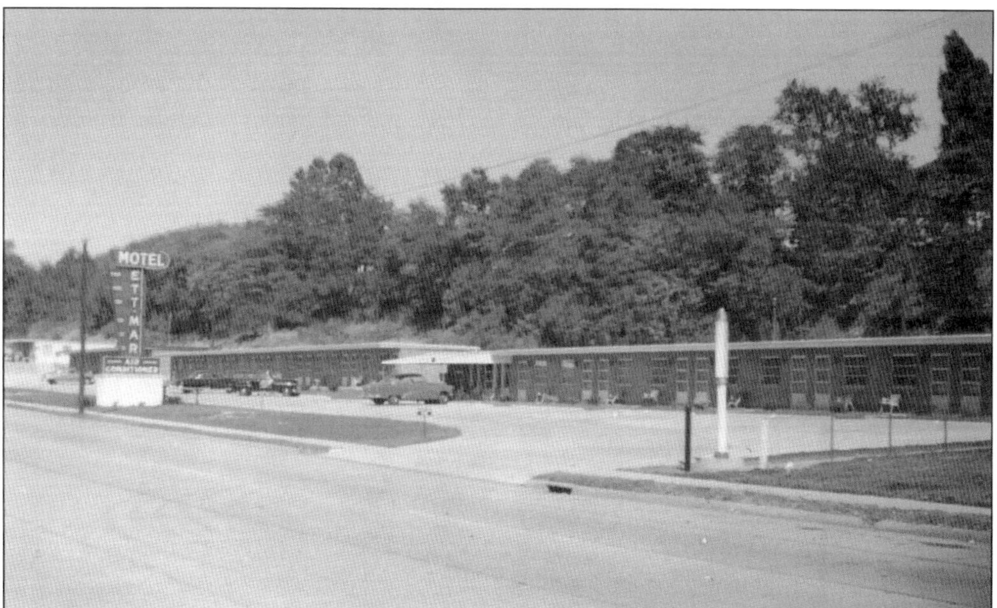

The Ett-Mar Motel opened in 1952 and was the first motel in Portsmouth. Located at 1600 Kendall Avenue, adjacent to Dreamland Pool, it advertised comforts not available at all motels, including air conditioning, electric heat, private telephones, and wall-to-wall carpeting. The building currently houses the Royal Inn Motel. (Paul O'Neill Collection.)

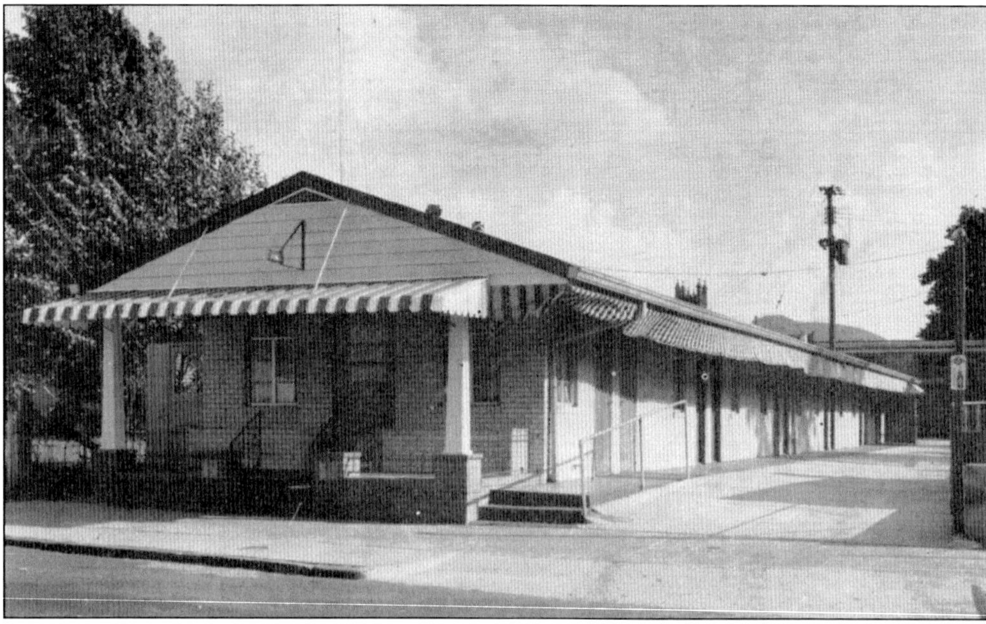

The Santa Maria Motel, constructed in 1957 at 1136 Eleventh Street, served tired travelers along US Route 52 East. Only three years after the motel opened, the thoroughfare was relocated, taking all the customers with it. The building was purchased by the Scioto County commissioners in 1987. Scioto Residential Services currently resides on the property. (Bill Glockner Collection.)

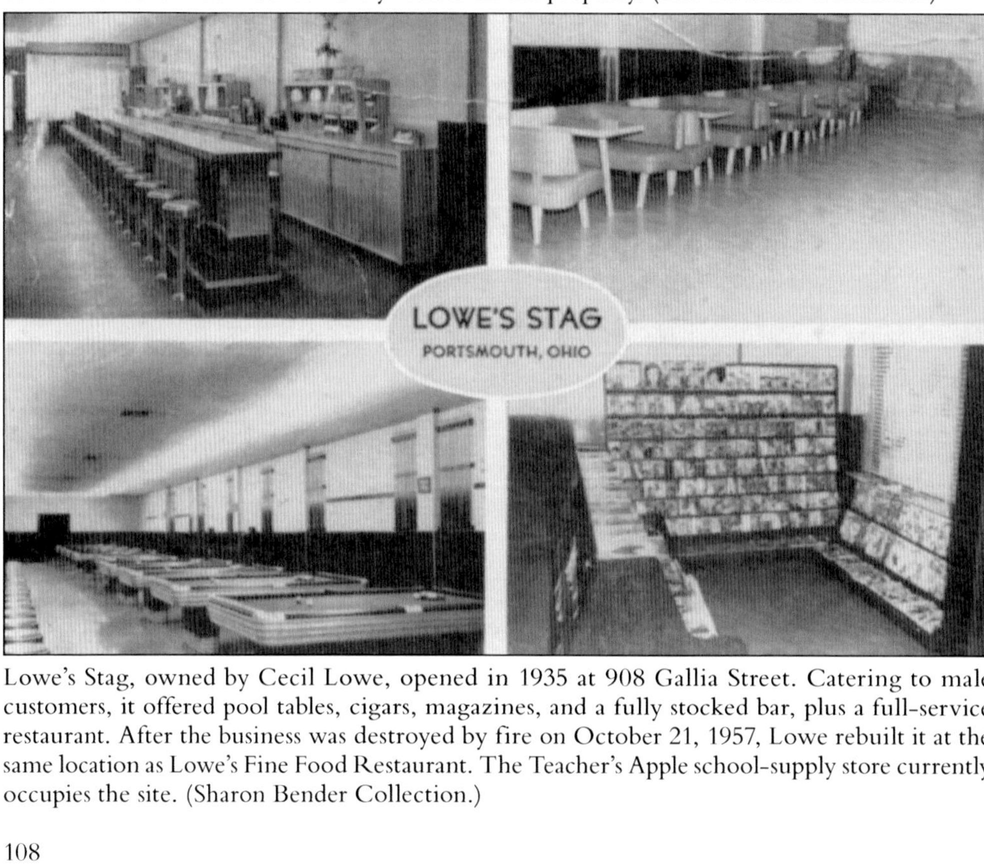

Lowe's Stag, owned by Cecil Lowe, opened in 1935 at 908 Gallia Street. Catering to male customers, it offered pool tables, cigars, magazines, and a fully stocked bar, plus a full-service restaurant. After the business was destroyed by fire on October 21, 1957, Lowe rebuilt it at the same location as Lowe's Fine Food Restaurant. The Teacher's Apple school-supply store currently occupies the site. (Sharon Bender Collection.)

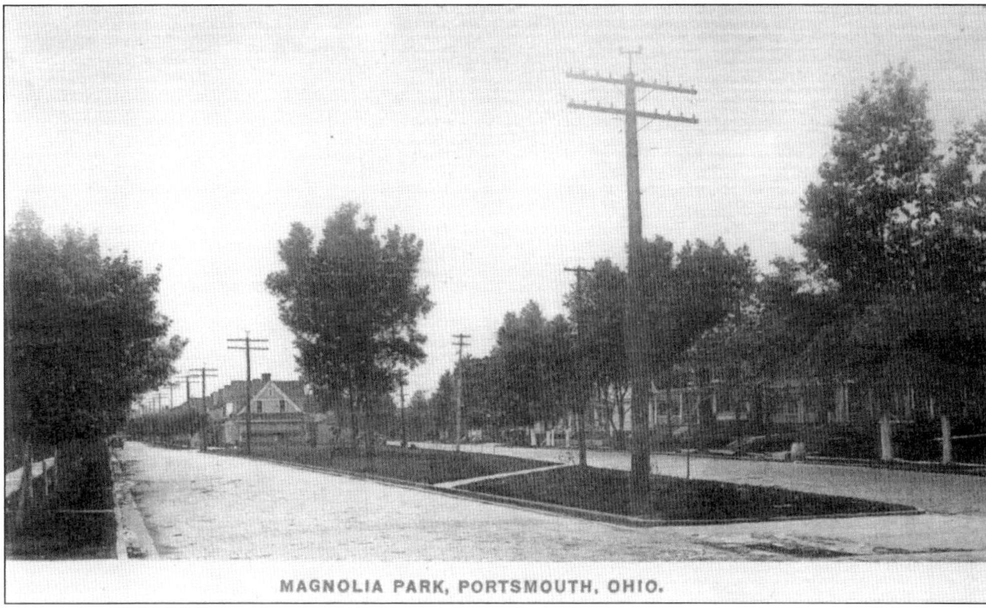

Magnolia Park, named for the many attractive magnolia trees in the area, was created by city council on November 20, 1919, and located at Twelfth Street and Robinson Avenue. Local citizens maintained the beautiful flowers, shrubs, and additional trees planted in honor of Portsmouth's World War I veterans. A realignment of US Route 52 in the 1960s nearly obliterated the park. (Sharon Bender Collection.)

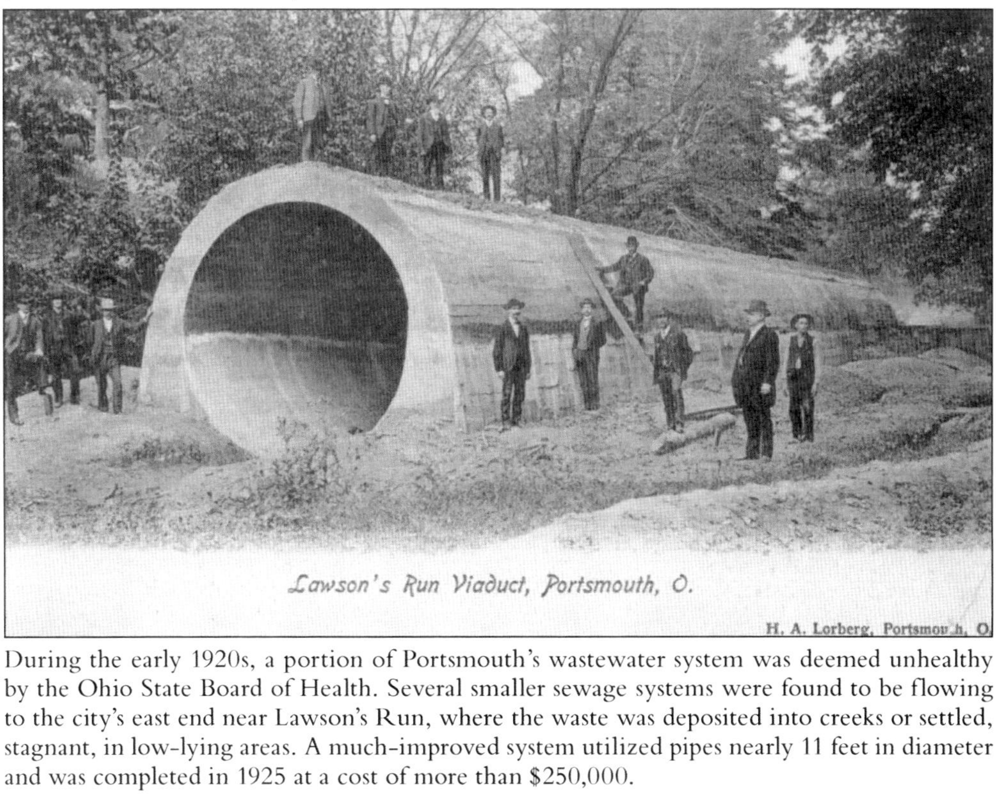

During the early 1920s, a portion of Portsmouth's wastewater system was deemed unhealthy by the Ohio State Board of Health. Several smaller sewage systems were found to be flowing to the city's east end near Lawson's Run, where the waste was deposited into creeks or settled, stagnant, in low-lying areas. A much-improved system utilized pipes nearly 11 feet in diameter and was completed in 1925 at a cost of more than $250,000.

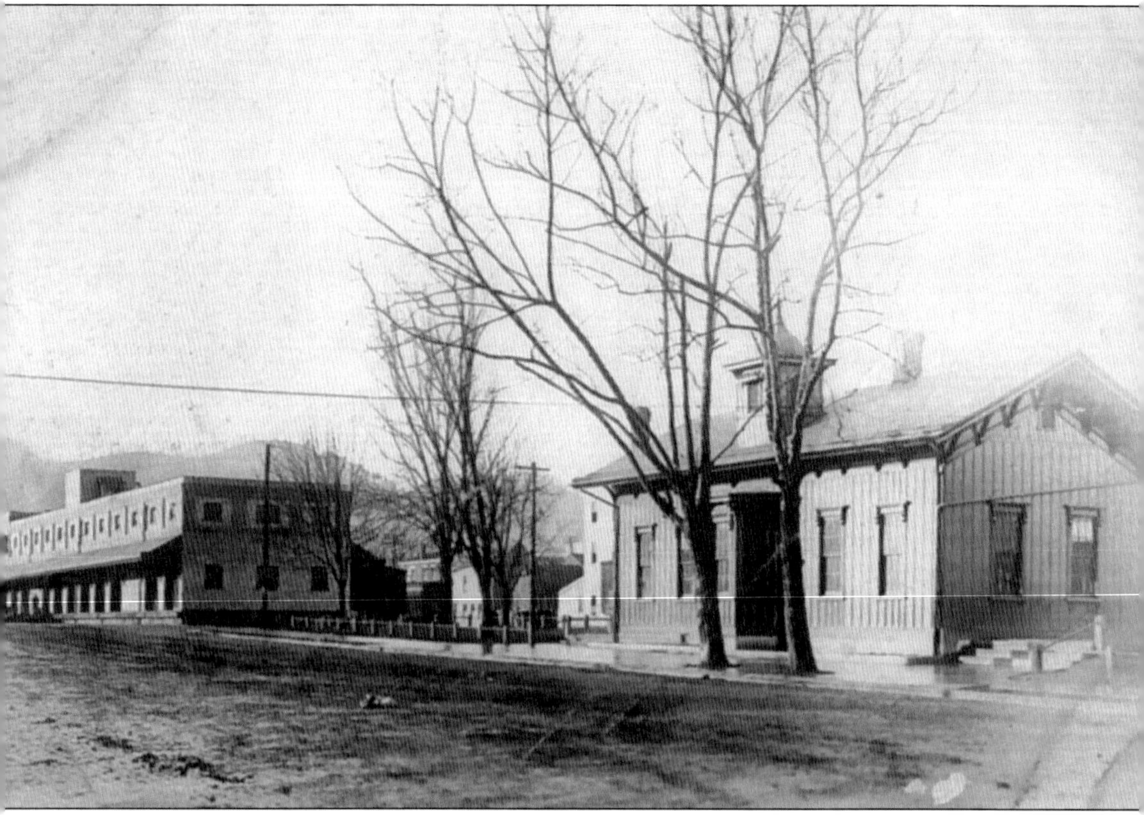

The Baltimore & Ohio Railroad's passenger depot (foreground) and freight house (background) are shown on this 1920 postcard looking south on Market Street. The B&O reached Portsmouth in 1852 and was the first railroad to operate in Scioto County. The depot was originally located a short distance to the west but was relocated around 1910 to allow for an expansion of the rail yards. A massive brick freight house was constructed to replace a smaller wooden one in anticipation of increased local business. While freight business did improve, it fell short of predictions, leaving much of the building seldom used. The adjacent J.P. Schaefer Grocery Store, which was heavily damaged in the 1937 flood, leased a large portion of the freight building in which to operate their business. The last passenger train ran through Portsmouth in December 1946, while freight trains continued to run until 1972. Parking lots now occupy the sites where these buildings once stood. (Bill Glockner Collection.)

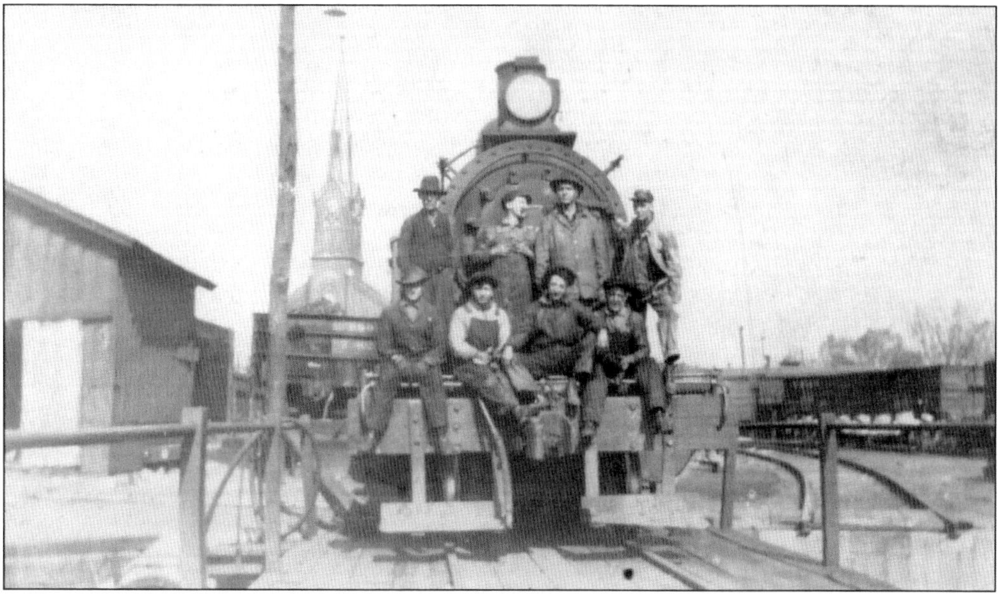

With the distinctive St. Mary's Church in the background, employees of the Baltimore & Ohio Railroad posed for this photograph around 1900. Located near Fourth and Market Streets, the rail yard remained in business for over a century before closing in the early 1970s. The property was acquired by Heck's Department Store in 1973, then by Wolohan Lumber in 1990. Ohio Valley Wholesale has occupied the property since 2000.

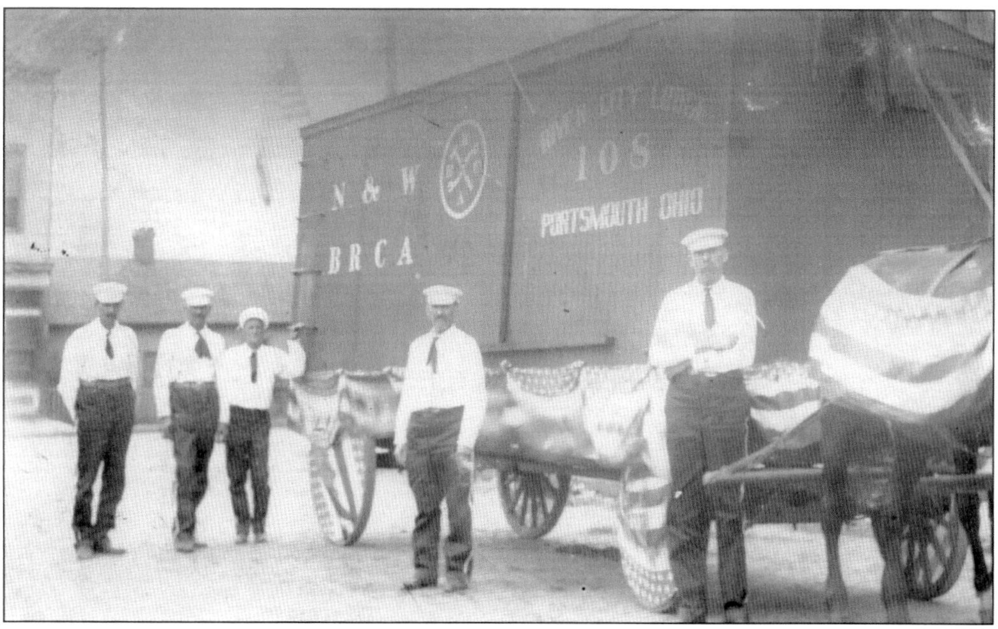

The Brotherhood of Railway Carmen of America River City Lodge No. 108 was one of the many labor unions in Scioto County. Consisting of nearly 200 employees of the Norfolk & Western Railway's car repair shop, the organization participated in many civic activities. In this c. 1915 postcard, BRCA members prepare to march in a Labor Day parade with their specially built boxcar float. (Paul O'Neill Collection.)

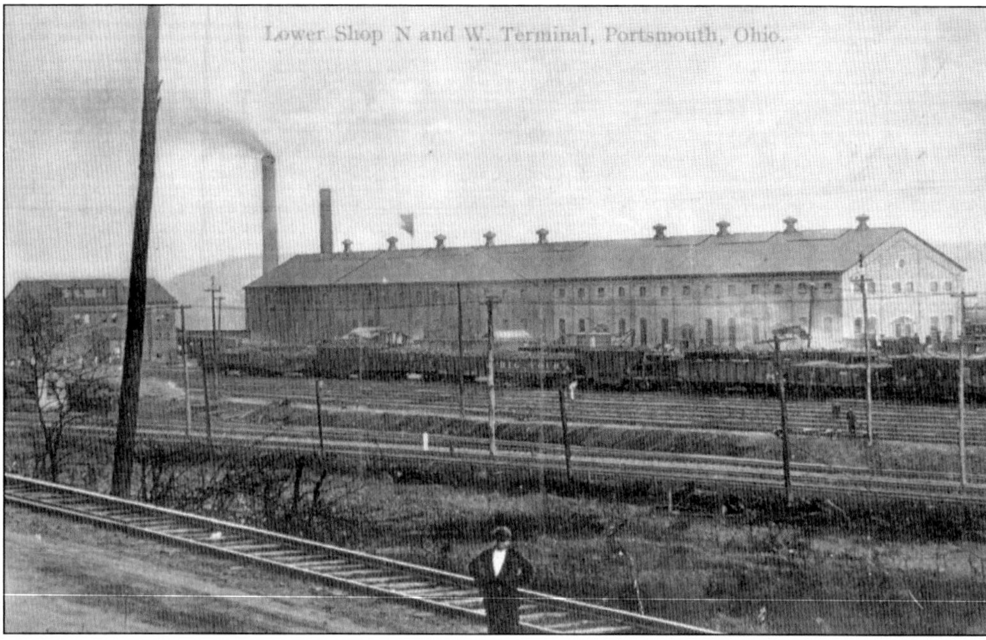

In 1902, the Norfolk & Western Railway began construction on the vast rail yards in East Portsmouth. Twenty-five years later, it had a total of 109 miles of track within 270 acres stretching across three miles. It soon handled more than 1.5 million railcars per month and was considered the largest single-owned railroad yard in the world in the late 1920s. (Bill Glockner Collection.)

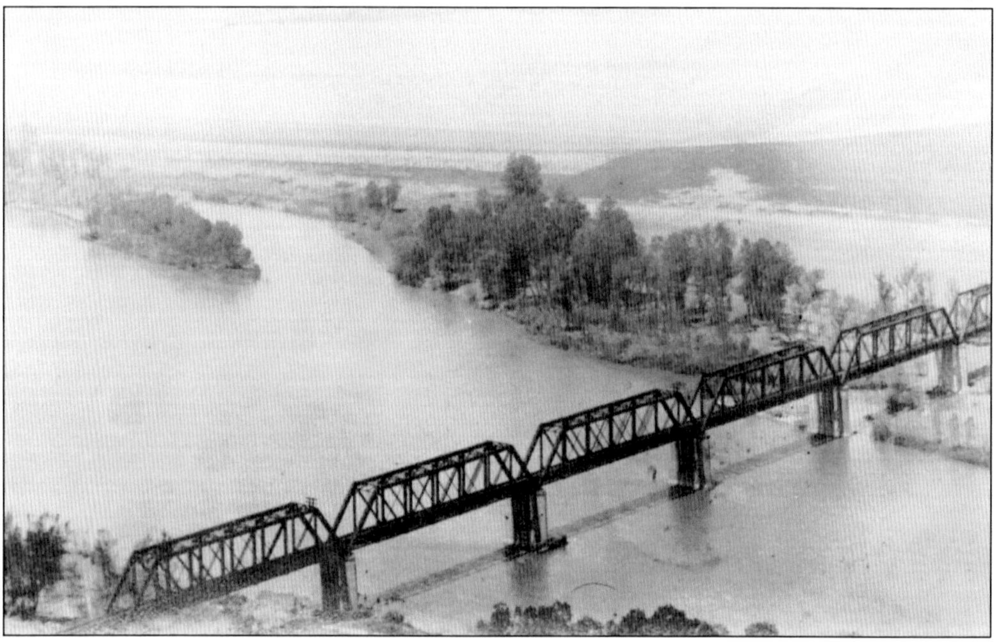

This well-known railroad bridge crosses the Scioto River at Portsmouth and was constructed by the Cincinnati & Eastern Railroad in 1884. After it was acquired by the Norfolk & Western Railway in 1901, its wooden span was replaced with steel (pictured) in 1904. Although it was nearly destroyed by the 1913 flood, it was repaired and remained in operation until May 2003. The bridge still stands today. (Bill Glockner Collection.)

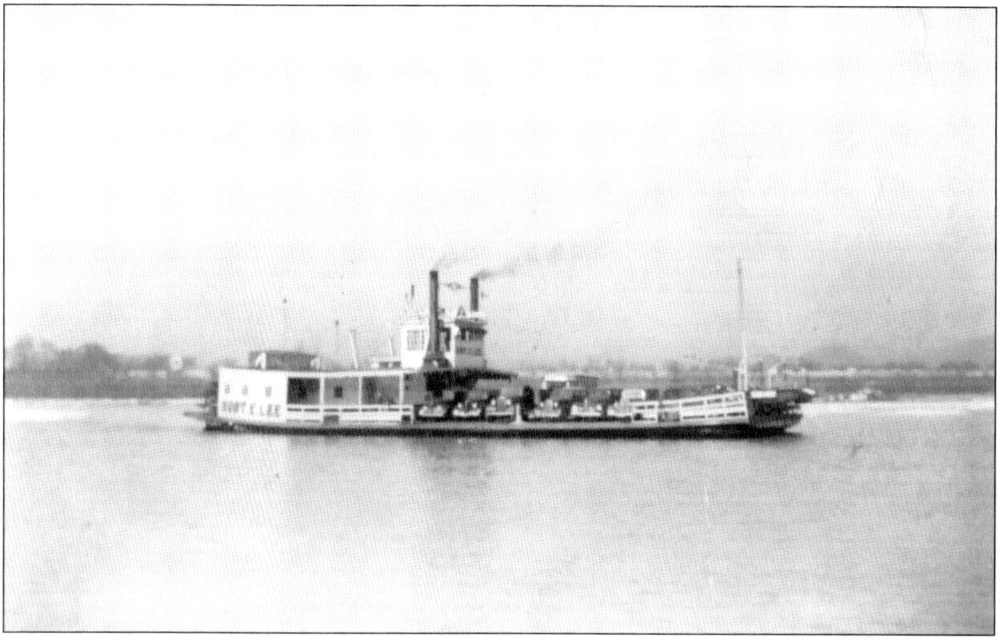

Constructed in 1939, the ferryboat *Robert E. Lee* operated between Portsmouth and Fullerton, Kentucky. It was appropriately named, as it was in direct competition with the U.S. Grant Bridge but charged a cheaper toll to cross the Ohio River. When the bridge closed in May 1939 for repairs that lasted for one year, the ferry continually worked at near capacity. The *Robert E. Lee* was destroyed in a collision with another ferryboat on February 4, 1947.

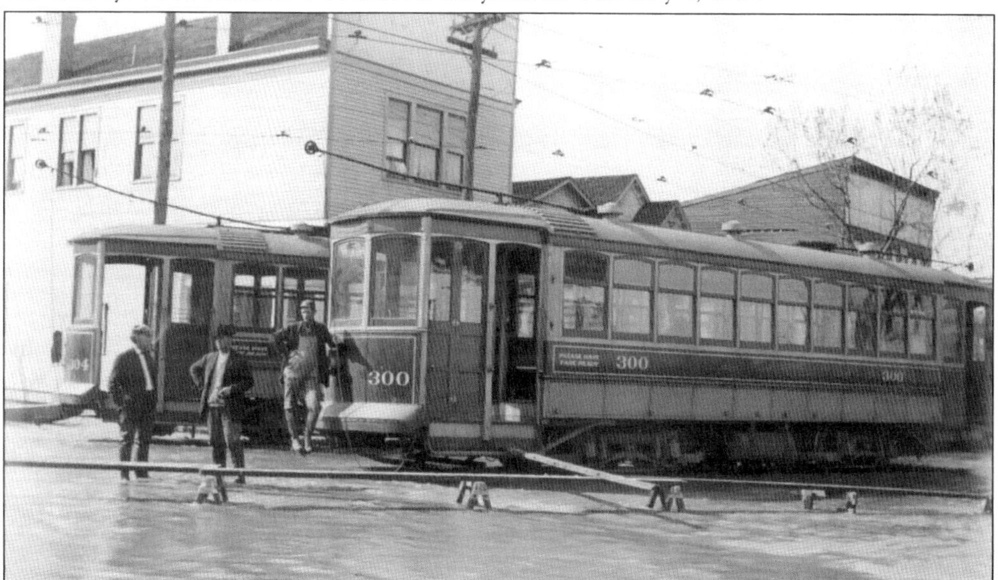

One of the many consequences of the 1937 Ohio River flood was the loss of electricity throughout much of the Portsmouth area. In this scene from the corner of Ninth and Offnere Streets, two streetcars had to remain in place, powerless, until the water receded and power could be restored. The gentlemen in the photograph appear to be ignoring the temporary wooden planks installed in an effort to keep pedestrians' feet dry. (Sharon Bender Collection.)

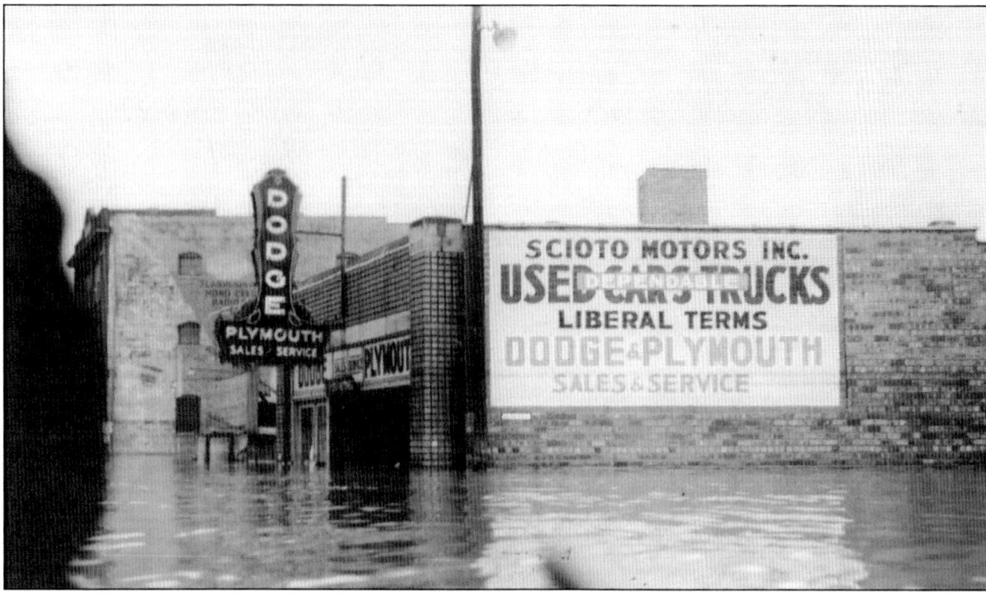

Scioto Motors opened their relocated Dodge-Plymouth dealership at 1508 Gallia Street in September 1936 with much fanfare. Four months later, the worst natural disaster ever to strike Portsmouth occurred when the Ohio River sent more than 12 feet of water over the protective floodwall. Although no vehicles were destroyed (they had been hastily moved to higher ground before the floodwaters arrived), the business sustained much damage, as shown above. Under the direction of young Henry Oberling, the business reopened a month later at the same location. Below, an unidentified man stands in front of the Fairtrace Shoe Company, located at 1015 Waller Street, as floodwaters recede. Owned by Henry Fairtrace, the popular shoe repair business was rebuilt at 1163 Ninth Street and remained in business for many more years.

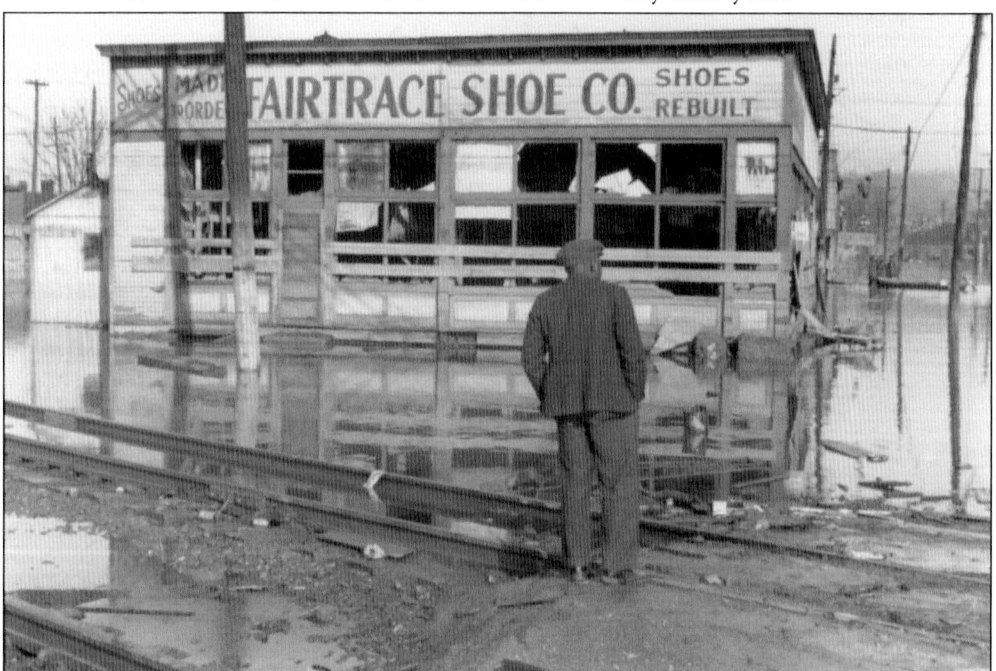

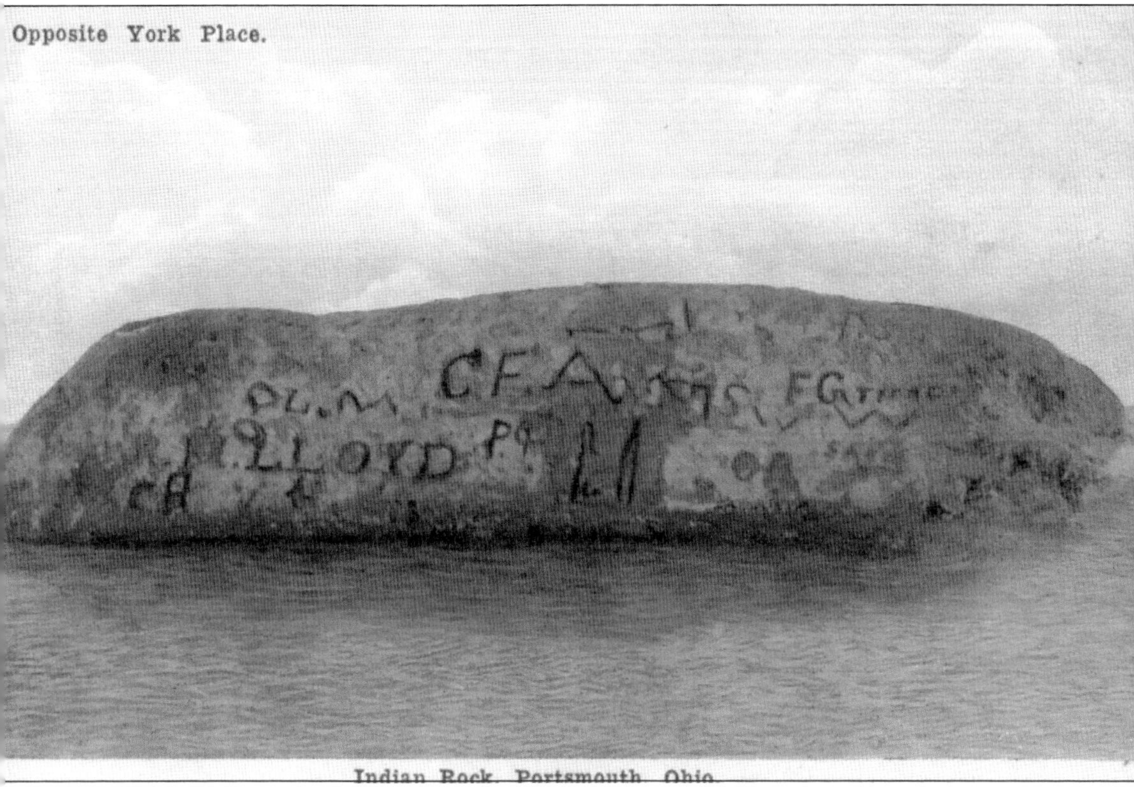

The eight-ton sandstone Indian Head Rock, lodged in the Ohio River between Portsmouth and Kentucky, was discovered in 1847. Named after a carving of a head believed to have been made by a Native American, Indian Head Rock was also decorated by early settlers who carved their names or initials into it. By 1920, dams on the river had completely submerged it, turning it into a legend for more than eight decades. In 2007, Ironton historian Steve Shaffer rediscovered the sunken rock and had it removed from the river and taken to Portsmouth with plans to put it on public display. The State of Kentucky claimed ownership of the rock, since that portion of the Ohio River is owned by the state. A three-year battle followed and involved politicians, judges, and courts from both states. As national media watched with both curiosity and amusement, the case was finally settled out of court. On November 4, 2010, Indian Head Rock was transferred to Greenup County, Kentucky. (Paul O'Neill Collection.)

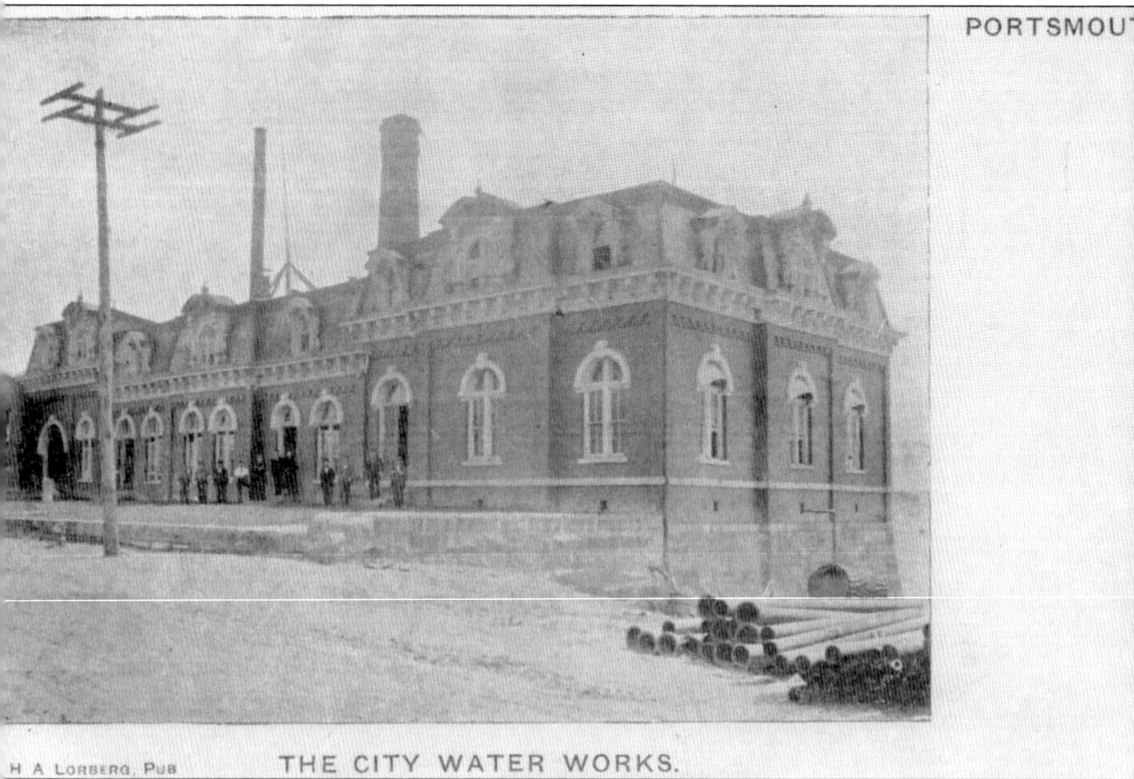

The first Portsmouth Water Works—located at Mill and Gay Streets, the current location of Shawnee State University— began operation in April 1872 and continued into the 1910s. Built at a cost of $132,000, the facility featured a 16-inch-diameter pipe that extended from the Ohio River to the pump house. A screen was placed on the end of the pipe in the river to help filter dirt and debris from entering the pumps. Divers were summoned to unclog the pipe when the screens became repeatedly clogged. With a capacity of two million gallons per day, the water works distributed water throughout the city via eight miles of pipes; 70 fire hydrants were also installed along its lines to assist in fire suppression. Water rates were based on yearly usage and were subject to the type of property one had; the owner of a small dwelling paid 4¢ per year, hotels paid $2 per room, banks were required to pay $10, and bakeries were charged $30. (Paul O'Neill Collection.)

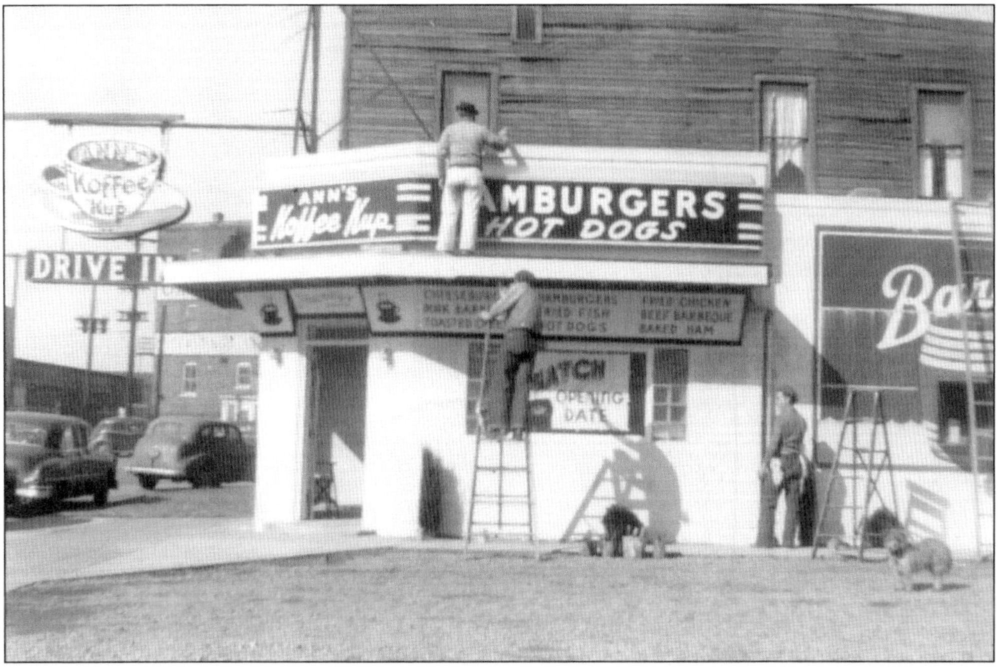

Ann's Koffee Kup, located at 1018 Chillicothe Street, is shown above preparing for its grand opening in 1950. Named after owner Anna Lee Arthur, it served hamburgers, hot dogs, and barbecue, which were delivered directly to customers in their vehicles by carhops on roller skates. Later that same year, Arthur sold the business to Retha Morton. Morton built a new structure in 1957 and changed the name to Morton's Restaurant (below), which featured home-cooked meals and a highly advertised "hamburger thru the garden." Morton's continued to operate until March 4, 2002, when poor health forced then-owner Peggy Morton to close the popular restaurant. The building then served various uses until it was razed in 2015 to make way for a CVS.

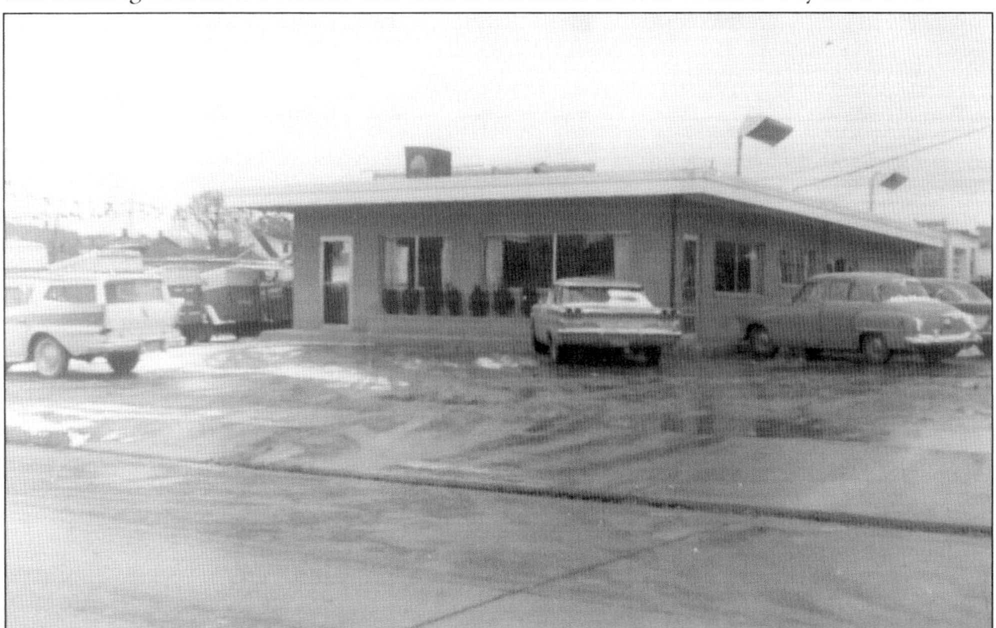

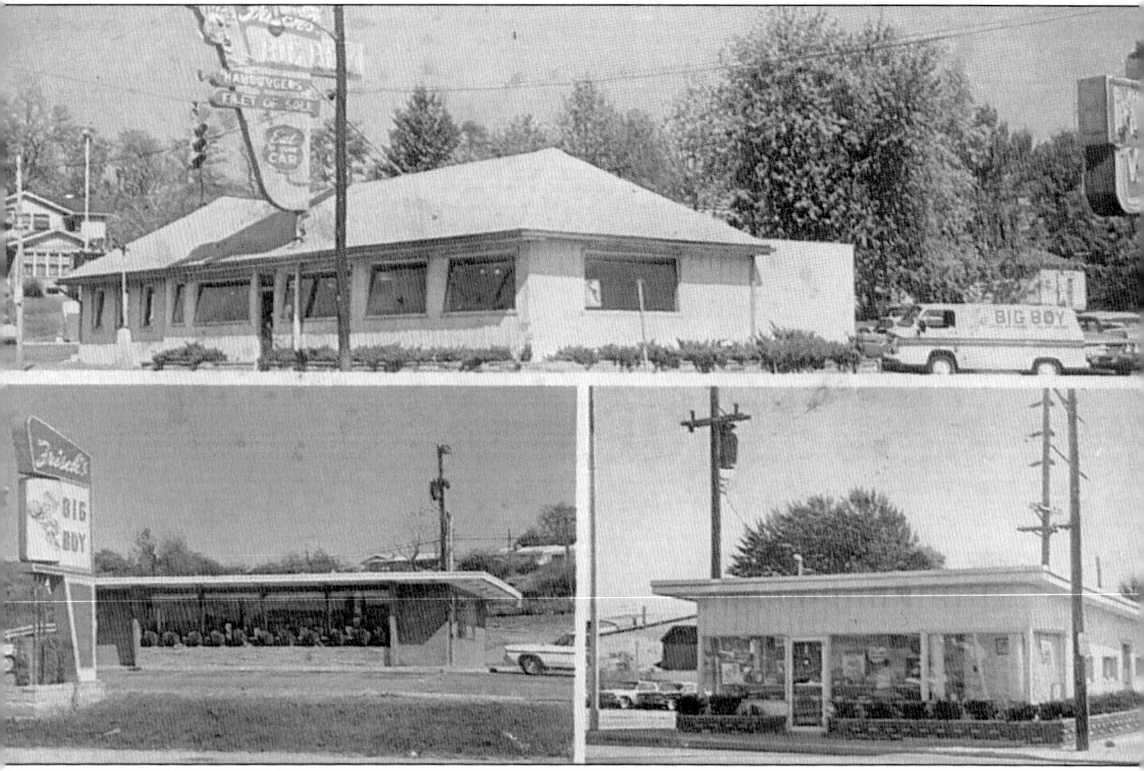

Frisch's Big Boy, which began in Cincinnati in 1948, is a popular Midwestern restaurant. The Portsmouth area has been home to four of the restaurants, three of which are shown in this early 1970s postcard. The Frisch's at the top was located at 2004 Scioto Trail, next to the Twin Motel. Originally a Moore's Restaurant, it was acquired by the chain around 1960. The Big Boy at lower left was situated on Route 23 in Rosemount and opened around 1965. The Big Boy at lower right—the oldest of the three pictured—opened in 1954 at 2348 Gallia Street on property that had previously been a used car lot. A fourth Frisch's was located at the corner of Twelfth and Offnere Streets after the company obtained the former Dale's Pharmacy building in 1965. Today, with all the Big Boy franchises gone, the only remaining structure is the Gallia Street building, which is the longtime home of the Jim Dandy Drive-In. (Bill Glockner Collection.)

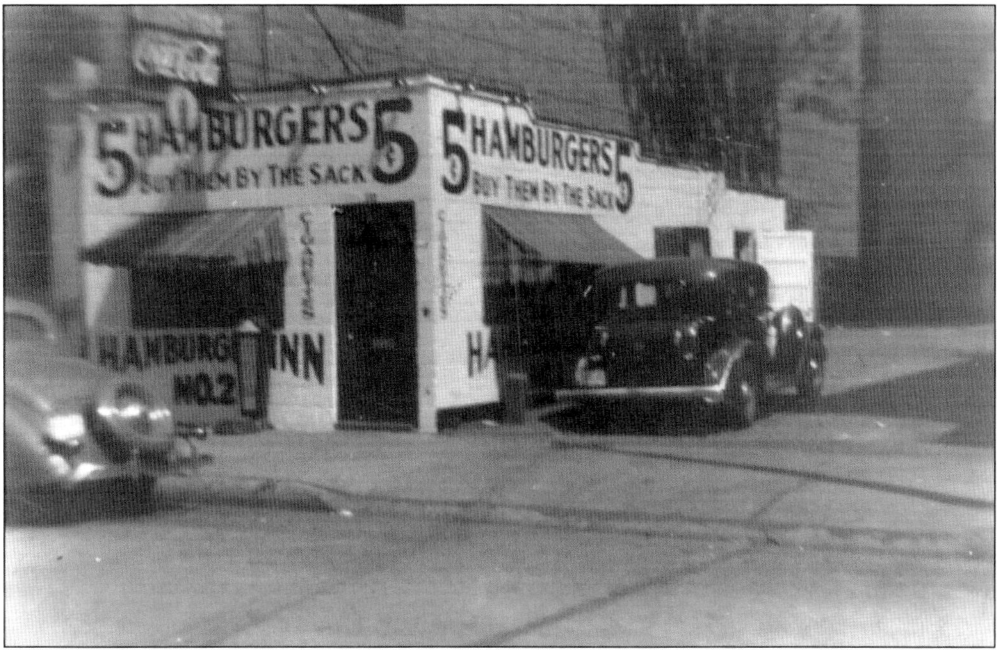

Scioto County residents have always had a love for a good hamburger, and that need was fulfilled by multiple eateries. While some may remember the White Front on Chillicothe Street or the Reese Hamburger Shop in Sciotoville, the Hamburger Inn is mentioned most often. Although Hamburger Inn had many locations, including those on Fifth Street (above) and Chillicothe Street (below), the original on Gallia Street outlasted them all. With hamburgers priced at 5¢, it was common to see people leaving with an entire bag full of deliciousness on payday. For a special treat, one could order a milkshake or a pie baked by Lewis Pies.

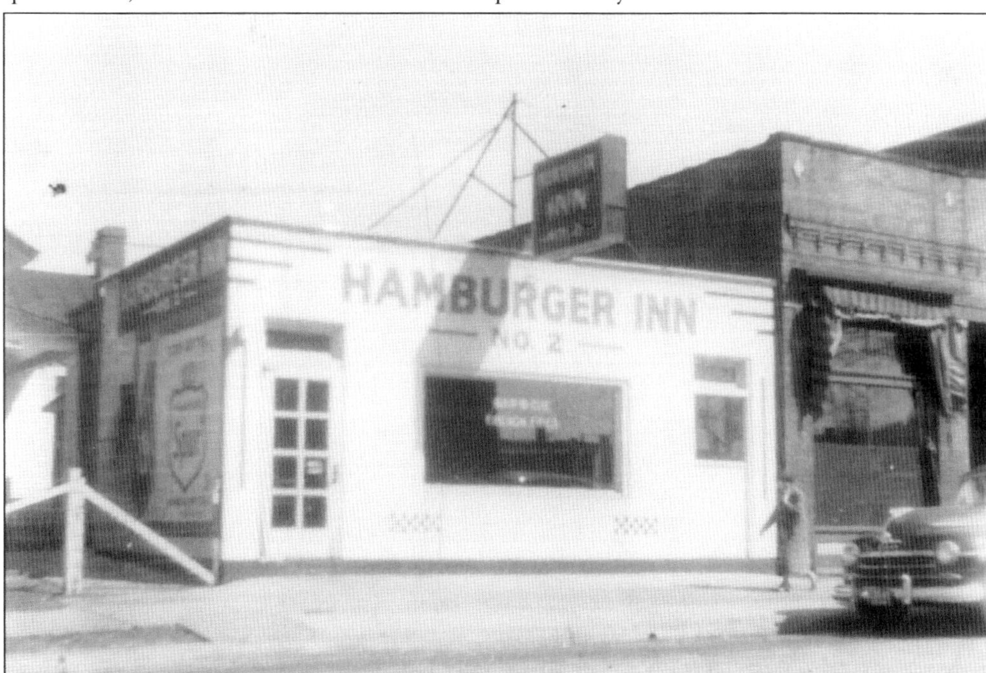

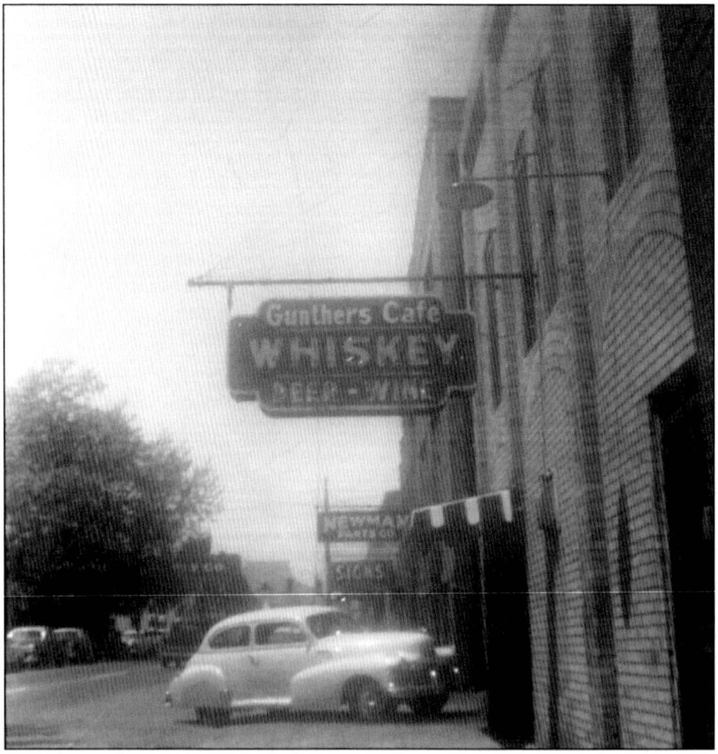

Harold Micklethwaite opened Gunther's Café at 1625 Eighth Street in 1960; he also owned the popular Harold's Restaurant within the same building. Gunther's was famous for its pizza and beer (served in frosty mugs). Following a disastrous fire in the early 1990s, the section of the building that was once Gunther's became a parking lot, while the portion that was Harold's Restaurant was acquired and remodeled by the Fraternal Order of the Eagles.

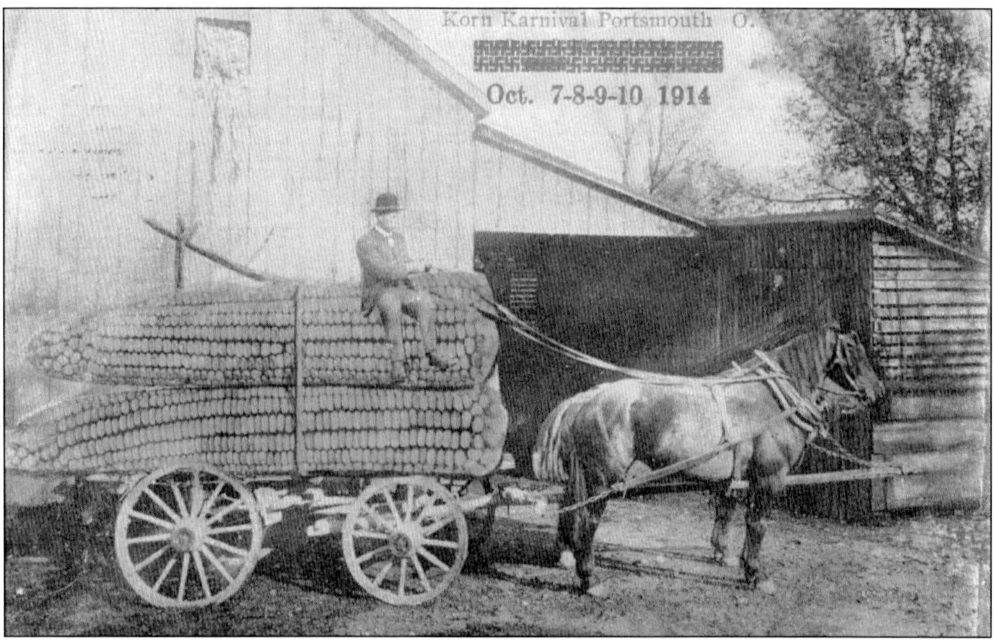

An unidentified gentleman sits upon what appear to be giant ears of corn in this 1914 advertisement for the Korn Karnival. The Kum Korn Karnival began in 1913, but its name was changed to Korn Karnival due to its initials. The annual four-day festival brought farmers and merchants together to display their merchandise. The carnival was suspended in 1916 due to World War I, and future attempts at reviving the tradition failed. (Sharon Bender Collection.)

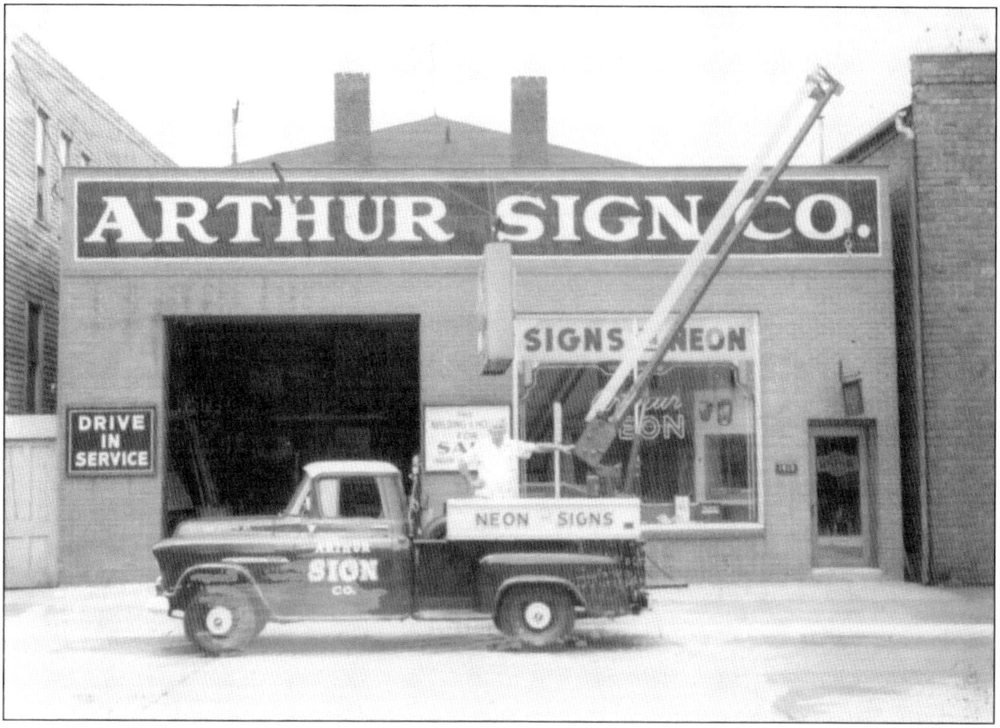

Arthur Sign Company, established in the mid-1930s, was owned by Kenneth Arthur. It was originally located on Chillicothe Street but relocated to 1613 Eighth Street (pictured). Arthur painted numerous signs in the Portsmouth area and between Ohio and Florida, where he spent his winters. Oak Tree Construction now occupies this building.

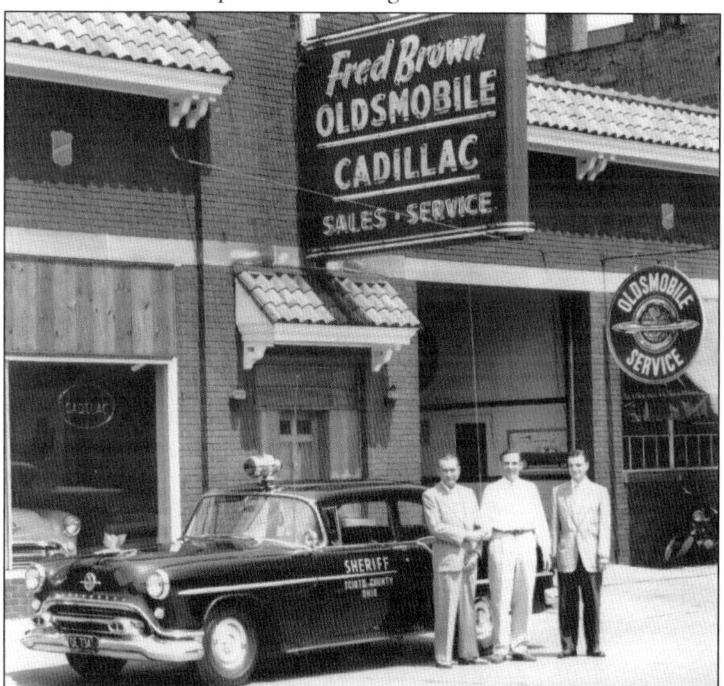

Scioto County sheriff Burl Justice (left) is shown with Fred Brown (center) accepting delivery of a new patrol car in the mid-1950s. Justice served as sheriff from 1949 until early 1958, when he was shot and later died after a tragic accident at the courthouse. His wife, Lucille, was appointed to finish his term in office, making her the first and only female sheriff in the history of Scioto County.

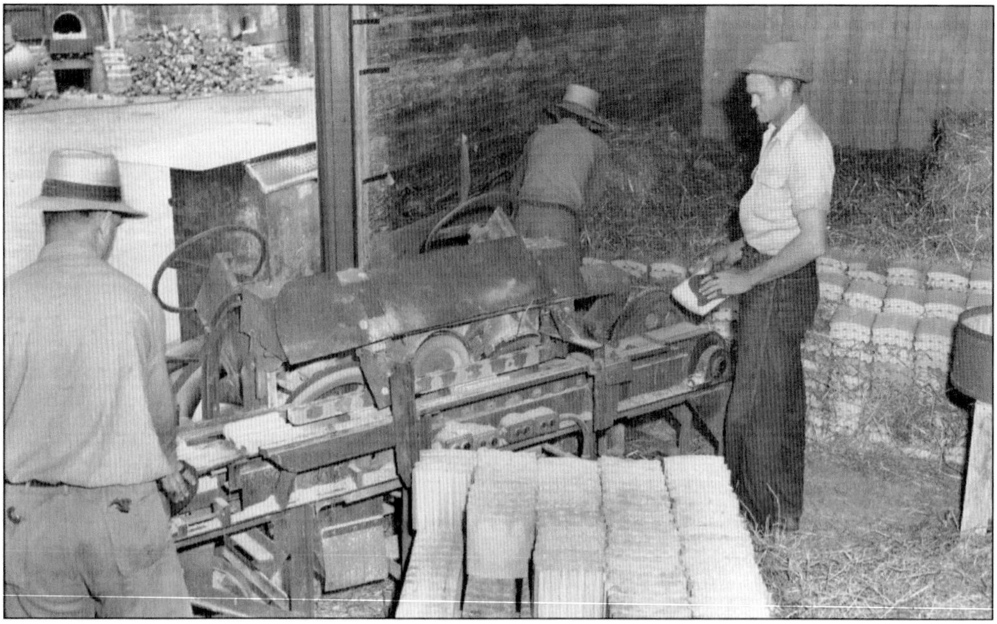

Located on a nine-acre parcel on Campbell Avenue, Harbison-Walker Refractories can trace its history back to 1881. Using special clay from southern Ohio and northern Kentucky, Harbison-Walker produced firebrick for furnace linings for more than a century. Refractory brick was previously manufactured on the same site by Hocking Valley Fire Brick Company, Portsmouth Fire Brick Company, and Kentucky Fire Brick Company. Dresser Industries acquired Harbison-Walker in 1967. Market conditions in the steel industry led to the plant closing in 1983. Above, workers are grinding firebrick before loading it onto a boxcar to be transported to a steel mill; below, men on the No. 2 power press are molding fresh brick.

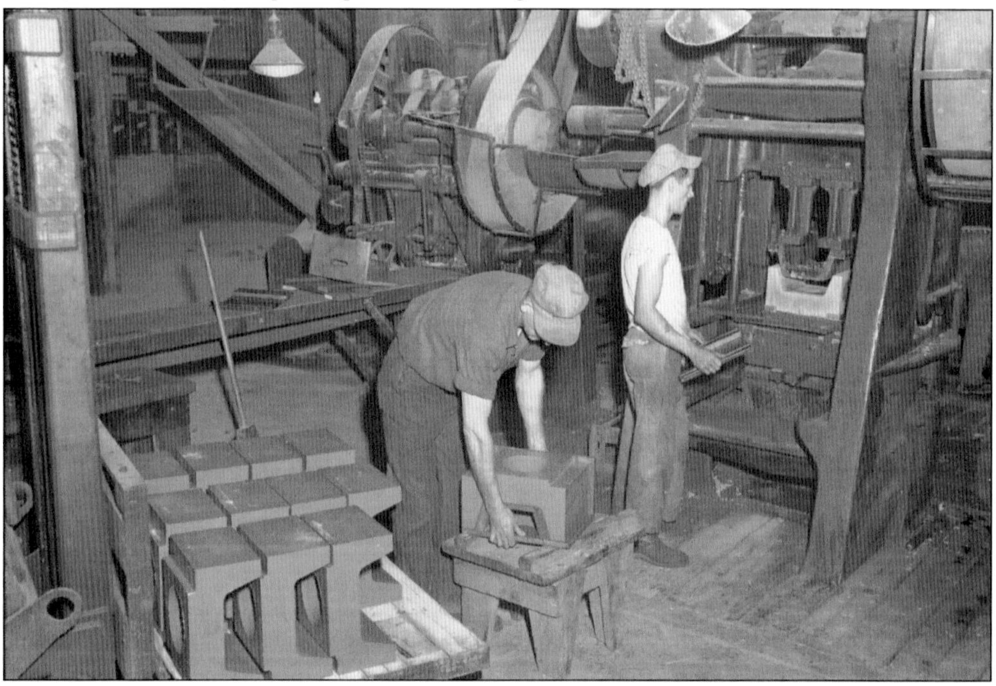

After many years of separate volunteer firefighting companies operating in the area, the Portsmouth Fire Department was formed in March 1871. Station No. 2, pictured here in the 1950s, was one of three fire stations that operated through the following years. This station opened on August 13, 1893, at Gallia and Lincoln Streets and remained in service until the Central Fire Station opened in 1978. The building remains standing today.

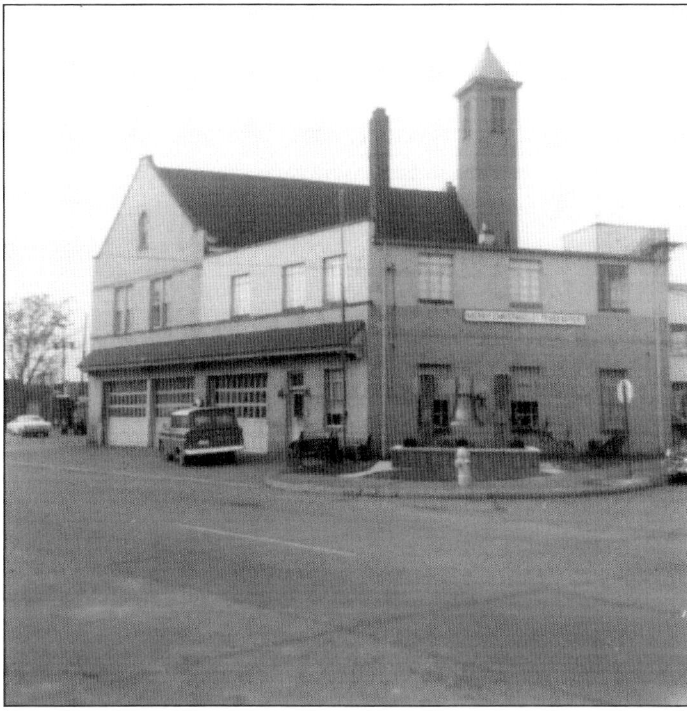

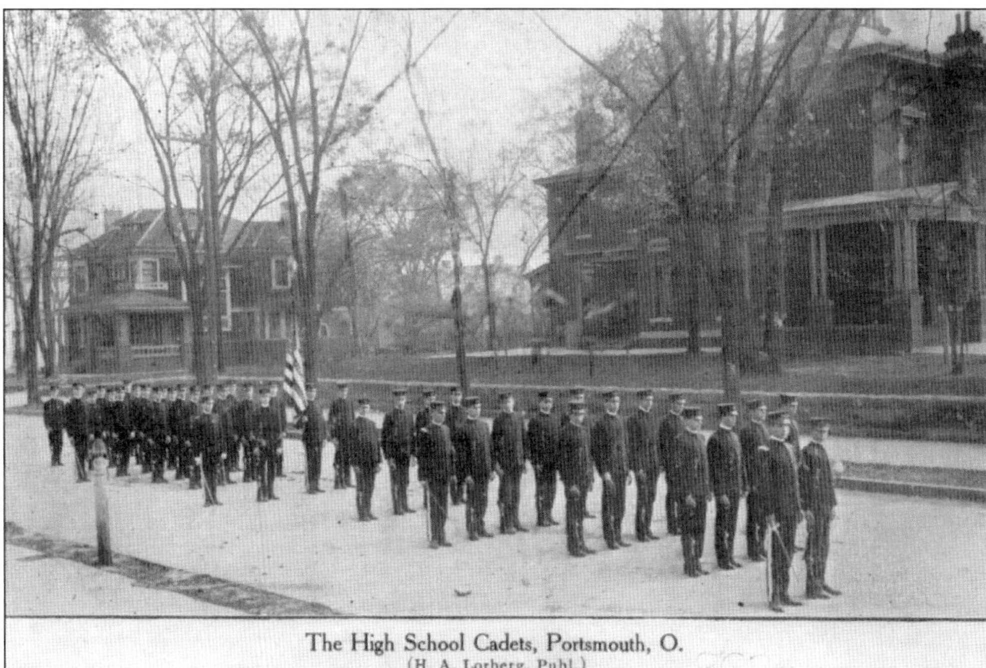

The Portsmouth High School Cadets group organized in May 1875 and consisted of school-age boys who were taught discipline and weaponry for possible future military service. Pictured on Waller Street in this 1907 postcard, the young men assembled at 6:50 a.m. every day before school to practice drills. They participated in many patriotic parades held in Portsmouth and remained active through World War I. (Sharon Bender Collection.)

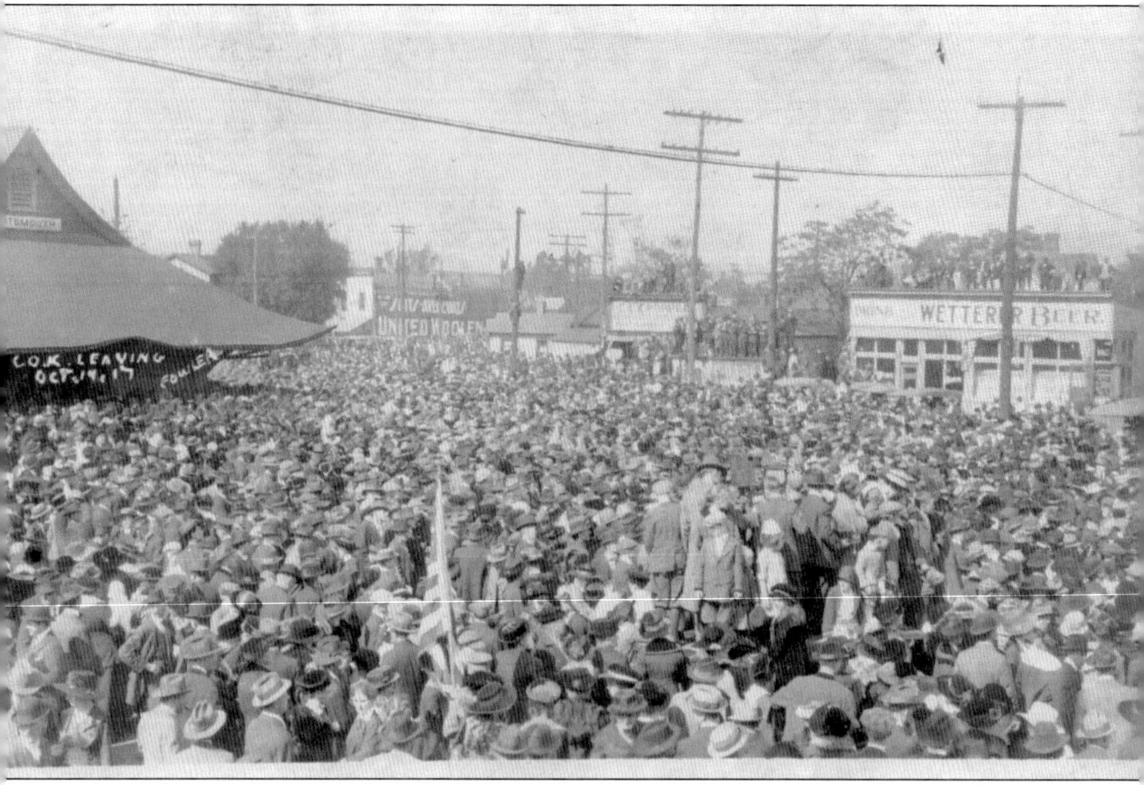

As shown in this stirring postcard image, hundreds of Portsmouth residents gathered at the Norfolk & Western station on Tenth Street to give a proper send-off to Company K of the 7th Ohio Infantry of the Ohio National Guard on October 14, 1917. The special train carrying the local soldiers is just out of view at right. During World War I, some guardsmen were deployed overseas to Europe while others were assigned to protect local potential enemy targets, such as the newly completed Chesapeake & Ohio Bridge in Sciotoville. On August 23, 1918, the local Red Cross opened a "canteen" inside the Norfolk & Western station to supply free bread, cakes, coffee, and soup to thousands of soldiers in order to make their travel toward an unknown fate a little easier. More than 70 area women volunteered their time to staff the Red Cross eatery, and a visiting US Navy official proclaimed it to be one of the best in the country. The beautiful Scioto County KIA–MIA (Killed in Action–Missing in Action) Memorial in Tracy Park lists the names of the Scioto County residents lost in all wars, including the 84 who gave the ultimate sacrifice during World War I. (Bill Glockner Collection.)

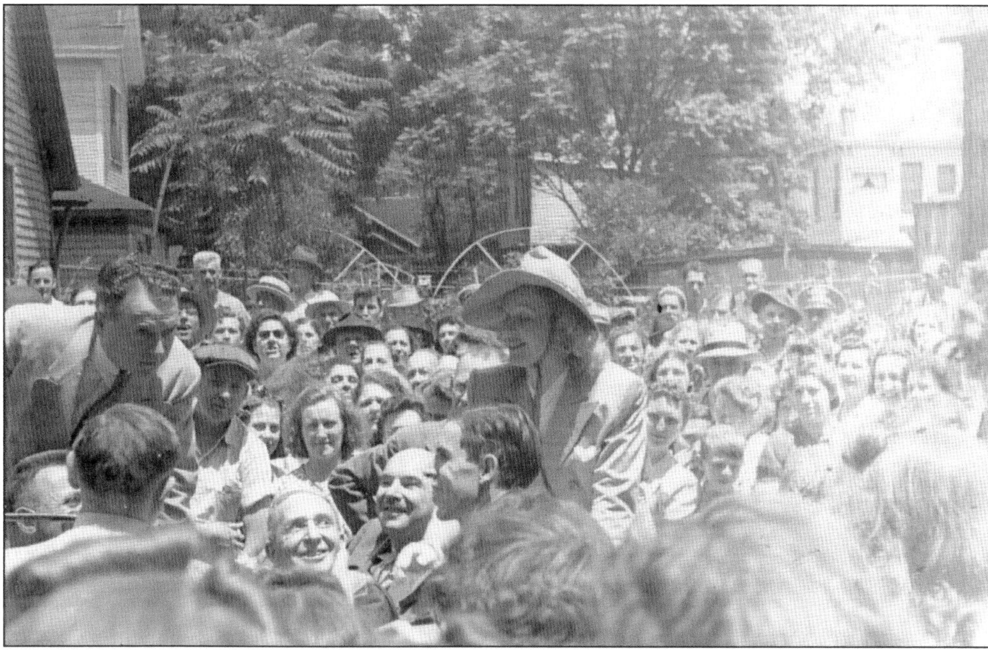

On June 24, 1942, Marlene Dietrich, the sultry movie star with the "bedroom eyes," arrived in Portsmouth to encourage the purchase of war bonds. While in town, Dietrich toured several factories and presented awards to businesses with 90 percent of employee enrollment in the war bond purchase program. During World War II, Portsmouth companies contributed over $1 million per year for war bonds. (Linda Rigsby Collection.)

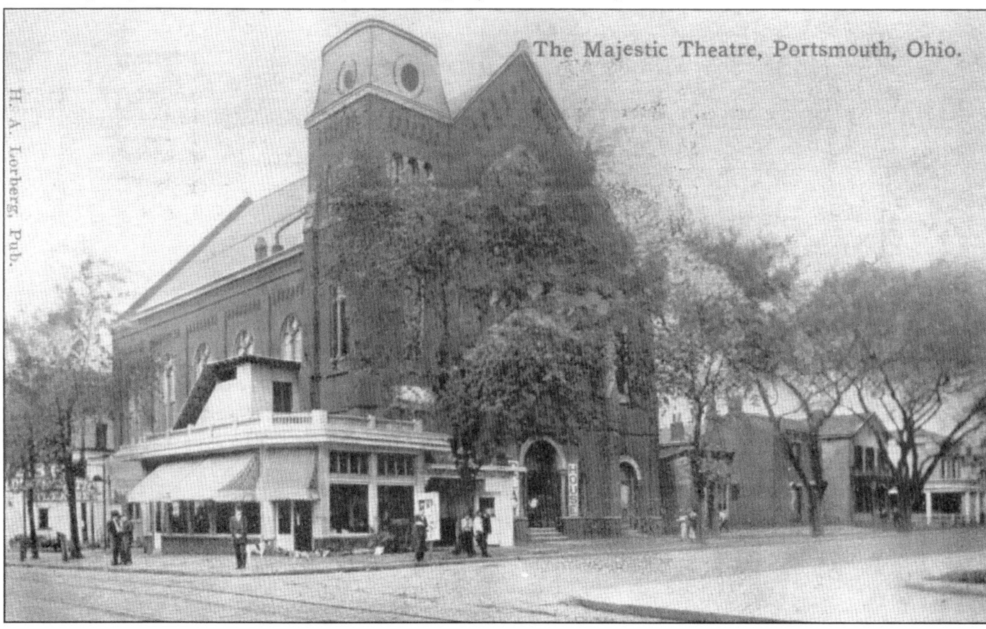

The corner of Sixth and Chillicothe Streets has been home to a wide variety of businesses. The first was the Sixth Street Methodist Church, which was remodeled into the Playhouse in 1915 after the church relocated. In 1918, it transformed once again into the Majestic Theater. The building was razed in the early 1920s to make way for the Masonic Temple. (Bill Glockner Collection.)

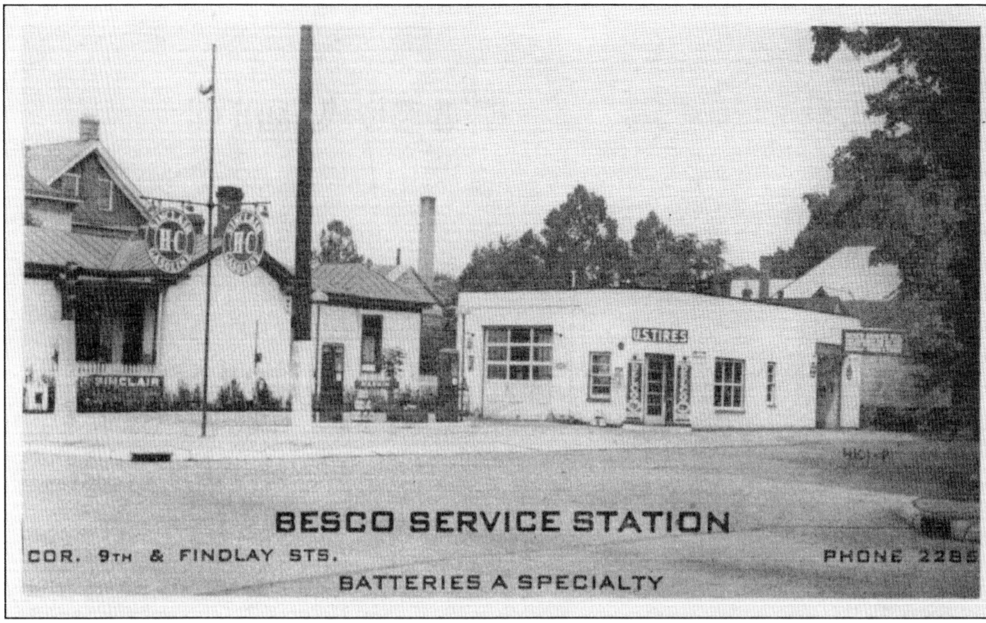

Besco Service Station was located on the corner of Ninth and Findlay Streets. Owner Theasel Besco opened the station in the late 1940s and offered gasoline, tires, and car batteries (for $1.85). When Besco passed away less than 10 years after opening the business, the space was home to Gordon's Garage and then Gibby's Service Center in the 1960s. It is now a parking lot for Daehler Funeral Home. (Bill Glockner Collection.)

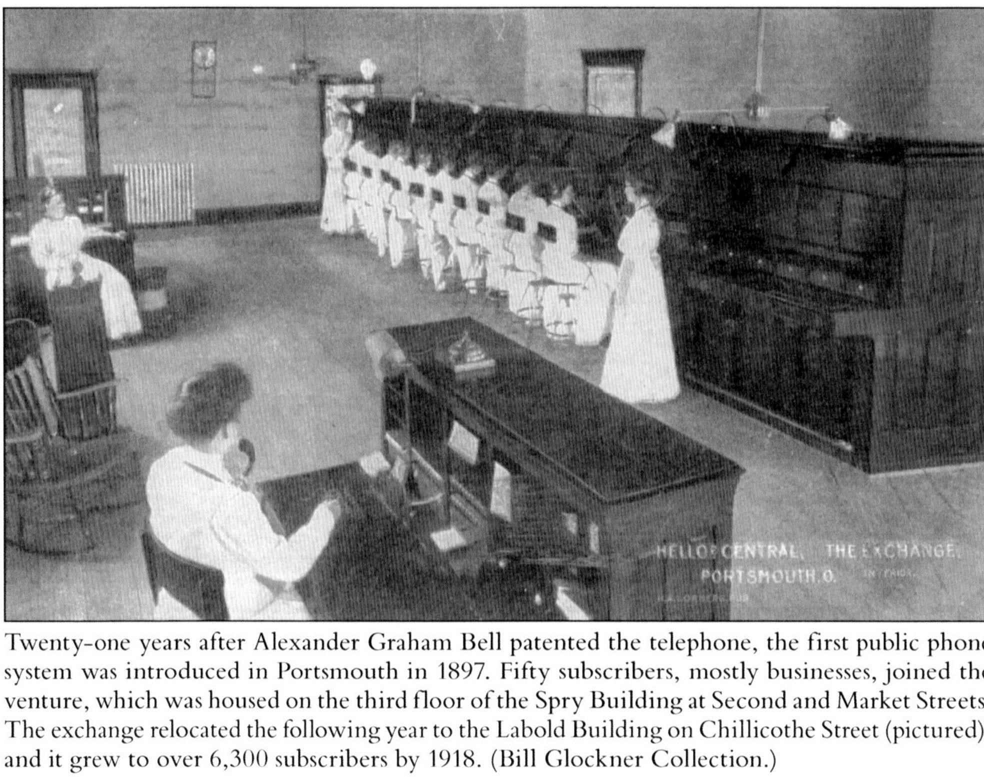

Twenty-one years after Alexander Graham Bell patented the telephone, the first public phone system was introduced in Portsmouth in 1897. Fifty subscribers, mostly businesses, joined the venture, which was housed on the third floor of the Spry Building at Second and Market Streets. The exchange relocated the following year to the Labold Building on Chillicothe Street (pictured), and it grew to over 6,300 subscribers by 1918. (Bill Glockner Collection.)

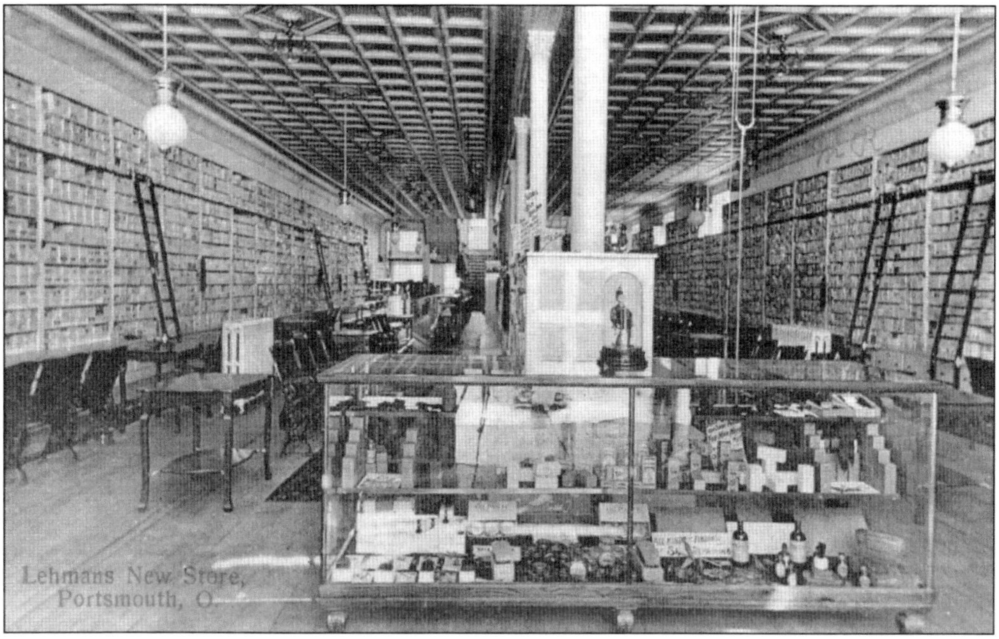

In 1882, Mose Lehman opened his first men's shoe store on Chillicothe Street. In 1895, he moved to a larger building on the same street and expanded his inventory to include women's and children's shoes. By April 1911, he had relocated once again, this time to a three-story building at 310 Chillicothe Street. The first floor (above) featured one of the area's largest selections of shoes, while the second floor primarily showcased men's work clothing and suits. Lehman's store survived the 1913 flood (below) and a tragic fire in March 1923, remaining in business until his retirement in 1926. The building then housed Grant's Department Store for many years. The structure remains standing today and is owned by Shawnee State University. (Above, Bill Glockner Collection; below, Sharon Bender Collection.)

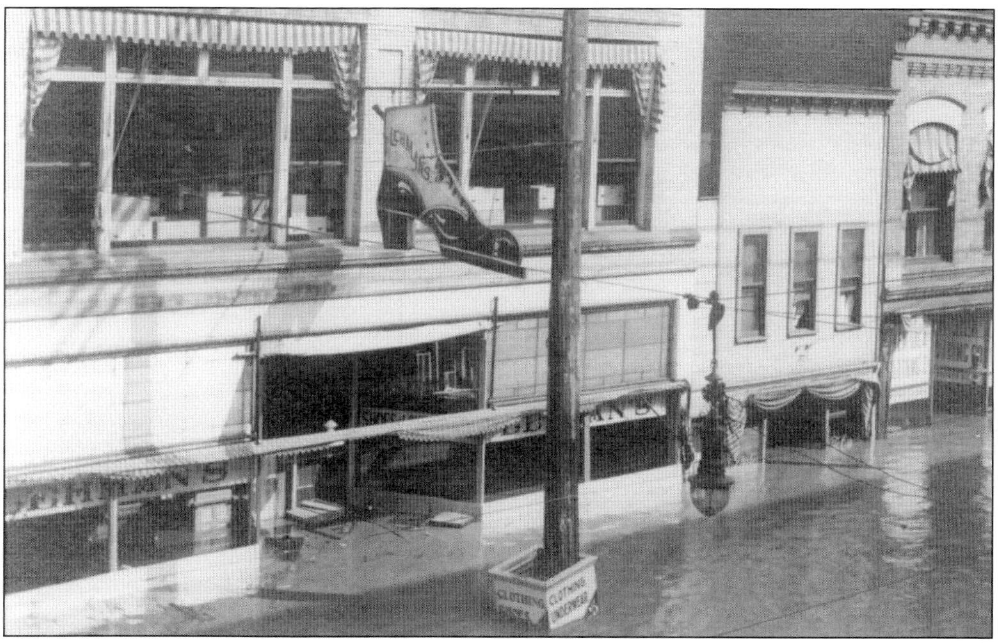

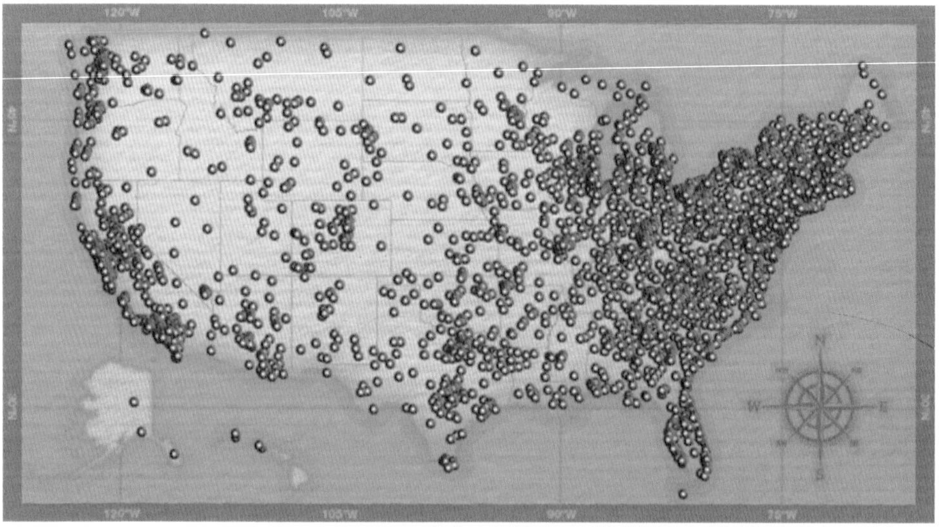